W9-DCC-572

Jaguar Books on Latin America

Series Editors

WILLIAM H. BEEZLEY, Neville G. Penrose Chair of Latin
 American Studies, Texas Christian University
COLIN M. MACLACHLAN, Professor, Department of History,
 Tulane University

Volumes Published

John E. Kicza, ed., *The Indian in Latin American History: Resistance,
 Resilience, and Acculturation* (1993). Cloth ISBN 0-8420-2421-2
 Paper ISBN 0-8420-2425-5

Susan E. Place, ed., *Tropical Rainforests: Latin American Nature and
 Society in Transition* (1993). Cloth ISBN 0-8420-2423-9
 Paper ISBN 0-8420-2427-1

Paul W. Drake, ed., *Money Doctors, Foreign Debts, and Economic
 Reforms in Latin America from the 1890s to the Present* (1994).
 Cloth ISBN 0-8420-2434-4 Paper ISBN 0-8420-2435-2

John A. Britton, ed., *Molding the Hearts and Minds: Education,
 Communications, and Social Change in Latin America* (1994).
 Cloth ISBN 0-8420-2489-1 Paper ISBN 0-8420-2490-5

Darién J. Davis, ed., *Slavery and Beyond: The African Impact on Latin
 America and the Caribbean* (1995). Cloth ISBN 0-8420-2484-0
 Paper ISBN 0-8420-2485-9

David J. Weber and Jane M. Rausch, eds., *Where Cultures Meet: Frontiers
 in Latin American History* (1994). Cloth ISBN 0-8420-2477-8
 Paper ISBN 0-8420-2478-6

Gertrude M. Yeager, ed., *Confronting Change, Challenging Tradition:
 Women in Latin American History* (1994). Cloth ISBN 0-8420-2479-4
 Paper ISBN 0-8420-2480-8

Linda Alexander Rodríguez, ed., *Rank and Privilege: The Military and
 Society in Latin America* (1994). Cloth ISBN 0-8420-2432-8
 Paper ISBN 0-8420-2433-6

Gilbert M. Joseph and Mark D. Szuchman, eds., *I Saw a City Invincible:
 Urban Portraits of Latin America* (1996). Cloth ISBN 0-8420-2495-6
 Paper ISBN 0-8420-2496-4

Roderic Ai Camp, ed., *Democracy in Latin America: Patterns and Cycles* (1996). Cloth ISBN 0-8420-2512-X   Paper ISBN 0-8420-2513-8

Oscar J. Martínez, ed., *U.S.-Mexico Borderlands: Historical and Contemporary Perspectives* (1996). Cloth ISBN 0-8420-2446-8 Paper ISBN 0-8420-2447-6

William O. Walker III, ed., *Drugs in the Western Hemisphere: An Odyssey of Cultures in Conflict* (1996). Cloth ISBN 0-8420-2422-0 Paper ISBN 0-8420-2426-3

Richard R. Cole, ed., *Communication in Latin America: Journalism, Mass Media, and Society* (1996). Cloth ISBN 0-8420-2558-8 Paper ISBN 0-8420-2559-6

David G. Gutiérrez, ed., *Between Two Worlds: Mexican Immigrants in the United States* (1996). Cloth ISBN 0-8420-2473-5 Paper ISBN 0-8420-2474-3

Communication
in Latin America

Communication
in Latin America
Journalism, Mass Media, and Society

Richard R. Cole
Editor

Jaguar Books on Latin America
Number 14

A Scholarly Resources Inc. Imprint
Wilmington, Delaware

Scholarly Resources Inc.
104 Greenhill Avenue
Wilmington, DE 19805-1897

Library of Congress Cataloging-in-Publication Data

Communication in Latin America : journalism, mass media,
  and society / Richard R. Cole, editor.
     p.   cm. — (Jaguar books on Latin America ; no. 14)
    Includes bibliographical references.
    ISBN 0-8420-2558-8 (cloth : alk. paper). — ISBN 0-8420-2559-6
(paper : alk. paper)
    1. Mass media—Latin America. 2. Journalism—Latin America.
I. Cole, Richard R. II. Series
P92.L3C54   1996
302.23'098—dc20   95-43170
                                           CIP

Acknowledgments

Three students in the master's program in the School of Journalism and Mass Communication at the University of North Carolina at Chapel Hill were exceedingly helpful in making this book possible: Miguel Casas, Patricia Richardson, and Karen Kemp. Miguel and Patricia, better known as Trish, were part of the project early on, and they never flagged in interest or accomplishment. Miguel was on the project the longest time; Karen joined us closer to the book's completion. All were excellent. My most sincere thanks to each of them.

Thanks also go to two pioneer U.S. professors in mass communication education with great interest in Latin America: Raymond B. Nixon of the University of Minnesota, who was my Ph.D. dissertation adviser way back in the early 1970s; and Mary A. Gardner of Michigan State University and, previously, of the University of Texas at Austin, where I took her classes in the mid-1960s. Both were giants in the field and were inspirations to me.

Since my undergraduate days, I have been intrigued with Latin America, especially the two countries to which I take students in my class in "Mass Communication in Mexico and Cuba." Students learn a great deal not only about the mass media in those nations but also about their political systems and national cultures. So many people in Mexico City, Havana, and elsewhere have been instrumental in making the classes a success, plus the exchange programs and other activities that have come about as a result of the classes. It is impossible to list them all. But I would like to acknowledge the support and wisdom that have come from these individuals in Mexico City, either in recent years or earlier: Juan Aranda López, a business and public relations consultant; Guillermo Chao Ebergenyi of *El Sol*; Luis Félix-Flores, who was with *The News* for many years and is now deceased; and Joe Nash, the famous travel writer who has written on Mexico for more than a half century. I also want to acknowledge the following faculty members or administrators currently or once associated with the Universidad de las Américas: Ellen Calmus, Francisco Giner, Dra. Margarita Gómez-Palacio Muñoz, Won-Ho Kim, Francisco Marmolejo, and Eduardo Vega. These members of the communication faculty at the University of Havana have been especially helpful: Dean Enma Fernández and current or former faculty members

María de los Angeles González Borges, Martha Campos Somavilla, and Carlos Sariol. I also wish to express my gratitude to Arnaldo Coro of Radio Havana Cuba, Miguel Núñez and José Ponce in the Cuban Interests Section in Washington, DC, and Patricia Boero at the John D. and Catherine T. MacArthur Foundation in Chicago.

Special appreciation goes to Jo Bass, my splendid assistant and secretary who has come to be a keen observer of Mexico and especially Cuba. And thanks for everything, as always, to my wife, Lynda.

Contents

0177181

Preface

Richard Cole, Miguel Casas,
and Patricia Richardson*

Mass communication, one of the most vital and dynamic fields in the modern world, is crucial to societies today as never before. It will continue to grow as an occupational field everywhere, as new media arise, as societies become increasingly complex, as populations continue to grow, and as knowledge maintains its relentless advance. All of these factors result in an enormous growth in specialized information. And the more specialized information there is, the more journalists and other communicators are sought—in business, research, government, and all walks of life. The communications media enable the specialists, and all of us, to talk with one another.

First, some basic terms:

Journalism refers to reporting, editing, and producing timely news accounts for the public. Interpreting the news and offering opinion are also basic to journalism.

Communication is simply the art of transmitting information and ideas from one person to another person.

Mass media are the institutions, businesses, or organizations that provide information to huge audiences or sometimes relatively small groups. The mass media include newspapers, radio and television stations, cable television channels, magazines, newsletters, motion pictures, compact discs, videos, interactive computer media, and on and on. Their business

*Miguel Casas, a native of Spain and a master's degree candidate at the University of North Carolina at Chapel Hill (UNC-CH), worked for six years as a financial reporter in Madrid and London before enrolling in the UNC-CH School of Journalism and Mass Communication, where he was a research assistant and in 1995 was the Dixie Davis Scholar in Washington, DC. Patricia Richardson has worked in print journalism and public relations and as a free-lance writer; she also taught English for eight years before enrolling in the master's program and then in the Ph.D. program in the UNC-CH School of Journalism and Mass Communication. She has also been assistant to the director of publications for the UNC-CH Bicentennial and administrative assistant to the UNC-CH faculty chairperson.

is providing audiences with information, opinion, and entertainment and, in countries with capitalistic economies, advertising. They are mass media as opposed to interpersonal media, where people talk back and forth in person or on the telephone, for example. The new interactive media, of course, do allow members of the audience to communicate with one another via computer but not face to face.

Mass communication, the broadest of these terms, embraces journalism and the mass media and more. It refers to the overall process of communication and includes all of its parts. It was defined cleanly and simply in the model put forth back in 1960 by Harold Lasswell, the famous pioneer researcher: Who? Says What? Over Which Channel? To Whom? With What Effect?[1] Over the years, other scholars have added elements to their own models or emphasized other parts of the communication process such as gatekeepers (the professional communicators who decide which information will be disseminated and which information will not be), regulators such as government agencies, and technological factors, to name only a few. But the term mass communication embraces them all.

This book considers mass communication in regard to the fascinating region of Latin America, with its huge and varied geography, peoples, languages, and cultures. Despite the enormous diversity from country to country (see table), however, some basic common factors affect mass communication dramatically over the entire region. Three factors in particular stand out, all of them interrelated:

Population. Latin America's annual population growth rate has been one of the world's highest for many years. In 1950, Latin America had 166 million people and accounted for 6.5 percent of the world's population; by 1990 its population had swollen to some 450 million and constituted 8.4 percent of the world's inhabitants.[2] Today the population of Latin America is roughly three times what it was in 1950. The growth continues at a dizzying pace for many reasons, including the high birth rate, improvements in medicine and treatment, a longer life span, the prevalence of Roman Catholicism and its strictures on birth control, the concept of machismo, and the tradition of large families. Mexico is only one example. Mexico had a population of about twenty-two million people in 1950; only two decades later its population had mushroomed to fifty million. Today, Mexico has a population of about ninety-three million, more than a 422 percent increase over 1950 and a 186 percent increase over 1970. The capital, Mexico City, which had about one million inhabitants a half century ago, now is the largest single city in the world, with roughly twenty-two million people, equal to the populations of North Carolina, South Carolina, Tennessee, and Georgia combined. The growing number of people throughout Latin America constitutes a huge burden on their societies, their governments, their economies, and their communication systems. As James Nelson Goodsell observed in early 1995: "It needs to be noted that the number of Latin Americans has increased in the last fifteen minutes by about two hundred. Two hundred more mouths to feed, bodies to clothe . . . babies to find housing for . . . to educate and to find jobs for . . . to provide them a better way of life than their parents. . . . This is what it is all about. We must never forget that."[3]

Poverty. The enormous growth in urbanization across Latin America has resulted in huge concentrations of poor people jammed into tin shacks around and within vast cities. A great proportion of the problems in every Latin American country—crime, violence, ignorance, sickness, poverty— festers in these urban agglomerations. Most Latin Americans by far are poor, although the annual per capita gross domestic product continues to climb. In 1970 it stood at the equivalent of $1,600 U.S.; by 1993 it had risen to $2,094.[4] A concomitant problem is illiteracy, which ranges from only 3.5 percent in cosmopolitan Uruguay to a staggering 53 percent in poverty-stricken Haiti. Poverty and illiteracy are elemental factors affecting how a nation can communicate with its people and how they communicate with one another. When most people in a country cannot read, newspapers are almost useless to them, even if they could afford to buy them. Poor countries must rely on the broadcasting media, particularly radio, to disseminate news and information.

Democracy and stability in government. The constitution of each country in Latin America espouses freedom of the press, but in reality the political regime in power has always had a more powerful effect on freedom of expression than any document has had. Military dictators used to be the cliché for Latin America, where uprisings and coups d'état were commonplace. Yet today democracy has flowered. Democratically elected governments are in place throughout the hemisphere except for the notable case of Cuba. Today's great increase in democratic government bodes well for national communication systems and for freedom of the press.

Generally, this book takes an optimistic view, recognizing that mass communication in Latin America, despite its serious problems, has undergone dramatic improvements in recent years and has a bright future. The mass media, particularly broadcasting, have multiplied and matured in content and technology. The printed press is influential among elites, if not the masses. Virtually everyone has access to radio. This book considers all the mass media, of course, but more pages are devoted to print than broadcasting for several reasons. Historically, the print media have been much more active in attempting to sway the people politically than

Latin American Mass Media by the Numbers

Country	Population (millions)	Per Capita Income (U.S. Dollars)	Percent Illiterate	Radio Stations	Radio Receivers per 1,000 Population	TV Stations	TV Sets per 1,000 Population	Daily Newspapers	Total Newspaper Circulation (millions)	Newspaper Circulation per 1,000 Population
Argentina	33.1	$2,370	4.7	190	683	42	221	194	2.6	82
Bolivia	7.5	$630	20.0	224	613	28	103	16	2.6	48
Brazil	146.6	$2,879	18.9	2,932	386	257	208	323	6.3	43
Chile	13.6	$1,940	5.2	405	344	48	210	39	0.8	67
Colombia	35.9	$1,500	18.3	587	177	52	117	32	1.9	49
Costa Rica	3.2	$2,342	7.2	84	258	12	141	4	0.3	106
Cuba	10.6	NA	6.0	184	345	34	162	3	0.4	40
Dominican Republic	7.5	$830	16.7	126	171	25	87	10	0.3	46
Ecuador	11.1	$980	14.2	321	318	16	85	26	0.9	34
El Salvador	5.4	$1,110	27.0	78	413	5	93	5	0.3	48

Guatemala	9.7	$900	44.9	109	66	6	52	5	0.2	19
Haiti	6.8	$370	53.1	37	47	4	4.7	4	0.02	4
Honduras	5.5	$590	26.9	184	387	39	73	4	0.2	30
Mexico	88.8	$2,680	12.4	693	255	82	149	286	10.5	119
Nicaragua	4.2	$380	27.0	72	262	7	66	4	0.08	18
Panama	2.5	$1,830	10.7	70	224	9	167	6	0.2	75
Paraguay	4.5	$1,568	9.9	49	171	5	82	5	0.2	44
Peru	22.6	$1,160	14.9	300	254	10	98	41	1.0	222
Uruguay	3.2	$4,115	3.5	99	604	26	232	33	0.7	224
Venezuela	20.2	$2,560	7.3	218	448	37	163	56	2.2	113

Sources: The primary source is the Inter American Press Association (IAPA)'s 1995 *Press Freedoms in the Americas*. IAPA staff members confirm the difficulty of obtaining accurate data and note that different sources in some countries often provide conflicting figures. The numbers of radio receivers and television sets come from *UNESCO Statistical Yearbook 1993*.

the broadcast media have been. Also, much more has been written about print than about broadcasting, and more research has been conducted on print.

Another cause for optimism is the media's role in educating their audiences. While most Latin American countries share a history of political instability and lack of long-standing democratic tradition, the media have played a central role in instilling democratic and civic values and supporting democratic institutions. Despite the great diversity from country to country in development, status, effectiveness, and level of maturity, the media of most Latin American nations are evolving toward standards of the Western mass communication model, with its emphasis on private enterprise and ownership, the prominent roles played by wealthy families who have controlled newspapers and other media, and the importance of advertising not only as the financial underpinning for the media but also for communicating the latest products, styles, and trends. As more stable democratic governments become the norm in Latin America, the media are also adopting a more professional approach to their role as the Fourth Estate in the political system. And we predict increased professionalization in the future.

The volume is organized into two parts: "Status of and Issues in Latin American Mass Communication" and "Case Studies of Mass Communication in Selected Latin American Countries." The first section opens with a cogent analysis of prominent and contrasting national mass communication systems followed by treatment of a number of important and timely issues: the role of women in the mass media, professional news organizations, journalism education, international propaganda in the stormy current case between Cuba and the United States, and the burning questions of whether journalists should be required to belong to professional organizations and have university degrees. These issues are among the most important in mass communication in the region. The second section of this book provides current analysis and commentary on some of the largest, most important, or most interesting national mass communication systems: those of Mexico, Cuba, Chile, Argentina, Brazil, and the Andean countries. These countries were chosen because of their international dominance in the region, as in the case of Mexico, or because of their uniqueness, as in the case of Cuba. The second section ends with overall conclusions and predictions for the future.

Notes

1. Harold D. Lasswell, "The Structure and Function of Communication in Society," in *Mass Communication*, ed. Wilbur Schramm (Urbana: University of Illinois Press, 1960), 117.

2. Department for Economic and Social Information and Policy Analysis, Statistical Division, *United Nations Statistical Yearbook 1990–1991* (New York: United Nations).

3. James Nelson Goodsell, "Observations on Changes in the Americas," remarks presented to the 12th annual Intercultural and International Communication Conference (February 3, 1995), School of Communication, University of Miami.

4. Economic Commission for Latin America and the Caribbean, *United Nations Statistical Yearbook for Latin America and the Caribbean 1994* (Chile: United Nations).

Some Milestones in Latin American Media History

1536

The first printing press operates (in Mexico).

1666

The paper *La Gaceta de México* starts publication.

1811

The first printing press arrives in Chile.

1812

The first regularly published newspaper starts: *La Aurora de Chile*.

1813

The first nonofficial newspaper in Latin America appears: *El Seminario Republicano* (Chile).

1826

The first newspaper with political cartoons is launched: *El Iris* (Mexico).

1829

The first daily newspaper appears: *El Mercurio de Valparaíso* (Chile). It is still the oldest continuously published Spanish-language daily in the world.

1934

The first college journalism program in the region is established at the Universidad de La Plata (Argentina).

1942

The National Association of Journalists (Colegio Nacional de Periodistas, or CNP) of Cuba becomes the first institution of this kind in Latin America.

1943

The Inter American Press Association (IAPA) is begun. Also known as Sociedad Interamericana de Prensa (SIP).

1950

On September 18 the first Latin American television broadcast takes place in Brazil.

1952

The IAPA and the International Broadcasting Association (IBA) join forces.

1954

The International Center of Advanced Studies in Journalism for Latin America (Centro Internacional de Estudios Superiores de Periodismo para América Latina, or CIESPAL) is established in Quito, Ecuador.

1957

Lenka Franulic, editor of the magazine *Ercilla*, becomes the first woman to win Chile's national journalism prize.

1962

The Asociación de Mujeres Periodistas del Cono Sur (Association of Women Journalists of the Southern Tip) is founded in Chile.

1976

The Latin American Federation of Press Workers (Federación Latinoamericana de Trabajadores de la Prensa, or FELAP) is established in Buenos Aires.

1985

The Inter-American Court of Human Rights issues an advisory opinion against compulsory licensing of journalists.

1990

Argentina passes a law supporting journalists' privilege to protect their sources. Mexico's newsprint monopoly, PIPSA (Productora e Importado de Papel, Sociedad Anónima), is abolished as compulsory.

1994

The Declaration of Chapultepec (Mexico City, March 11) sets forth ten principles on freedom of the press and expression.

The Declaration of Santiago (Santiago, Chile, May 6) states that access to the practice of journalism must be free.

I

Status of and Issues in Latin American Mass Communication

1

Current Status of the Mass Media in Latin America

Robert T. Buckman

More diverse than homogeneous, Latin America has vast differences among its lands and peoples. Even defining the region depends upon what criteria are selected. This book takes Latin America to be twenty independent nations in the Western Hemisphere that were greatly influenced by Latin cultural traditions from southern Europe, especially Spain and Portugal. Geographically, the area covers the seventeen nations occupying the huge land mass south of the United States, from the Rio Grande in the north to Tierra del Fuego in the south—except for Belize, Guyana, Suriname, and French Guiana—plus the three Caribbean nations of Cuba, the Dominican Republic, and Haiti.

Just as those twenty nations are enormously different geographically, culturally, and economically, so are their mass communication systems, both historically and currently. Freedom of the press everywhere depends upon a nation's culture, general political development, and the particular political administration in power at the time. With the new wave of democracy in Latin America in recent years has come increased press freedom, but it is important to remember that mass communication and press freedom there are somewhat different concepts from what they are in the United States. One general difference historically is that the Latin American press has had a more political character. Latin American newspaper editors have tended to be more political than their counterparts in the United States, but perhaps no more so than in southern Europe, the source of many of their media traditions. In addition, in the mainstream media, news often has been colored conservatively toward the status quo; members of the Latin American media have historically hesitated in showing desacato *(disrespect) toward those in power.*

In this chapter, Robert Buckman provides a masterful synthesis of the mass media situation for Latin America generally and for several individual countries in particular. He sees significantly expanded freedom of expression today, and he is optimistic for press freedom in the future.

Professor Buckman teaches journalism at the University of Southwestern Louisiana in Lafayette, specializing in public affairs reporting, feature writing, and international communication with an emphasis on Latin America. He has worked in the media as a reporter and editor for more than twenty years, with frequent assignments in Latin America, where he has also taught. He has contributed to many books and journals on the region's press. Professor Buckman coauthored the chapter on Latin America and the Caribbean in John Merrill's Global Journalism *(1990), and he has written numerous articles on the Latin American press for* Editor & Publisher. *His study of the cultural content of the area's newspapers and magazines appeared in* Latin American Research Review *(1990).*

Something unprecedented in Latin American history occurred between February 7 and September 30, 1991. Between the former date, when Jean-Bertrand Aristide was inaugurated as Haiti's first democratically elected president, and the latter, when the military overthrew Aristide, nineteen of the twenty Latin American republics were governed by duly elected civilian heads of state. With Aristide's return on October 15, 1994, Fidel Castro's Cuba remains the hemisphere's lone holdout.

This new wave of democracy in Latin America closely parallels that in Eastern Europe and elsewhere in the 1980s, and it ushered in with it the hope for expanded freedom of expression and of the press. Like toppling dominoes, military dictatorships yielded to free elections and constitutional civilian rule: Ecuador in 1978, Peru in 1980, Bolivia, El Salvador, and Honduras in 1982, Argentina in 1983, and Brazil, Uruguay, and Guatemala in 1985. The trend continued in October 1988, when Chile's General Augusto Pinochet lost a plebiscite that would have extended his rule until 1997. He called free presidential elections for December 1989 and turned over the presidential sash to Patricio Aylwin in March 1990, in the process restoring the press freedom Chileans traditionally had enjoyed before the 1973 coup.

Even the hemisphere's longest-ruling despot, Paraguay's General Alfredo Stroessner, who seized power in 1954, fell in February 1989 in a coup led by General Andrés Rodríguez. At first, it was assumed that Rodríguez would continue Paraguay's tradition of one-man rule, but one of his first acts was to lift the five-year-old ban on what had been the country's leading daily newspaper, *ABC Color*. Rodríguez also surprised everyone by subjecting himself to a free election and stepping down when his four-year term was up in 1993. And, in February 1990, Sandinista President Daniel Ortega of Nicaragua was defeated for reelection by, and duly relinquished power to, Violeta Barrios de Chamorro, owner of the daily *La Prensa*, which had felt the heavy hand of repression under both the Sandinistas and the Somoza dictatorship that they toppled in 1979.

Finally, Panama's General Manuel Noriega was ousted from power by the U.S. military intervention in December 1989, and Guillermo Endara, whose election Noriega had nullified the previous May, assumed office. Within days, *La Prensa*, the opposition daily that Noriega's operatives had vandalized and padlocked in 1987, began publishing again, as did another independent daily, *El Siglo*. Two other newspapers, *El Panamá América* and *Crítica*, which had been expropriated by the government of the late strongman Omar Torrijos in 1968, were returned to their rightful owners, the children of their late founder, Harmodio Arias, although it has taken years of litigation to confirm ownership because of the debts incurred during government ownership. *Crítica* was optimistically renamed *Crítica Libre* (Free criticism).

Clearly, democracy is in its ascendancy in Latin America. But does this trend toward popular rule translate into respect for freedom of the press? There have been setbacks and scares, and not only in Haiti, whose media never had been either free or sophisticated. Elected civilian government, it must be pointed out, is not a firm guarantee that press freedom will be respected; politicians and journalists, after all, are by nature adversaries. In several cases in recent years, elected civilian presidents have sought to curtail the media—Venezuela, Peru, and Guatemala being the most dramatic instances. Moreover, journalists and news organizations throughout Latin America still are the frequent targets of assassinations, beatings, lawsuits, vandalism, and other forms of intimidation, whether by government officials, political extremists, or common criminals, whose motive is to cow the media into submission.

The Latin American republics may be likened to twenty planets revolving around a distant star, all different sizes and moving at different speeds. Perhaps once in a thousand years they are in alignment. Such a phenomenon seems to be taking place as the countries become more democratic, although Cuba, with its party-controlled newspapers, government-operated propagandistic broadcast stations, and jailing of dissidents, remains on the far side of the star. Whether this unprecedented alignment of constitutional civilian rule is merely a transitory phenomenon or the harbinger of a permanent order remains to be seen at this writing. Even if it proves to be durable, however, genuine press freedom still is proving elusive.

In examining the media of Latin America, the first step is to discard the North American stereotype of the region as geographically, ethnically, linguistically, culturally, and economically homogenous. Geographically,

Latin America encompasses the deserts of Mexico and Chile; the tropical rain forests of Central America, Colombia, Venezuela, Ecuador, and Brazil; the rarefied atmosphere of the Andean altiplano of Peru and Bolivia; the lush, temperate grasslands and wheat-producing areas of Uruguay, Argentina, and southern Brazil; the rocky, arid Gran Chaco of Paraguay and Bolivia; the California-like Mediterranean climate of central Chile; the dense forests and fjords of southern Chile; and the tundra and glaciers of Patagonia and Tierra del Fuego.

Although most Latin American republics are predominantly mestizo, a blend of European and native American blood, Costa Rica, Argentina, Brazil, and Uruguay are overwhelmingly Caucasian, while the indigenous race is dominant in Guatemala, Peru, and Bolivia. There are significant African-American minorities in Brazil, the Dominican Republic, Cuba, Venezuela, and Panama. Linguistically, the majority of the population of the South American continent is composed of Portuguese-speaking Brazilians, and Spanish remains a secondary language to Quiché in parts of Guatemala, to Quechua in the Peruvian highlands and parts of Bolivia, to Aymara in the rest of Bolivia and to Guaraní in rural Paraguay. Even among Spanish speakers, accent and slang sharply differentiate Mexicans from Argentines, Cubans from Chileans, Venezuelans from Uruguayans. To paraphrase George Bernard Shaw's observation of the British and Americans, the Spanish-speaking Latin Americans are eighteen peoples separated by a common language. In Haiti, French is the lingua franca, but a Creole dialect is the language of the masses.

Culturally, the music, dress, cuisine, and customs vary sharply from one country to another. The hybridization of the indigenous American, colonial European, African American, and the diversity of later immigrants from the Middle East and Asia gave each country a discrete cultural thumbprint, according to how the mix was measured. If there has been any unifying factor in Latin America, it has been the near-universal influence of the Roman Catholic Church over five hundred years, and the characteristically Iberian fondness for authoritarian rule and obsequiousness toward authority.

The North American economic stereotype of Latin America is of an impoverished, backward region. To be sure, Haiti, Honduras, Nicaragua, Peru, and Bolivia are among the most destitute countries on earth, and pockets of squalor stubbornly persist in the major urban areas of some of the more affluent countries, defying economic assimilation into the ever-expanding middle class. That expansion has been uneven but inexorable throughout the region. Latin America's economic growth has been stimulated by investment in the new technological infrastructure, and this growth in turn has had the inevitable impact on the communication media. Symbolic of the march toward the twenty-first century is the 150-meter-tall Entel Tower that dominates Avenida Bernardo O'Higgins in Santiago, Chile, just two blocks from the four-hundred-year-old Moneda Palace. The tower represents the capital city's voice, video, and data links via microwave and satellite with the rest of the country and the world beyond the Andes and the Pacific, the geographic barriers which always had kept Chile isolated. Such modernization is now evident throughout the hemisphere.

The purpose of this examination of the region's diversity is to emphasize that the Latin American media cannot be viewed as a homogenous entity any more than can the other variables just discussed. Media systems are inextricably linked to the political, economic, cultural, and social systems in which they operate. The Latin American media range from the multitude of newspapers and slick magazines and the state-of-the-art radio and television broadcasting systems in affluent and highly literate Argentina, to the primitively written, edited, and published newspapers, the dearth of radio stations or receivers, and the government-owned, elite-oriented television station in dirt-poor, overwhelmingly illiterate Haiti. Those parameters having been established, it also should be stated that any study of the discrete Latin American media must be approached by examining two fundamental subvariables: the social and political milieux in which the media operate and the extent of free expression they are afforded; and the degree of technological advancement and economic viability of the media.

Social and Political Milieux

Virtually all of the political constitutions of Latin America pay lip service to freedom of the press, even in Cuba, but in reality the Iberian legacy of executive-heavy government resulted in a climate in which free expression was deemed of secondary importance to the interests of the state —which was to say, of the man at the top. Censorship and sanctions were the rule in the region rather than the exception. Although the press developed in private hands, it was not unusual for the government to publish an official gazette that guaranteed the reigning strongman a loyal mouthpiece. Even today, Guatemala's *Diario de Centroamérica*, Mexico's *El Nacional*, and Chile's *La Nación* have been in government hands for a succession of presidents of various ideological shades, though the governments of Mexico and Chile now are seeking to privatize their papers. Other newspapers were, and some still are, published by political parties, labor unions, and the Catholic Church. Until the second half of the twentieth century, the only countries where journalists traditionally were allowed to practice their profession in a relatively unfettered environment were Uruguay and Chile, both of which fell under military rule in the early 1970s but which now again enjoy virtually complete press freedom.

Argentina and Brazil wobbled back and forth between democratic and military regimes, including such elected but heavy-handed strongmen as Getulio Vargas in Brazil and Juan Perón in Argentina. Although the press was highly developed in those countries, it endured years of repression. Argentina's *La Prensa*, owned by the Gainza family, and *O Estado de São Paulo*, owned by the Mesquita family, were especially courageous in denouncing their country's respective dictators, and both papers were closed for a time. During the early years of Brazil's military regime of 1964–1985, prior censorship of the major dailies was a way of life. During the Argentine military government of 1976–1983, authorities seized the daily *La Opinión* for alleged ties to leftist guerrillas; its editor, Jacobo Timerman, was jailed, tortured, and finally exiled to Israel in 1979.[1]

Mexico has been ruled since 1929 by the Institutional Revolutionary Party (Partido Revolucionario Institucional, or PRI), a one-party dominant system not unlike that of Alfredo Stroessner's Colorado Party in Paraguay in terms of control and patronage. Unlike in Paraguay, however, Mexican presidents are elected for a six-year term and cannot seek reelection, but even so Mexican democracy has been illusionary at best. The outgoing president simply anointed his successor, and the ruling party went along. In those areas where opposition parties seriously threatened the PRI's dominance, vote fraud was employed to ensure victory.

As for the media, an old-boy network traditionally existed between political leaders and powerful owners of media outlets or chains of media properties, such as Televisa owner Rómulo O'Farrill and newspaper tycoon Mario Vásquez Raña. For publications less willing to accept the status quo, the government wielded an especially convincing cudgel called PIPSA (Productora e Importado de Papel, Sociedad Anónima), the state-owned and subsidized newsprint monopoly. PIPSA sold paper to newspapers and magazines at below cost, a seemingly irresistible deal. But those publications that were overly critical of the PRI and its system often found themselves cut off. In a celebrated case late in the 1970–1976 administration of President Luis Echeverría, government pressure forced the ouster of Julio Scherer García, a persistent critic of Echeverría, as editor of the influential daily *Excélsior*. When García sought to establish the weekly newsmagazine *Proceso*, PIPSA refused to sell him newsprint. Undaunted, García purchased the needed paper at much higher prices on the open market, and *Proceso* appeared and remains a success today.

Another tawdry aspect of Mexican journalism is *la mordida*, a type of bribe to underpaid journalists in exchange for ensuring the publication of information, often paid by the government itself.[2] Rigid broadcast regulation has provided an equally effective brake on criticism from the electronic media.[3] When all else failed, journalists sometimes were murdered. Probably the most celebrated such victim was Manuel Buendía, who wrote a Jack Anderson-style investigative column that appeared each day on the front page of *Excélsior*. He regularly attacked the United States and the CIA, but another favorite target was government corruption. On May 31, 1984, he was gunned down on the street at point-blank range as he left his office. Some abuses have been corrected in Mexico, but physical attacks on journalists remain rampant today.

Colombia and Venezuela both endured more years of dictatorship than democracy until 1958, when the dictatorships of Gustavo Rojas de Pinilla of Colombia and Marcos Pérez Jiménez of Venezuela both fell. Since then, both countries have been characterized by plural democracy in which two major parties regularly alternate in power. In Colombia, newspaper publishers frequently have used their positions as springboards into politics, of both the Liberal and Conservative Parties. The press in Venezuela takes pride in its ostensible neutrality; traditionally, newspapers do not even endorse candidates.[4] In each country the print media have attained some level of sophistication, but the practice of journalism has not enjoyed the same degree of freedom as in Chile or Argentina. Today in Venezuela the pressures derive from officialdom, while in Colombia the threats come from physical violence against journalists from leftist guerrillas and drug traffickers.

Chile's tradition of press freedom and respect for ideas was sorely tested during the elected, but minority, Marxist regime of Salvador Allende in 1970–1973. As public opinion became sharply polarized, so, too, did the press. Previously respectable newspapers began engaging in sensational, often fraudulent reporting to support or condemn one side or the other. After General Augusto Pinochet's military coup on September 11, 1973, all pro-Marxist dailies were banned. The only dailies that remained in the capital were the venerable *El Mercurio, Ultimas Noticias*, and *La Segunda*, all owned by the Edwards family, and *La Tercera de la Hora*, the country's circulation leader, owned by the Picó family. All were generally supportive of the Pinochet regime. The only meaningful opposition came from three opinion magazines, *Apsi, Mensajes*, and *Análisis*, and a weekly newsmagazine, *Hoy*, which Emilio Filippi, the respected former editor of the pro-Pinochet newsmagazine *Ercilla*, launched in 1977. All four opposition magazines were closed for brief periods at one time or another.[5] After a court struggle, Filippi was allowed to establish a daily newspaper, *La Epoca*, in 1987, and it played a leading role in the victory of the "No" forces in the plebiscite of 1988.[6]

In Bolivia and Peru, a brief springtime of democracy and press freedom in the 1950s and 1960s, following decades of quintessential Latin American strongmen, was cut short by the military coups of 1964 and 1968, respectively. The left-leaning military regime in Peru expropriated all the daily newspapers in the capital city of Lima and assigned each to one of the country's "social forces," such as labor unions and intellectuals.[7] When President Fernando Belaunde Terry was elected in 1980, his first act as president was to return the newspapers to their rightful owners. The press in Bolivia remained in private hands, but far from free.

Cuba is an especially tragic case. Ruled by Spain for four centuries until the Spanish-American War of 1898, administered by the United States until its independence in 1903, and economically and politically dominated by the United States thereafter, Cuba was marked by a series of ineffectual and corrupt "democratically" elected presidents. Sergeant Fulgencio Batista seized power in a barracks revolt in 1933 and ruled with a stern hand until 1940, when he relinquished power to a constitutionally elected president. But when Batista ran for president in 1952, he again seized power when defeat appeared imminent. Tolerance of press criticism was not in his nature, although the conservative publishers generally were docile. When Fidel Castro's rebels drove Batista from power on New Year's Day 1959, the situation of the press went from bad to worse. Cuba boasted a number of highly professional newspapers, such as *Diario de la Marina*, but all were closed by the Castro regime by 1961. In their place appeared the Communist Party mouthpiece, *Granma*, named for the boat that brought Castro and his rebels to Cuba in 1956. The popular prerevolution weekly magazine, *Bohemia*, was continued under government control. The broadcast media, of course, also are propaganda vehicles in the Marxist-Leninist model.[8]

The remaining countries of the region—the Dominican Republic, Haiti, Ecuador, Paraguay, and the Central American states—had only fleeting encounters, if any, with democracy or freedom of expression. Most experienced lengthy rule under a despotic strongman: Rafael Leónidas Trujillo in the Dominican Republic (1930–1961); François "Papa Doc" Duvalier in Haiti (1957–1971), followed by his son Jean-Claude "Baby Doc" Duvalier (1971–1986); the elder Anastasio Somoza in Nicaragua (1936–1956) and his like-named son (1967–1979); Jorge Ubico in Guatemala (1931–1944); and Alfredo Stroessner in Paraguay (1954–1989). Honduras, Ecuador, Panama, and Nicaragua all had experience with competing political parties, but the civilian presidents they produced were ousted regularly by the military. In El Salvador and Guatemala, the military had their own political vehicles, and they assured the victory of their candidates through rigged elections.

Independent newspapers did develop, some of them quite respectable, such as *El Imparcial* in Guatemala; *Listín Diario* and *El Caribe* in the Dominican Republic; *El Comercio* and its evening sister paper *Ultimas Noticias* in Quito, and *El Universo* in Guayaquil, Ecuador; *La Tribuna* in Paraguay; and *La Estrella de Panamá* in Panama. However, the ground always was too infertile for meaningful press freedom, if by that term one means an aggressive, investigative press that can editorially criticize the regime without fear of reprisal.

Guatemala, for example, has known only eighteen years of press freedom in 173 years of independence: the liberal period of 1944–1954, and of 1986 to the present. Journalists found themselves caught in the crossfire of a protracted guerrilla war throughout the 1960s and 1970s. Journalists with establishment newspapers often were kidnapped or murdered by left-wing guerrillas; Isidoro Zarco, cofounder of the country's leading daily, *Prensa Libre*, was so murdered in 1970. Left-leaning newspeople, meanwhile, were slain by death squads at the service of the military, and those who sought to be objective ran the risk of incurring the enmity of both sides. More than forty journalists were killed during that period, and a monument to them stands in Guatemala City. Despite the current high degree of press freedom there, journalists continue to be killed.[9]

In Nicaragua, the Chamorro family probably was the most prominent in the country except for the Somozas. *La Prensa*, owned and edited by Pedro Joaquín Chamorro, was a nagging thorn in the side of both the elder and younger Somoza. When Chamorro was gunned down on his way to work in 1978, the assassination galvanized public opinion in favor of the Sandinista guerrillas, and Somoza fell from power a year and a half later. One of Chamorro's sons, also named Pedro, took over *La Prensa*, and soon it was attacking the Marxist excesses of the new order as diligently as it had opposed the misrule of Somoza. Ironically, another Chamorro son became editor of the official Sandinista daily, *Barricada*, while the elder Chamorro's brother, Xavier, established an independent but pro-Sandinista daily, *El Nuevo Diario*. At first, *La Prensa* was spared reprisal out of deference to the elder Chamorro's martyrdom, but eventually legal and extralegal pressures were brought to bear against the paper.[10] These attacks continued until Mrs. Chamorro was elected president in 1990.

Democracy never took firm root in Panama, either. The country gained independence from Colombia in 1903 through the intrigues of U.S. president Theodore Roosevelt, who quickly won exclusive territorial rights to construct the Panama Canal. Although civilian presidents frequently were elected, the military often intervened to remove them. The press was in private hands, and the daily *La Estrella de Panamá* dates to 1853, one of the hemisphere's oldest. When Omar Torrijos seized power in 1968, he allowed *La Estrella* to remain in the hands of the Altamirano Duque family, provided it followed a supportive editorial line, and he expropriated two newspapers, *El Panamá América* and *Crítica,* owned by Harmodio Arias. *La Prensa*, launched by businessman I. Roberto Eisenmann in 1980, and its staff were subjected to intimidation and vandalism during both the Torrijos and Noriega regimes. Eisenmann was exiled twice, once forcibly by Torrijos and once voluntarily because of death threats from Noriega henchmen. Noriega ordered *La Prensa* (not connected with the Nicaraguan paper of the same name) closed in July 1987. The regime also shut down another daily, *El Siglo*, and several radio stations and cowed the two privately owned television channels into submission. The civilian president himself controlled one television station, and the armed forces another.[11]

In the Dominican Republic, a period of turbulence followed the assassination of Trujillo in 1961, leading to U.S. military intervention in 1965. The following year, Joaquín Balaguer was elected president, and he has dominated Dominican politics ever since. He was reelected in 1970 and 1974. When the election returns went against him in 1978, he sought to suspend vote-counting, but pressure from the Carter administration forced him to respect the verdict at the polls. After two intervening presidents, Balaguer reclaimed the presidency in 1986 and was reelected in 1990 and 1994. The press is generally free, although it seldom seems to criticize Balaguer.

Paraguay represents an intriguing case of a press struggling first to exist and then to survive in an impoverished, isolated, and autocratic country. Aldo Zucolillo, a businessman, established an attractive, colorful tabloid named *ABC Color* in 1967, and it soon replaced the venerable *La Tribuna* as the country's principal newspaper. *La Tribuna* folded, then reappeared, and two other dailies joined the market in the 1970s: *Hoy*, owned by Humberto Domínguez Dibb, dictator Alfredo Stroessner's son-in-law, and *Ultima Hora*, an evening tabloid owned by Demetrio Rojas. This writer, then a government employee stationed at the U.S. embassy in Asunción, watched from the sidelines as these dailies, emboldened by the human rights initiatives of U.S. president Jimmy Carter, began engaging in unprecedented investigative reporting; there was much to investigate! After Domínguez Dibb separated from Stroessner's daughter, even *Hoy* began digging up dirt on the regime. Stroessner's onerous interior minister, Sabino Montanaro, closed *La Tribuna* and *Ultima Hora* for thirty days in 1979. *ABC Color* became the leading critic of the dictatorship. One of its columnists, Alcibiades González Delvalle, was twice arrested, and Stroessner had the paper closed in April 1984. In its place soon appeared a new daily, *El Diario*, launched by a car dealer and Stroessner confidant, Nicolás Bo, who went on to open Paraguay's first private television station. The presses of *ABC Color* remained silent for five years, until Stroessner was ousted and exiled to Brazil in 1989.

Although the trend now is toward democracy in the region, there are some troubling legacies of the authoritarian past that linger stubbornly. The attempts by the elected civilian presidents of Peru, Venezuela, and Guatemala to collar the press, always in the name of preservation of order, were only the most overt efforts. But Latin American governments have long had subtle legal measures that they can use to cow a recalcitrant publication or broadcast station in lieu of outright seizure or censorship or, in the more draconian cases, the jailing, exile, or murder of journalists. These measures include tax audits on corporate or personal income, property taxes, and value-added taxes on the sales of publications or advertising; building inspections; the granting or withholding of advertising for government-owned institutions such as public utilities, mass transit, or national lotteries; broadcast licensing; the statutory licensing of journalists, requiring them to have a journalism degree and to hold membership in a *colegio*, or guild; libel suits by public officials and right-of-reply laws that require newspapers to give equal time to someone criticized in print; and in the case of Mexico until fairly recently, a government monopoly on the sale of newsprint, which could be withheld selectively.[12]

The growing tolerance by governments toward the exercise of aggressive, independent journalism does not mean, unfortunately, that it is now safer to practice the profession than before. Dozens of Latin American journalists are slain every year, not by the order of high-level government officials but by political extremists, drug traffickers and other organized criminals, robber barons, local political bosses, renegade members of public security forces, in short, anyone who perceives a threat from the spotlight of journalistic scrutiny. The worst such violence has come in Colombia, Peru, Mexico, and Guatemala.

For a current assessment of the media climate in Latin America, the best source is the Miami-based Inter American Press Association (IAPA), which is composed of thirteen hundred member newspapers in North and South America, including the United States, Canada, and the English-speaking countries of the Caribbean. Twice each year, at its general assembly and midyear meeting, the IAPA issues its *Freedom of the Press Report*, which provides a detailed overview of the state of press freedom in each country. Even the United States is taken to task for cases of reporters' being jailed for contempt for refusing to divulge news sources.

Among the twenty Latin American republics, the highest marks in the *Freedom of the Press Reports* of 1990–1994 go to Argentina, Bolivia, Chile, the Dominican Republic, Ecuador, Honduras, Nicaragua, Paraguay, and Uruguay. Here, the IAPA has concluded, the press generally operates without restrictions, although the organization faults them for sporadic individual cases of taxation laws, harassing libel suits, nongovernmental intimidation, and the like. Of these, Nicaragua and Paraguay deserve special mention; no countries in the region have shown more dramatic progress, evolving from situations characterized by the most severe repression into press systems that operate freely and effectively with far fewer problems than might be expected given their level of underdevelopment and their lack of experience with democratic institutions.

In the remaining countries, and even in those just mentioned, there are various official and extra-official restrictions on the practice of journalism, ranging from harassing lawsuits to assassination at the hands of killers in the service of public officials, guerrillas, or criminals. Whichever tactic is employed, and whoever is responsible for violent acts against journalists, the effect is the same: intimidation to prevent information from being freely disseminated. In some cases, notably Mexico, Colombia, and Peru, the pressure on the media comes from both flanks. As will be seen in the following examination (based on the IAPA's *Freedom of the Press Reports* for the past five years unless otherwise noted), no two countries have the same fingerprint. What follows is a discussion of significant recent events in thirteen countries, in descending order from the most promising to the least promising outlook for press freedom.

Argentina. Although press freedom is highly respected here and jealously protected, one troubling event was the reappearance in 1993 of Argentina's *desacato* statute, a kind of criminal libel. It provides up to five days in jail for lawyers, litigants, and "other persons" who in writing or other types of communication "impugn the authority or dignity or decorum" of judges. Although journalists are not specifically mentioned, the threat against them is tangible. On the positive side, Argentine law since 1990 has honored their privilege to protect confidential sources— for which journalists in other countries, including the United States, frequently are held in contempt—and has given them immunity from liability for erroneous news reports if they are unaware that the reports are false, a guarantee patterned after the "reckless disregard" provision in the 1964 U.S. Supreme Court decision in *New York Times v. Sullivan*. The Argentine Supreme Court recognized a "right of reply" in a 1992 decision, but President Carlos Menem has voiced his disagreement and said he would introduce no enabling legislation. For the most part, the Argentine press is as free as, and in some cases freer than, its counterparts in North America and Europe.

Chile. A law proposed by President Patricio Aylwin that would have required a university degree to practice journalism became stalled in the Congress, and Aylwin's successor, Eduardo Frei, appears uninterested in pushing it. Had such a law been in effect in the 1960s, Isabel Allende, Chile's world-renowned novelist, would have been unable to get her start in magazine journalism. On the down side, a military court ordered the seizure of copies of the Santiago daily *La Epoca* for carrying information on the investigation into the 1976 murder of Spanish diplomat Carmelo Soria, allegedly by members of the security forces. Except for these notable cases, Chile's press has reclaimed the liberty that was once a beacon for the rest of the region.

One of the most dramatic changes in the Chilean mass media has come to its unique television broadcasting model. The first three television stations in the early 1960s were licensed neither to the government nor to private investors but to major universities. That system still exists today; the University of Chile owns Channel 11, Catholic University of Chile has Channel 13 (the country's dominant station) and Catholic University of Valparaiso operates Channel 5. The government of the elder President Eduardo Frei licensed a government station, TV Nacional, on Channel 7 in 1969, and this mixed model endured during both the Marxist government of Salvador Allende and the military regime of Augusto Pinochet. Shortly before relinquishing power, Pinochet granted licenses for the first two privately owned stations. Steamship magnate Ricardo Claro owns Megavisión on Channel 9, and Alvaro Saieh, a banker who owns the country's two largest dailies and the newsmagazine *Que Pasa*, launched La Red on Channel 4.[13] Economic reverses of the University of Chile's station forced TV Nacional to assume operational control in 1991. The civilian government recently has expressed an interest in privatizing TV Nacional and the government-owned daily newspaper, *La Nación*. Although it is government-owned, TV Nacional has proven itself to be highly professional and objective in its news coverage since the end of the Pinochet era, much like the BBC in Britain.

Brazil. Because of its transition to democracy and press freedom since 1985 and because of the aggressive role of its press in exposing the corruption that led to the impeachment and removal from office of President Fernando Collor de Melo in 1992, Brazil is an intriguing case. In 1990, the daily *Folha de São Paulo* was invaded by federal auditors who examined the company's books, apparently in retaliation for a series of articles alleging that Collor had awarded two advertising agencies lucrative government contracts without advertising for bids as a means of retiring some of Collor's U.S. $70-$80 million campaign debt. The president also filed a defamation suit.

Collor is gone, but the travails of the press continue. The IAPA has complained that although the new 1988 constitution prohibits any restrictions on the press, the old press law of the military regime remains on the books like a Sword of Damocles. Libel and defamation suits are favorite weapons by public officials against the press, and under the old press law, truth is not a defense. In 1990, Otavio Frias Filho, managing editor of *Folha de São Paulo*, was sentenced to seven months in jail and fined three months' pay after a federal deputy sued him for defamation over the wording of headlines used to describe him. The sentence later was suspended on condition that the editor perform community service. Two other journalists were sentenced to six and eight months of confinement for defaming a former Supreme Court president, although in March 1993 the sentence was reduced to a fine. The country's new president, Itamar Franco, filed a libel suit in April 1993 against a columnist for *Folha de São Paulo* who alleged that the president granted favoritism in awarding bids for privatization of the state-owned steel company. Since then several other journalists have been sued by public officials for perceived insults against their integrity, and a judge in Rio Grande do Sul state proscribed the publication of a column in the newspaper *Diario da Manhã* in Passo Fundo that reported on local commissioners voting on a Christmas bonus for themselves.

Other legal measures have had a chilling effect on the free exercise of journalism. The IAPA is troubled by Brazil's Child and Adolescent Statute, which allows courts to seize newspapers or to suspend broadcast stations that report the names of juvenile offenders. The police also investigated two journalists with *Folha de São Paulo* for "illegally" practicing their profession because they lacked university degrees, but the courts dropped the investigation. Finally, there have been numerous incidents of death threats against journalists, and at least one outspoken newsman, João Alberto Ferreira Souto, owner of *Jornal de Estado* in Bahia state, was murdered in February 1994. He had been highly critical of local politicians.

Costa Rica. This near-idyllic little country threw off its long-standing military yoke in 1949, abolished the army, and encouraged a free marketplace of ideas, becoming an enclave of two-party democracy and stability in a region of despotism and turbulence. Costa Rica today holds the record in Latin America for the longest uninterrupted period of constitutional rule. Yet, since 1969, journalists have been required to hold a degree and to belong to a *colegio*, and they frequently are subjected to government coercion and lawsuits. In January 1993, for example, the editor of a provincial newspaper was sentenced to ten days in jail and fined U.S. $900 for libeling a former congressman by reporting on mysterious landings and takeoffs by light planes on his property, implying that they were involved in illegal activity. And, in December 1992, a journalist with the government-owned National Radio and Television System (SINART) alleged that her scheduled program on Channel 13 had been canceled because a group of panelists would be critical of the government's garbage collection program in the capital of San José. The newly appointed SINART general director denied the allegations, but the journalist's contract with the station was not renewed. She went to court and was ordered reinstated.

In January 1994 a journalist with the program *Telenoticias* on Channel 7 was summarily fired, allegedly because of political pressure from aides to winning presidential candidate José María Figueres. The program was about to air allegations by his opponent that Figueres was guilty of banking irregularities. The program's editor and four other journalists resigned to protest her firing.

Colombia. The principal danger to journalists in Colombia is physical, traditionally coming not from the government but from drug lords and leftist guerrillas. In one of the most celebrated acts of violence, Guillermo Cano, the respected editor of the Bogotá daily *El Espectador*, was gunned down on December 17, 1986, while driving near his office, a reprisal for his attacks on drug kingpin Pablo Escobar of the infamous Medellín cartel. The cartel bombed the office of *El Espectador* in September 1989.[14] The government had formally charged Escobar with Cano's murder before Escobar himself was slain by security forces in December 1993.

The cartel's war on journalists reached a crescendo in 1990, when members of the cartel threatened to execute members of the Cano family. *El Espectador* suspended all editorials for two weeks to protest the government's failure to provide adequate safeguards. In August, Diana Turbay, publisher of the newspaper *Hoy por Hoy* and the daughter of former president Julio César Turbay Ayala, was kidnapped; she was killed during a police rescue operation the following January. In September 1990, the Medellín cartel kidnapped Francisco Santos Calderón, news editor of the prestigious *El Tiempo* in Bogotá; he was released the following May. The violence continued into 1992, when six journalists were slain during a six-month period.

By 1994, after Escobar's death and the virtual dissolution of the Medellín cartel, the attacks on journalists had dissipated dramatically and were coming almost exclusively from guerrillas, with at least one death attributed to five members of the army. The still-powerful Cali cartel, allegedly headed by the Rodríguez Orejuela brothers, Gilberto and Miguel, generally has eschewed violence, preferring instead to bribe politicians or journalists as well as to control various communication media. According to *Forbes*, the Rodríguez Orejuelas own twenty-eight radio stations.[15] Although the Cali cartel has not generally been known to murder Colombian journalists, the third leading figure in the Cali cartel, José Santacruz Londoño, allegedly ordered the March 11, 1992, assassination in New York City of Manuel de Dios Unanue, a muckraking journalist and editor who had exposed the Cali cartel's operations in New York.[16] But the danger persists, and the press apparently has even more enemies. In January 1994 a journalist in Cúcuta whose radio program was known for airing public complaints was killed as he entered the station, and in April a reporter and a photographer for *El Espectador* were murdered in the village of Segovia, where they had gone to report on the violence. It was unclear whether the murders were the work of guerrillas or paramilitary groups.

Obviously, then, journalism remains a high-risk occupation in Colombia. In addition to the violence, there are increasing legal pressures coming from the Colombian government, especially the use of the "legal protection measure," or injunction, provided in the country's new constitution. In numerous instances, government agencies have obtained such injunctions against print and broadcast media, both gag orders and orders requiring rectifications of news reports. In one case, a Barranquilla court ordered three newspapers to pay the debts of a dead singer after the papers had violated an order not to report on the singer's alleged extramarital activities. The Constitutional Court, meanwhile, decreed that newspaper cartoonists must "eliminate abuses and exaggerations," which strikes at the very modus operandi of political satire. Perhaps the most chilling restriction came in the form of a new law, enacted in 1993, that prohibits the broadcast media from airing interviews with terrorists or drug traffickers without first obtaining permission from the Ministry of Information. The law, which is to be in effect for two years, also bans the live airing of terrorist or subversive acts in progress.

Mexico. Perhaps in no other country of the region is the gap between press freedom promised and press freedom fulfilled more apparent than in Mexico. New hope came with the narrow, and still suspect, election in 1988 of reform-minded President Carlos Salinas de Gortari, who became the first president to honor PRI electoral defeats for state governorships rather than resorting to vote fraud. His most lasting reform in terms of the media was the abolition of the fifty-four-year-old newsprint monopoly on April 20, 1990. The following year, Salinas announced plans to privatize two of the four state-owned television stations, with the other two being placed in the control of universities or intellectual groups, as well as to sell the official government newspaper, *El Nacional.* In his dealings with the media, Salinas has proven to be refreshingly accessible and cognizant of the press's role.

There still are dark, ominous clouds in Mexico. As the IAPA noted in its 1990 *Freedom of the Press Report,* "the press in Mexico oscillates between the president's pledge to respect it and the desire of some bureaucrats to prevent it, at times violently." The 1984 assassination of Manuel Buendía, the investigative columnist for *Excélsior,* already has been noted. In January 1993, two former officials of the Dirección Federal de Seguridad, the Mexican equivalent of the FBI, and three policemen were arrested and subsequently convicted of Buendía's murder. The government officially closed the case with the conviction, but Mexican journalists continue to raise doubts whether the intellectual perpetrators behind the crime were among those convicted.

Buendía was merely the most prominent journalist to become a victim of violence. Each year, the IAPA chronicles a lengthy list of journalists who have been murdered, wounded, beaten, arrested, or threatened, and media entities that have been closed, bombed, or vandalized, usually by middle- and lower-level federal and state officials, including military and police. Many media have been intimidated into a form of self-censorship. To cite one example in 1993, unknown persons confiscated copies of the daily *La Jornada* in La Paz, Baja California, apparently because of a photograph of the local federal deputy sleeping during a congressional debate. There were numerous attempts to squelch media coverage of the peasant rebellion in Chiapas state early in 1994. Though the level of physical violence against journalists is not as grave as in Colombia, the climate of intimidation is palpable. The situation prompted Interior Minister Patrocino González Garrido to comment in December 1993: "We cannot guarantee in Mexico that nothing will ever happen to a journalist. What is important is that nothing happens as a result of carrying out his or her duties, for the truths the journalist expresses and maintains." Unfortunately, that is precisely what is happening.

Panama. As in Brazil, Panama's press, despite the collapse of the military dictatorship, until recently had continued to live under the old press law adopted during the Torrijos regime, which, among other things, provided for criminal sanctions for alleged defamation.[17] President Endara, not known for his thick skin, sued a political cartoonist at *La Prensa* in 1991 after publication of a cartoon that implied that he had taken a bribe for releasing two Noriega henchmen on bail. Nothing came of the suit, but it was a reminder that the climate for freedom of expression remained chilly.[18] When Ernesto Pérez Balladares, the candidate of Noriega's old political vehicle, was elected to succeed Endara in May 1994, the outlook for press freedom suddenly seemed even bleaker. But two days after the election, Balladares announced that he would repeal the old press laws. "I don't believe we should stay with a law that gives discretionary powers to the minister of interior and justice, and I feel anyone who thinks he has been damaged by a journalist should use civil remedies, not penal ones," Balladares proclaimed.[19] Coincidentally or not, one of Balladares's two vice presidents is Tomás Gabriel Altamirano Duque, the publisher of *La Estrella de Panamá*, whom Torrijos had coerced into editorial obsequiousness in 1968.

El Salvador. The Salvadoran press was caught in the cross fire of the 1979–1992 civil war. Right-wing death squads targeted leftist journalists, while the left-wing guerrillas carried out attacks against the conservative, mainstream media, such as the daily newspaper *El Diario de Hoy*, or physical attacks against their journalists. In 1991 a left-wing daily, *Diario Latino*, was torched by apparent arsonists.[20]

The government and the guerrillas signed a peace accord in January 1992, and the press has begun to function with some degree of normality. But the IAPA is concerned over the country's outdated press laws and new legislation, such as the electoral code, that threatens to restrict press freedom by banning the publication or broadcasting of certain types of propaganda and even party advertising during campaigns. The press and society of El Salvador both have a long way to go and many lessons to learn, but considering the bloodletting from which they have just emerged, the outlook there must be described as optimistic.

Venezuela. In one of the three worst cases of governmental attacks on the press in recent years, President Pérez imposed prior censorship in the wake of two coup attempts in February and November 1992, ostensibly to preserve the constitutional order but also apparently to thwart interviews with coup leaders and, in the first crackdown, even to prevent local coverage of his own press conference with foreign journalists.[21] In June that same year, army troops invaded the daily *El Nacional* in Caracas and established a military court that began interrogating the newspaper staff. The head of the Supreme Court of Justice ordered the detention of Diógenes Carillo of the newspaper *El Nuevo País* and of Radio Rumbos for criticizing, in his opinion column, the judge's assertion that he had no jurisdiction in the case of suspected corruption by Pérez. In late August, the television program of prominent commentator José Vicente Rangel on Channel 10 was suspended for a week. After the November coup attempt, Radio Rumbos was taken off the air for seven days, allegedly for inciting rebellion. Congress also enacted the Law on Protection of Privacy on Information, seen as an effort to quell investigative reporting, by which journalists who reported on the contents of private telephone conversations would face up to four years' imprisonment. It also amended the constitution to include a right of reply clause and to prohibit exclusive ownership of the news media in a specific geographic area.

Other attacks on the Venezuelan press that turbulent year were more violent. In January, even before the first coup attempt, journalist María Verónica Tessari was killed when a policeman hit her in the head with a tear gas canister. In September, Jean Hope Phelps, cofounder of the newspaper *Diario de Caracas*, was shot in the head by three armed men near her home. Other executives of the paper had received death threats prior to the attack, which was reported to the authorities, but no action was taken. As of this writing two years later, she remains in a coma, and the crime remains unsolved. Military or intelligence personnel were suspected in the deaths of three other journalists during 1992. In February 1993 opposition deputies in Congress released an "enemies list" of Pérez opponents, including Rangel and at least three other prominent journalists, who had become targets of government harassment.

Critics of Pérez charged that he was motivated primarily by mounting press reportage of alleged corruption in his administration. These changes turned out to be true, and Pérez was impeached and removed from office late in 1993. Nor was Pérez, a member of the Democratic Action Party, the first Venezuelan president to prove thin-skinned over press cri-ticism. In 1980, President Luis Herrera Campíns of the Social Christian Party, also known by its old acronym COPEI, refused to grant permission for a ship to dock that was carrying newsprint for a newspaper that had been harshly critical of the president. Only when the paper's management agreed to tone down the attacks was the newsprint offloaded.[22]

The post-Pérez climate appears somewhat more promising. Rafael Poleo, owner and editor of *El Nuevo País* and of the weekly magazines *Zeta* and *Auténtico*, returned to Caracas in June 1993 after two years in self-imposed exile in Miami, the result of death threats following his publications' attacks on the corruption of the Pérez regime. However, the administration of President Rafael Caldera of the COPEI Party got off to an inauspicious start in February 1994 when three journalists were severely beaten by members of the presidential guard during the inauguration ceremony. Moreover, a bill proposed by the Venezuelan *colegio* that would require a university degree to practice journalism and mandatory licensing by the *colegio* was pending in Congress in mid-1994.

Peru. In the second major case of a civilian president clamping down on the media in the name of law and order, President Alberto Fujimori briefly imposed draconian restrictions on the media, including censorship, when he staged his self-coup in April 1992. In a case that caused an international stir, Gustavo Gorriti, local correspondent for Spain's *El País* and a specialist on the Sendero Luminoso (Shining Path) guerrillas, was held under house arrest for two days without charges, and his computer and personal files were seized. The computer was returned but with its hard drive erased. Gorriti accused Vladimiro Montesinos, a presidential assistant, of instigating the seizure because of a critical article he had written about Montesinos for the Peruvian newsmagazine *Caretas*. Whether the charge was true or not, Montesinos sued *Caretas* editor Enrique Zileri for libel for having referred to him several months earlier as a "Rasputin." The Supreme Court upheld lower court judgments against Zileri and blocked publication of a cover story on Montesinos.

After visiting the offices of the influential daily *El Comercio*, Fujimori lifted the censorship after only two days, and since then he generally has permitted the media to function normally. However, the IAPA has taken Fujimori to task for the slow pace of the prosecution of two military men linked to the 1988 murder of Hugo Bustíos of *Caretas*. Several journalists have been arrested on various charges, held without trial, and then released. In a case reminiscent of General William Westmoreland's lawsuit against CBS, retired General Clemente Noel, former commander of the Ayacucho emergency zone, sued two journalists, one Peruvian and one Spaniard, over a television report in which he was accused of witnessing the torture of suspected terrorists in 1982. The Spaniard, César Hildebrandt, failed to return to Peru to appear in court and was found in contempt; the Peruvian, Cecilia Valenzuela, was sentenced to a year of "conditional prison" in 1993. The IAPA also complains that a number of laws remain on the books in Peru that either restrict the media or are subtle threats against them. As in Colombia, the overt threat to journalists continues to come from drug traffickers and guerrillas, particularly Sendero Luminoso. At least thirty-five journalists were slain in Peru during the height of the violence from 1980 through 1992. In 1995, President Fujimori was overwhelmingly reelected.

Guatemala. In the third case of a civilian leader suspending constitutional guarantees, President Jorge Serrano suddenly declared a state of emergency and ordered prior censorship of both print and broadcast media in May 1993. His ostensible justification was much like Fujimori's: the country's economic plight and a protracted guerrilla war required a strong hand unencumbered by constitutional niceties. The capital city's four highly competitive dailies suddenly found common cause in opposing this attack on their newly won freedom. When the censors arrived at *Prensa Libre*, the leading daily, its director, Mario Antonio Sandoval, cowed them by handing them a black marker and the page proofs and threatening to publish the paper with their marks on the pages. They left, but early the next morning armed police surrounded the building to prevent distribution of that day's edition. A few copies were smuggled out, and thousands were disseminated using copy machines and faxes. Another daily, *El Gráfico*, agreed to self-censorship but ran blank opinion columns on its editorial page. A third daily, *Siglo Veintiuno* (Twenty-first century) changed its flag to read *Siglo Catorce—Era de Oscurantismo* (Fourteenth century—the Dark Ages). When the board of directors of *Prensa Libre* met with President Serrano and agreed to self-censorship, Sandoval resigned in protest, arguing that prior censorship makes it possible to outwit the censors. Public protests also mounted against Serrano, and after seven days he was forced to step down. The congress elected Ramiro de León Carpio, a human rights champion, as his successor. De León Carpio immediately restored full press freedom and has continued to respect it.[23]

Physical attacks on journalists or members of their families have been widespread in Guatemala both before and after Serrano's abortive self-coup. In one incident in November 1990, Byron Barrera, cofounder with his brother of the Acen Siag news agency and vice president of the Guatemalan Association of Journalists, was severely wounded in an ambush while driving in his car with his wife. He survived; she did not. The murder remains unsolved, and he lives in exile in Costa Rica. The wife and daughter of Marco Vinicio Mejía, a journalist and political satirist, were kidnapped and murdered. Víctor Manuel Cruz, a reporter for Radio Sonora, was gunned down in a similar fashion in December 1993. The most prominent victim was Jorge Carpio Nicolle, owner of *El Gráfico*, a losing presidential candidate in 1985 and 1990, and first cousin of President de León Carpio. He was wounded and bled to death in a northern city in July 1993 in what appeared at first to have been a routine robbery. But his widow has since charged before a meeting of the United Nations (UN) Human Rights Commission in Geneva that he was slain by a group of vigilantes allegedly receiving government support. The case is unsolved. There have been numerous other threats or attempts against journalists' lives.

Haiti. Little promising can be said about Haiti. Its people are so poor and illiterate that neither print nor broadcast media have developed there beyond the most rudimentary form, and a succession of dictatorships have either controlled or intimidated the few media that do exist. Although Aristide is a democratically elected president, journalists who have been critical of him have received threats, and his government has taken little or no action to protect members of the media from such intimidation.

The UN economic sanctions in effect at this writing also have an adverse effect on the continued functioning of the media. The most exciting development in Haiti is the recent appearance of a clandestine station, Radio Sole Leve, which carries provocative programs and news reports opposing the military government. While the establishment media publish or broadcast in French, Radio Sole Leve broadcasts in Creole, the language of the masses.[24]

Cuba. The wrenching economic changes that have beset Cuba since even before the fall of its primary benefactor, the Soviet Union, have been profoundly manifested in the island's totalitarian media apparatus. The official daily newspaper, *Granma*, was forced to cut back from six issues a week to five outside Havana in 1990 because of newsprint shortages. That same year, *Juventud Rebelde*, the Communist Party's youth newspaper, and *Trabajadores*, the workers' organ, switched from daily to weekly publication. *Bohemia* was cut severely in number of pages, while *Bastión*, the armed forces newspaper, was discontinued. According to information published in the Mexican newsmagazine *Proceso*, which cites Cuban sources, a few years after the cut-off of Soviet aid the supply of newsprint had decreased from 24,000 to 6,000 metric tons for newspapers and from 12,000 to 3,200 tons for magazines. Fuel shortages, meanwhile, had forced a 35 percent reduction in broadcast time. More than 1,100 journalists had been reassigned or laid off. The situation for the mass media, especially print, has continued to deteriorate as the Cuban economy has suffered.

It is Cuba's appalling disregard for human rights, however, that most profoundly sets it apart from its sister republics of Latin America. During 1988–1990 there were stirrings of what at first appeared to be a Cuban-style glasnost. Occasional objective and even provocative articles began appearing in *Juventud Rebelde* and the magazine *Revolución y Cultura*, published by the Writers and Artists Union, which the IAPA interpreted as the beginnings of intellectual debate. Moreover, the authorities tolerated the appearance of an underground publication, *Religión en Cuba*. Another underground publication, *Criterio Alternativo*, appeared in 1990, published on a mimeograph machine. An underground magazine called *Franqueza* also began circulating. Huber Jerez Mariño, a former writer for the official magazines *Verde Olivo* and *Bohemia*, organized the Cuban Association of Independent Journalists (Asociación de Periodistas Independientes de Cuba, or APIC). Perhaps the most tantalizing indicator of possible reform came from Julio García Luis, president of the official journalists' union, who said in a *Juventud Rebelde* interview that the state-

and party-controlled media model "no longer has anything to offer us Cubans" and denounced the use of propaganda over genuine news. He advocated "authentic journalism, but within the guidelines of the sole party."

Alas, the hope that freedom of expression was blooming in Cuba was quickly dashed. *Religión en Cuba* ceased publication before the year was out after its publisher, Enrique López Oliva, received threats from the authorities. APIC was banned in 1990. Jerez Mariño and two other dissident journalists, Elizardo Sánchez Santa Cruz and Hiram Abi Cobas, were sentenced to two years in prison in 1989 for talking with U.S. reporters about the execution of two Cuban officers for treason. When Jerez Mariño began circulating a one-page, handwritten publication called *La Bartolina* among his fellow prisoners, he was transferred to the maximum-security Kilo 7 prison in Camagüey Province and placed in solitary confinement. For forty-two days he received only half his normal rations in reprisal for a letter he wrote to the Nicaraguan president Violeta Chamorro. When he was released in February 1991, he reported to the Coordinating Committee of Human Rights about the beating of three dissidents in prison who had refused to wear the prison garb of common criminals.

Franqueza publisher Samuel Martínez Lara, who also was general secretary of the dissident Human Rights Party, was arrested in March 1990. Roberto Luque Escalona, author of the book *Fidel: The Judgment of History*, published in Mexico, was fired from his post at the University of Havana and later arrested for voicing criticism of the government. He was allowed to leave for Mexico in 1992, but his teenaged son was not allowed to join him, although he had been granted an exit visa. In 1993 various Latin American artists and musicians wrote a letter urging the Cuban government to allow Luque's son, Ernesto, also a musician, to leave the country.

In 1992, APIC boldly requested official recognition, leading to a campaign of intimidation against its handful of members. APIC's new president, Néstor S. Baguer, and a vice president, Elías Valentín Noa, were arrested on August 3 that year, questioned for several hours about APIC's activities, and informed that the organization was illegal and would not be tolerated. Fifteen days later, as he was walking down a street, Baguer received a karate chop from a passing cyclist that required three stitches to his head. Noa was allowed to leave Cuba on August 28. Baguer was assaulted a second time in February 1993 by two men who beat him up as he left his house. Mobs of so-called Rapid Response Brigades held Baguer under virtual house arrest, and his telephone was bugged. In February 1994 two men entered Baguer's house, beat him, ripped the telephone from the wall, and left with it. Baguer was seventy-two at the time.

These were just some of the more visible cases. Other cases abound, and Cuban journalists continue to risk unemployment, physical harm, or imprisonment for advocating greater freedom of expression. The few foreign correspondents based in Cuba also faced tighter restrictions. Authorities began granting fewer visas to other foreign journalists, and those who entered Cuba with tourist visas were expelled. In its 1991 *Freedom of the Press Report*, the IAPA listed thirty dissident journalists and writers known to be in prison for expressing opinions, and two years later the number had risen to more than fifty. Its 1992 report stated that forty-eight journalists and intellectuals had been fired for participating in or collaborating with such groups as APIC or for publicly advocating democratic reforms. The following year the IAPA reported that "the tiny space that dissident journalists and foreign correspondents had to operate within Cuba through 1992 has been shrunk even more, if that is imaginable." Discontent has been growing even within the ranks of the Union of Cuban Journalists and Writers, and at least three prominent journalists sought political asylum in November 1993 and February 1994 while traveling abroad, two in Puerto Rico and one in Rome. Cuba has become a kind of international waiting game, with speculation rife on when the Castro regime will fall. When or if it does, there appears to be a cadre of reform-minded journalists eager to bring Cuba's media system into concert with the rest of Latin America.

In March 1994, after a year of preparatory work, an eclectic assemblage of editors, journalists, writers, scholars, constitutional law experts, and political leaders met for three days at Chapultepec Palace overlooking Mexico City for the historic Hemisphere Conference on Free Speech. Former UN secretary-general Javier Pérez de Cuellar of Peru chaired the conference. On March 11 the participants signed the Declaration of Chapultepec, which sets forth ten principles on freedom of the press and expression which all the countries of the hemisphere have been called upon to endorse. (Most of the text of the Declaration appears in the Conclusions section of this book).

A few years ago such a declaration would have been little more than wishful thinking, but as more and more Latin American governments have abandoned their traditional intolerance to criticism, and as support has grown for the free interchange of ideas, the principles outlined at Chapultepec are closer to being realized than at any period in Latin American history. As this chapter has demonstrated, these principles will continue to fall on some deaf ears—Fidel Castro, the Haitian strongmen, drug traffickers, guerrillas, local political bosses, and midlevel public officials—but there is no mistaking that the trend now favors the forces of democracy for the first time.

Economic and Technological Factors

In some respects the print media of various Latin American countries are reminiscent of those of the United States three or four decades ago. It is common today to have a multitude of daily newspapers published in the capital cities and even to have two or more competing papers in large provincial capitals. Unlike in the United States, however, many of these capital city newspapers are circulated nationally rather than locally. The reason why newspaper diversity is still common in Latin America while one-newspaper cities are the norm in the United States is simply explained: much lower labor costs and, until recently, relatively low overhead expenses.

This situation began changing in the early 1980s, as the pressure for modernization in the computer age began to take its toll on papers with marginal financial situations. Two of the hemisphere's oldest and most respected newspapers, *El Imparcial* of Guatemala and *La Prensa* of Peru, folded during this period. Latin America's pioneer weekly newsmagazine, Chile's *Ercilla*, succumbed in November 1991 to the new economic realities of high-cost hardware and increased competition for finite advertising revenue.[25] New newspapers and magazines continue to appear, however, and some of them take root but not without adequate capitalization. In most cases, this means that newspapers and magazines still are primarily in the hands of the elite, and that Latin America is facing the same social dilemma as the United States—lack of access to the mass media for the entire population.

The publications that do survive are, for the most part, highly professional in appearance, with quality writing and state-of-the art color and graphics. Others, especially those in the less-developed countries, are more primitive, but the fact that they exist and serve the needs of an audience is what is important. Some of the more successful slick magazines enjoy a circulation in neighboring countries, such as Brazil's *Manchete*, whose photography compensates for the language barrier, Colombia's *Cromos*, and Argentina's *La Semana*. Latin America's broadcasting systems are a peculiar hybrid of the U.S. model of privately owned, commercially supported, entertainment-based stations and the European model of state-owned and subsidized public service-oriented stations. In many countries, these two models have existed side by side and even overlapped.

Radio broadcasting began simultaneously with that in Europe and the United States, and, in some countries such as Brazil, it was U.S. giants such as Westinghouse and General Electric that paved the way. In other countries, such as Mexico, Peru, and Uruguay, the public sector picked up from those beginnings and established stations and networks, only later permitting private stations to enter the field. In Argentina, Chile, and Cuba, it was entrepreneurs who pioneered radio and later television broadcasting, with the government following on their heels. Brazil was a unique case, beginning with privately owned, noncommercial radio stations.[26]

As might be expected in an underdeveloped region, television broadcasting began slowly, and as with radio, it sometimes was advanced by the private sector and in other countries by the public sector. As mentioned earlier, the first three television stations in Chile were licensed to major universities, and they still control them today, although a government channel and two private channels now compete with them. Color programming came at a glacial pace, and, because of the high costs involved with program productions, stations throughout the region relied heavily on dubbed imports, mostly from the United States, such as the omnipresent *I Love Lucy*.

Brazil and Mexico were the first to break the dependency on imported programs in the 1970s, and their domestically produced programs became increasingly more sophisticated and of higher quality, to the point that they began exporting them to the rest of Latin America.[27] The most popular export remains the *telenovela*, or soap opera, second only to soccer in popularity on Latin American television. It was also in Brazil and Mexico where two privately owned networks arose that have become giants in the region: Televisa in Mexico, and Brazil's TV Globo, regarded as the most-watched commercial television network in the world with sixty million to eighty million viewers nightly.[28] In the 1980s, Argentina, Colombia, Venezuela, and Chile began to produce more programs for domestic consumption as well as for export. These six countries also have developed creditable motion picture industries. The remaining countries are still too impoverished or lack sufficient population to invest in major domestic television industries with the sophisticated satellite links and increasingly costly production and transmission equipment that have become essential.

Either despite or because of the burgeoning technological demands on the broadcast media, particularly television, Latin America's electronic media are subject to the same marketplace pressures as the print media. In fact, print and broadcast media must compete with each other as well. This pressure is felt even on the state-subsidized stations and networks, such as in Mexico, Argentina, Chile, Colombia, Peru, Costa Rica, and Venezuela, and even government-owned stations frequently are commercially supported to remain economically viable.

For a regionwide approach, it is useful to employ John Merrill and Ralph Lowenstein's "Elite-Popular-Specialized Curve of Media Development."[29] Simply stated, the average audience of the print or broadcast media progresses from an elite stage, in which only the society's elite have access to the media, along a sharply ascending curve through the popular stage, and finally into a specialized stage, characterized by increasingly specialized media and a larger number of media products, resulting in a declining average audience for each. Two barriers impede the progression from the elite to the popular stage: poverty, which restricts the development of television and movies, and illiteracy, which hinders the print media. To pass from the popular to the specialized stage, a country must possess four "specialization accelerators": a population of ten million to fifteen million, higher education, affluence, and leisure time. Radio, they note, has a "leapfrog effect" over the barriers of both poverty and illiteracy, because both transmitters and receivers are less expensive than television, because receivers do not require access to an electrical power grid, and because a radio listener need not be literate. The greater range of radio signals offers an additional advantage over television, especially in inaccessible, mountainous hinterlands.

Latin America is a useful test case of this three-stage curve. Abstract terms such as poverty, affluence, and illiteracy can best be gauged through per capita gross domestic product and literacy figures provided by the UN, although such figures always are subject to dispute. In some countries, "literate" means a person who can write his name, not pore over a weekly newsmagazine. Table 1 provides these figures, and Table 2 indicates the number of daily newspaper copies and radio and television receivers per thousand members of the population.

Table 1. Actions against Journalists and Media, October 1988–October 1993

Country	Murders	Assaults	Kid-nappings	Arrests	Attacks on Media	Exiles/ Expulsions
Argentina	0	53	0	2	9	0
Bolivia	0	6	0	0	2	0
Brazil	5	15	0	2	9	0
Chile	2	8	1	3	1	0
Colombia	47	102	30	1	15	3
Costa Rica	0	1	0	0	0	0
Cuba	0	25	0	54	0	18
Dominican Republic	0	0	0	0	0	0
Ecuador	2	4	0	0	5	0
El Salvador	16	48	0	18	3	1
Guatemala	6	70	0	0	17	3

Haiti	4	35	1	11	13	1
Honduras	0	12	0	0	0	1
Mexico	12	96	3	1	8	0
Nicaragua	0	13	0	0	6	1
Panama	0	31	0	3	2	24
Paraguay	1	17	0	14	2	2
Peru	18	55	3	32	44	0
Uruguay	0	0	0	0	1	0
Venezuela	5	104	0	48	5	1
Totals	118	695	38	189	143	55

Source: Press Freedom in the Americas: 1994 Annual Report (Miami: Inter American Press Association, 1994).

Most Latin American countries clearly are within the popular stage. Anyone who has visited Mexico City, Rio de Janeiro, Buenos Aires, Caracas, or Santiago and has seen the multitude of newspapers and magazines for sale likely would agree. Some countries, however, still are languishing in the elite stage: Haiti, Guatemala, Honduras, Nicaragua, Bolivia, and, arguably, Peru. It is a topic for constructive intellectual debate among Latin Americanists whether Argentina, Brazil, Mexico, and Venezuela could be deemed to have met the criteria for entering the specialized stage. The best case can be made for Argentina, where the middle class is larger and there is more equitable distribution of that theoretical per capita income than in Brazil and Mexico, where highly developed media systems cannot compensate for some truly appalling pockets of squalor.

Table 2. Major Media in Twenty Latin American Countries

Country	Per Capita Income	Percent Literate	Daily Newspapers	Radio Transmitters	Television Transmitters
Argentina	$2,370	95.3	194	190	247
Bolivia	$630	77.5	16	204	42
Brazil	$2,680	81.1	366	1,300	113
Chile	$1,940	93.4	39	171	134
Colombia	$1,260	86.7	45	440	56
Costa Rica	$1,900	92.8	4	84	12
Cuba	NA	94.0	1	175	78
Dominican Republic	$830	83.3	10	126	17
Ecuador	$980	85.8	26	302	10
El Salvador	$1,100	73.0	5	78	5

Guatemala	$900	55.1	5	110	25
Haiti	$370	53.0	4	37	4
Honduras	$590	73.1	4	184	39
Mexico	$2,490	87.3	286	790	430
Nicaragua	NA	57.5	3	46	7
Panama	$1,830	88.1	6	85	14
Paraguay	$1,100	90.1	5	47	5
Peru	$1,160	85.1	12	451	185
Uruguay	$2,560	96.2	33	110	NA
Venezuela	$2,560	88.1	56	204	63

Source: *World Media Handbook*, 1992–1994 ed. (New York: United Nations Department of Public Information).

Latin America also is a textbook case for the so-called leapfrog effect of radio. Tables 2 and 3 provide the figures for the three major media. A Spearman's rank-order correlation of the Latin American countries' literacy rates and per capita income figures yield a *rho* of .950. When literacy is rank-ordered with newspaper circulation per thousand, the figure is .946, and with literacy and television receivers per thousand it is an even higher .959. The *rho* for per capita income and newspaper circulation is .964, for income and television receivers an even higher .978. But the *rho* for income and radio receivers per thousand drops to .904, and for literacy and radios, .898.

Table 3. Newspapers and Radio and Television Sets per 1,000 People

Country	Newspaper Circulation per 1,000	Television Receivers per 1,000	Radio Receivers per 1,000
Argentina	82	219.3	673
Bolivia	48	98.4	574
Brazil	53	203.6	373
Chile	67	200.6	340
Colombia	49	108.1	167
Costa Rica	106	136.1	259
Cuba	40	203.4	343
Dominican Republic	46	81.9	168
Ecuador	84	82.3	314
El Salvador	48	87.1	403
Guatemala	19	44.7	64
Haiti	4	4.5	42
Honduras	30	70.3	384

Mexico	119	126.8	242
Nicaragua	29	61.4	247
Panama	75	164.6	222
Paraguay	44	48.2	169
Peru	46	94.6	251
Uruguay	224	227.2	600
Venezuela	113	156.0	432

Source: *World Media Handbook*, 1992–1994 ed. (New York: United Nations Department of Public Information).

All are significant beyond the .01 level. The correlation between radio on the one hand and literacy and income on the other is still significantly high because countries at the two poles of the income ranking show a close correlation. Highly affluent Argentina and Uruguay have the most radios per thousand; desperately poor Guatemala and Haiti have the least. But, in between, the correlation is not as evident: Bolivia, for example, ranks sixteenth in income but third in the number of radio receivers per thousand inhabitants; El Salvador ties with Paraguay for eleventh place on the income scale but ranks fifth in radios per thousand; Honduras ranks next to the bottom in income but sixth in radios per thousand. Conversely, Mexico ranks fourth in income but twelfth on the radio ladder; Colombia ranks ninth in income but sixteenth in radios; Costa Rica and Panama are seventh and eighth in income but tenth and thirteenth in radios, respectively.

The reason for this phenomenon is relatively simple. As affluence increases and there is greater access to television, the popularity of radio wanes, much as it did in the United States during the 1950s. The less the affluence, the greater the dependence on radio as an affordable mass medium. Another factor that must be taken into consideration is the size of the average Latin American family, especially among the poor. One radio in a family may serve three generations at once, numbering from a minimum of four people per receiver. Thus, a figure of 574 radios per thousand people in Bolivia, or 403 in El Salvador, represents virtually universal access. Moreover, in every country but Argentina, the number of radio transmitters far outnumbers the number of television transmitters and daily newspapers. Few familiar with Latin American life would dispute that radio is the most important mass medium in the region. Radio is regarded as a companion by the masses. It is used by governments, capitalists, political parties, labor unions, religious groups, and others to convey ideas, inform, market products, proselytize, entertain, and promote education, culture, and national development. Juan and Eva Perón were quick to discover its value as a powerful propaganda instrument, and guerrilla movements of later years have employed clandestine radio skillfully to further their ends. An amusing case in point came prior to the U.S. intervention in Haiti in September 1994. U.S. planes first dropped propaganda leaflets in a classic psychological warfare maneuver. Apparently, someone in the chain of command was advised that the overwhelming majority of Haitians are illiterate, and the planes then began parachuting boxes of cheap transistor radios!

It is not surprising that when coups were staged in Latin America, radio was a high-priority target to seize. The recent Haitian intervention is another case in point. U.S. forces seized the radio and television studios after the military government continued to use them to air anti-Aristide messages. The fact that many stations carry programming in indigenous Indian languages further boosts listenership. Radio is as ubiquitous in Latin America as it was in the United States at the advent of television. As long as there are stubborn pockets of poverty and isolated areas unreached by television signals, radio will remain the pervasive medium of Latin America.

Table 4. Satellite Earth Stations in Latin America

Country	Intelsat	Domestic
Argentina	2	40
Bolivia	1	0
Brazil	3	64
Chile	2	3
Colombia	2	11
Costa Rica	1	0
Cuba	1	0
Dominican Republic	1	0
Ecuador	1	0
El Salvador	1	0
Guatemala	1	0
Haiti	1	0
Honduras	2	0
Mexico	5	120
Nicaragua	1	0
Panama	2	0
Paraguay	1	0
Peru	2	12
Uruguay	2	0
Venezuela	1	3

Source: *The World Factbook* (Washington, DC: Central Intelligence Agency, 1993).

As the economies of Latin America expand, as the masses become more literate and accumulate more disposable income, it is inevitable that more and more investment will be poured into the mass communication infrastructure—satellite systems (see Table 4), cable television, fiber optics, sophisticated computer hardware and software, high-resolution color photographic reproduction, state-of-the-art broadcast production, recording and transmission equipment—to reach these audiences. Communication is, after all, a growth industry of the future. It is not unusual to see newspapers even in impoverished countries such as Guatemala that are fully computerized, with full-color graphics. The same is true of television production.

As the pace of technological advance accelerates, many systems in which struggling Latin American media have invested precious resources will become obsolete almost overnight, and consequently some media entities will lag behind, while others will perish. As it is with the case of press freedom, the trend in economic and technological viability of the media in Latin America is encouraging. Some venerable publications and broadcast stations may fail to keep pace with the changing technological realities and fall by the wayside, and some new media ntities will fail to establish a niche. But it is more optimistic to conclude that for the Latin American media as a whole, the glass should be viewed as half full rather than half empty.

Notes

1. Marvin Alisky, *Latin American Media: Guidance and Censorship* (Ames: Iowa State University Press, 1981), 89–119, 166–89; Robert N. Pierce, *Keeping the Flame: Media and Government in Latin America* (New York: Hastings House, 1979), 3–22, 23–54.

2. Alisky, *Latin American Media*, 28–50; Pierce, *Keeping the Flame*, 96–118.

3. Alisky, *Latin American Media*, 51–63; Elizabeth Mahan, "Mexican Broadcasting: Reassessing the Industry-State Relationship," *Journal of Communication* 35 (Winter 1985): 60–75.

4. Alisky, *Latin American Media*, 123–51; Pierce, *Keeping the Flame*, 146–77.

5. Pierce, *Keeping the Flame*, 55–79.

6. Robert Buckman, "Survivor in Santiago," *Editor & Publisher*, May 5, 1990, 22–23, 38–39; J. W. Knudson, "The Chilean Press since Allende," *Gazette* 27 (1981): 5–20.

7. Alisky, *Latin American Media*, 67–86; Pierce, *Keeping the Flame*, 119–45; Rita Atwood and S. Mattos, "Mass Media Reform and Social Change: The Peruvian Experience," *Journal of Communication* 32 (Spring 1982): 34–45.

8. Alisky, *Latin American Media*, 153–64; John Spicer Nichols, "Cuba: Right Arm of Revolution," in Pierce, *Keeping the Flame*, 80–95.

9. Robert Buckman, "Guatemalan Press Withstands Throwback to Dictatorship," *Editor & Publisher*, July 31, 1993, 14–15, 35.

10. Alisky, *Latin American Media*, 217–22; Bonnie J. Brownlee, "The Nicaraguan Press: Revolutionary, Developmental, or Socially Responsible?" *Gazette* 33 (1984): 155–72; D. Kunale, "Nicaragua's *La Prensa*: Capitalist Thorn in Socialist Flesh," *Media, Culture, and Society* 6 (April 1984): 151–76; J. E. Maslow, "Letter from Nicaragua: The Junta and the Press: A Family Affair," *Columbia Journalism Review* 19 (March–April 1981): 46–47.

11. Alisky, *Latin American Media*, 223–24; Robert Buckman, "The Editor and the Dictator," *The Quill* 76 (January 1988): 14–21.

12. Pierce, *Keeping the Flame*, 181–99.

13. Robert Buckman, "Multimedia Conglomerate," *Editor & Publisher*, December 5, 1992, 16–17, 38.

14. Peter Eisner, "Colombia's Killing Fields," *The Quill* 78 (September 1990): 14–18.

15. "Cocaine & Co.," *Forbes*, July 22, 1991, 12.

16. Joseph P. Fried, "A Localized Look at the Cali Drug Cartel," *New York Times*, February 20, 1994, 43. See also Joseph P. Fried, "Youth Guilty in Slaying of Editor," ibid., March 10, 1994.

17. Robert Buckman, "Free at Last: The Rebirth of Panama's *La Prensa,*" *The Quill* 78 (March 1990): 24–27.

18. Robert Buckman, "Panamanian President Sues Political Cartoonist," *Editor & Publisher*, September 21, 1991, 16–17.

19. Associated Press report, May 9, 1994.

20. Robert Buckman, "IAPA Delegation to Investigate Salvadoran Newspaper Fire," *Editor & Publisher*, March 2, 1991, 16, 40; Robert Buckman, "IAPA Team Critical of Salvadoran Government," ibid., April 13, 1991, 15, 42.

21. Robert Buckman, "Venezuelan President Cracks Down on Press," ibid., March 7, 1992, 18–19.

22. Ibid.

23. Buckman, "Guatemalan Press Withstands Throwback," 14–15, 35.

24. Kathie Klarreich, "Haiti's Sunrise Radio Friend to Masses, Foe to Military," *Houston Chronicle*, May 15, 1994.

25. Robert Buckman, "Media Shake-up in Chile," *Editor & Publisher,* December 28, 1991, 16–17, 32.

26. James Schwoch, *The American Radio Industry and Its Latin American Activities, 1900–1939* (Urbana: University of Illinois Press, 1990), 96–116.

27. Joseph D. Straubhaar, "Brazilian TV: The Decline of American Influence," *Communication Research* 11 (April 1984): 221–40.

28. Edward Jay Whetmore, *Mediamerica, Mediaworld*, 5th ed. (Belmont, CA: Wadsworth, 1993), 391.

29. John C. Merrill and Ralph L. Lowenstein, *Media, Messages, and Men* (New York: David McKay Company, 1971), 34.

2

The Role of Women in Latin American Mass Media

Louise Montgomery

Latin America has always been a macho society, where men occupy the powerful public roles and women have stayed in the home. That organization of gender is now changing in journalism, with more women entering the craft, and with some rising to top positions. Unfortunately, women in the highest executive posts in the media remain the exception. In this chapter, Louise Montgomery discusses the general situation and relates the personal success stories of several female journalists.

Professor Montgomery, whose newspaper experience includes the Dallas Morning News *and the* Miami Herald, *specializes in Latin America at the University of Arkansas, where she teaches journalism. She taught investigative reporting as a Fulbright Fellow at the Catholic University in Santiago, Chile, during the 1989 presidential campaign. Montgomery also has edited a handbook,* Journalists on Dangerous Assignment: A Guide to Staying Alive *(1987).*

Women are absent in most books about Latin American journalism, but the 1980s and early 1990s have brought about rapid change in the journalistic careers of many Latinas. Women are flocking to journalism throughout Latin America, inspiring hope that their presence in the newsroom and in journalism schools will heighten interest in human rights and democracy. Their experiences as journalists in Latin America, one of the world's most traditional regions in terms of women's roles, augur well for the future of the area and for women themselves. Over the past two decades, women across the region are making a difference. In Central America, female radio and print journalists teamed up with others in persistently but patiently demanding less violence. In the Southern Cone of Chile, Latinas appear traditional on the outside in public, but they are modern and indefatigable in investigating corruption and demanding rights.

To be sure, the improved lives of women—journalists and non-journalists—in many parts of Latin America have been greatly affected by political events, timing, their expectations, and their fate around the world. But not everyone agrees that women's lives and their journalistic experiences have improved in Latin America. Two female journalists in the same country may report greatly different experiences, with one depressed by women's failures to achieve freedom and equality, and the other having experienced no discrimination in her career in journalism.

Despite the contradictions in these testimonies, female journalists indisputably have greater visibility in Latin America than ever before, although their achievements have come at a great price, particularly to the generation whose often unrecognized successes opened the way for a better-educated, more liberated group of women with higher expectations. Whether women's progress is secure and whether their newfound positions in media boardrooms will bring them real power remain for history to determine as the region's dynamic sociopolitical institutions adjust to the fast, often unpredictable, pace of the late twentieth century.

In the mid-1990s, Latin American women from privileged backgrounds—educated and well-positioned socially—continue advancing in television, magazine, and newspaper newsrooms, expanding and solidifying gains made in the 1980s. Another group, which includes some upper-class women, operates on the fringes of traditional media and advocates faster, more radical change in societies that are undoubtedly too conservative, too sexist. Some women have operated from within leftist organizations such as Nicaragua's Sandinista organization, while others worked in opposition to military rulers such as Chile's Augusto Pinochet. All in all, Latin American female journalists are elevating the region's journalism, and, as they advance, they are garnering international prizes and praise from their male editors and publishers. What old-fashioned, hard-boiled male editors once considered weak, feminine traits—empathy, intuition, concern for the poor—have become recognized as valuable journalistic tools.

Some women at the top, however, testify that the road has been long and hard. One consequence is insecurity that the gains may be short-lived, a fear that men, society, or fate will take away the little leverage they have gained. Some women fear that they could be pushed back, especially once men realize that they could become a threat. An indication of this insecurity is that many female journalists pass up opportunities to talk about their roles, just as one group of Latin American female educators hesitated to use the nonsexist textbooks that they produced in work-

shops. They feared they would lose power at home if they gained it outside the home and that their men would be ridiculed if they helped with
housework. Finally, women educators feared that men's failures would
be blamed on them.[1]

It is clear, however, that women are making gains. In a region where
the few female journalists historically have been wives or daughters in
elite family publishing empires or widows trying to maintain a family
newspaper, today many women unrelated to family oligarchies are in management positions and are undergirded by growing numbers of female
reporters and editors. These gains in journalism, not surprisingly, occurred
in tandem with more general ones for women and followed decades of
grass-roots organizing, pan beating, and other forms of demonstrations
of woman-power. Employment of women outside the home in Latin
America more than doubled in the twenty-five years ending in 1992, ex-
ceeding growth in male employment but still keeping the region ahead of
only the Middle East in the percentage of the labor force made up of
women.[2] Women in the Latin American labor force reached 27 percent in
1990, up from 18 percent in 1950. From the 1950s to the 1980s, the percentage of labor force participation by women below age twenty dropped
in all Latin American countries except Mexico and Brazil. This bodes
well for Latinas, who are being educated in increasing numbers throughout the region. From Brazil northward, women as a percentage of school
enrollment have increased throughout the hemisphere.[3]

Caution is in order, however. Despite the percentage gains in female
employment outside the home and the increasing education for women,
they remain "hemmed in by a *machista* culture."[4] The common expectation is that their place is in the home, not beside men in the workplace or,
even more important, in politics. The "public woman" in many countries
is still a euphemism for prostitute. In books about Latin American journalism, women are mentioned mainly as widows who take over the family newspaper upon their husband's death.

No organization seems to maintain regional data on women in journalistic positions, and few countries have associations of female journalists. Statistics on women in journalism are not available for most Latin
American countries. Scanning the *Guide to Central American Communication Media*,[5] however, reveals the names of numerous women. The organization that published the guide—the Latin American Journalism
Program at Florida International University in Miami—strives to train as
many women as men. All in all, the experiences of many female journalists suggest that the late twentieth century is an ideal time for them
to be journalists in Mexico, Chile, Colombia, and probably throughout
the region, but we should not forget those working outside the

mainstream who suffer disillusionment when media-assisted strategies fail to correct historic abuses of women.

The experiences of several outstanding female journalists are recounted below, along with comments of other journalists on how they see their profession. This information was gathered by searching databases that collect material from mass-circulation media as well as from academic sources; the author also interviewed prize-winning journalists by telephone. Several Chilean female journalists were identified and interviewed or asked by Chilean journalist Mariela Vallejo to submit information. In an attempt to reach a diverse audience, a survey was broadcast to electronic mail addresses throughout the region, with the request that the addressee forward the survey to a journalist or journalism educator. As a result, several questionnaires were returned. Material from those surveys is identified below and is included without attempting to verify the authenticity of the authors' experiences. Each woman's account is a valid and important one from which others can learn.

Sofía Montenegro in Nicaragua. "Because you're a woman."[6] For that reason, Sofía Montenegro's mother and father said, she could not talk politics and had to wash and iron her own clothing and that of her brothers. Montenegro's rebellious spirit was not quieted by several years of high school in West Palm Beach, Florida, where she was sent with the expectation that her foolish notion of being her brothers' equal would be replaced by more traditional attitudes. Instead, back in Nicaragua, she passed college entrance exams while one of her brothers did not. When the family decided to educate him and not her, "I cried. I kicked. I asked my father, who loved me, how he could do this to me. And I'll never forget his response—that same old phrase, 'Because you're a woman.' "[7] The more she heard those words, the more radicalized she became. Her anger, mixed with leftist politics, led to her joining the Sandinista effort to overthrow the corrupt Somoza regime. Nicaragua turned to a Cuban-style communism in the Sandinista period.

"As a woman, it seemed to me that the only real weapon I had was my mouth, my writing hand," Montenegro says. She studied journalism in college and, while translating for foreign journalists, started writing for a newspaper published by a group she described as the ultraleft Maoist Popular Action Movement (Movimiento de Acción Popular, or MAP). She found her way to *Barricada*, the Sandinista newspaper run by Carlos Fernando Chamorro, the Sandinista son of the famed newspaperman martyred in the early days of the struggle, Pedro Joaquín Chamorro. The Chamorro family, like Montenegro's, was split politically. In both cases, some members stayed with the traditional parties, while others became Sandinistas.

Torn ideologically between factions of the left, estranged from her mother, and troubled by some Sandinista rulers' abuse of power and of women, Montenegro collapsed. When she recovered, Chamorro took her back at *Barricada* despite what they called her "bad attitude." She was punished for rejecting the Sandinista Party but was allowed to come back to the party's newspaper "to do all the work that none of the other journalists wanted," she said. "And, of course, I was forbidden to hold a position of any importance. [Sandinista leader] Bayardo Arce's idea was that I humbly work my way back up again, from the very bottom." Her work won a prize in a contest in Cuba, but she soon was in trouble again. She and others protested Daniel Ortega's abuse of power and were fired. *Barricada* went into a crisis at about the time the Sandinistas lost their bid for reelection, and Chamorro once more asked her to return, this time as editor of the editorial page. *Barricada* was transformed into an independent newspaper after Nicaragua's return to an anti-Communist government. Chamorro's mother, Violeta, headed the new government, and Montenegro stayed on at *Barricada* as the respected editor of *Gente*, a weekly intellectual supplement to the newspaper aimed at women and youth.

In post-Sandinista Nicaragua, Montenegro has concentrated on her job and on feminism. "Here in Nicaragua, at least insofar as Sandinism is concerned, the thinking was always done by the men," she says. "There were nine male leaders who took it upon themselves to do the thinking for the rest of us. It's time we women learn how to think for ourselves." She has worked toward democratization through the Frente Sandinista de Liberación Nacional, although she claims that "the left's model didn't work. The only ideology that remains standing in today's world is feminism. . . . Feminists have been critical of socialism as we've known it, and of the left, for thirty years or more. And the socialists and the left never paid any attention to our criticism."

Cristiana Chamorro in Nicaragua. The daughter of Violeta, Cristiana has made a mark in Nicaraguan journalism as well. With other family members, she continued operating the family newspaper, the conservative *La Prensa*, throughout the Sandinista decade despite constant harassment by Sandinista censors and declines in revenue. Cristiana has served on the awards committee of the Inter American Press Association, a staunchly anti-Communist champion of private ownership and press freedom in Latin America.

Chilean women journalists. Just as the Sandinista period created opportunities for female journalists in Nicaragua, an opportunity arose in Chile as well, even though its history is quite different. Chile, the oldest democracy in South America, with close to a 100 percent literacy rate,

elected a socialist president, Salvador Allende. The turmoil accompany-
ing Allende's assassination and the coup that put General Augusto Pinochet
in power gave women special opportunities to excel. Many outstanding
female journalists opted to stay within existing institutions, particularly
higher education and opposition, but not fringe, magazines. Chilean
women moved to "seize the journalism field as their own" in a "quiet but
profound and potentially far-reaching revolution," write Lucía Castellón
and Alejandro Guillier.[8]

Whereas many socialist-inspired feminists embraced freedom from
traditional roles, Chilean women moved into leadership roles in journalism education, magazines, newspapers, and television while maintaining
their traditional roles at home. Castellón, dean of the College of Communication and Information Sciences at the Universidad Diego Portales in
Santiago, and Guillier, a journalism educator and television anchor, stress
that women journalists strove to "avoid excess." An example of the
Chilean woman journalist who successfully maintained both roles—that
of a full-time professional and a full-time wife and mother—is another
female journalism educator, Silvia Pellegrini, now dean of the faculty at
the Universidad Católica de Chile. As her husband studied for a doctorate in Germany, Pellegrini earned her doctorate—studying in German—
while also maintaining her role as a mother. When the family returned to
Chile, she expanded the journalism program at the Universidad, reaching
out to visiting scholars from abroad while maintaining a traditional family life. As Castellón and Guillier note, "Chilean women have not resorted
to feminist war cries to force room for themselves in the nation's journalistic circles. Both recognizing and comfortable with their 'womanness,'
they bring to the professional sphere talents that have helped women succeed in Chilean journalism as in few other areas in Latin America. The
recent impact of women on Chilean society in public debate over social
issues and policy formation, in governance and in journalism, is indisputable; it is in the last of these areas—the media and journalism education—that women have perhaps had the greatest impact."[9] Even so, most
Chileans would acknowledge that their male-dominated society has a
deeply rooted prejudice against women who leave the home for careers,
and those who do are expected to continue performing the traditional duties
of a wife and mother. Most men are unconcerned about women as rivals,
they say, until a woman is unexpectedly successful, and "then they begin
to worry."[10]

However, women's gains in Chile cannot be denied. In the mid-1990s
women head the six most important university schools of journalism. A
woman won the most prestigious national award in journalism in 1991,
and Chile is one of the few countries in Latin America with a women's

journalism association. Now called the Association of Women Journalists of the Southern Tip, the group was formed in 1962, five years after Lenka Franulic, editor of the magazine *Ercilla*, became the first woman to win the national journalism prize, and eleven years before the coup that put a nonelected military man at the head of the government for sixteen years.

Feminists often expect that women's progress in one sector of society moves apace with other sectors, but in Chile journalism is ahead of such fields as medicine and law. Not until 1992 did a woman become a member of the Academy of Medicine, and no woman has served on the Supreme Court. Yet female journalists distinguished themselves early in the sixteen years of military rule. For example, Raquel Correa interviewed generals who participated in the coup, and women such as Patricia Politzer, María Olivia Mockeberg, and Mónica González exposed abuses of the military rulers.

In the wake created by stars such as Mockeberg and González have come scores of female journalists, particularly in magazines and on television. According to Castellón and Guillier, in the mid-1990s, 31 of the 60 top magazine executives in Chile were women, while 38 percent of the 413 newspaper journalists in Santiago were women. As in many countries, most journalism students—sometimes 70 percent—are female.

Journalism in Chile draws women from elite families, Castellón and Guillier say, bringing journalists new access to business boardrooms and more prestige to the field. These journalists are socially, culturally, and intellectually better prepared than those of the past, leading Dean Pellegrini, the first female director of a Santiago journalism school, to credit women with changing the image of journalists: "Out of a journalism whose chief symbol was a bohemian way of life, there has evolved a professional activity framed in a conventional family life."[11] In addition, according to *La Nación*'s Abraham Santibáñez, women excel at interviewing because they are more empathetic and more intuitive than their male counterparts. Moreover, women, more than men, are drawn to journalism by an "inner vocation," says Cristián Zegers, who recruited a team of virtually all women editors and reporters to *El Segunda*, the evening daily he heads.[12]

Carolina Rossetti. Since earning a journalism degree at the University of Chile, Carolina Rossetti has been employed as a press attaché for the Chilean embassy in Paris and as a journalist in various media. She has worked with two male journalists to produce the news program *Domicilio Conocido* on Santiago's Channel 11 and did three radio interviews per week on Radio Tierra, the feminist radio station. Although there are more female journalists in Chile and they are more visible, she contends that they are exploited:

> Women have no power. The increased presence of women has not implied an increase in power; nor has it brought more equality in the media. Even when more than 50 percent of the reporters are women, more than 90 percent of the editors are men.
>
> In Chile, women direct magazines for women, but they have no presence as editors of news programs on TV or in newspapers. . . . Two women of great quality were candidates for general editor of *La Nación*, but the board elected a man. If a woman had been chosen, she would have been the first to direct a newspaper in this country. This is a clear example of discrimination. Men do not leave space for women even if the women journalists are devoted and brave and sometimes more efficient than men.
>
> What happens in this country is that the journalism field reflects what happens in society. Women journalists are those responsible for the public relations of men, so they can continue keeping power. But the women have not achieved power.[13]

Rossetti, who calls herself progressive and a rebel who avoids organizations and political parties, says that many women do not want responsibility. "Some women are afraid of power. And women rarely help other women." Her male coworkers at Channel 11 have treated her as an equal, Rossetti said, although that was not true in her earlier jobs. Even now, she states:

> They don't listen to me. I have to raise my voice above the others so they hear my proposals. Often they end up doing what I have proposed, but after long discussion and negotiation. Men have a hard time accepting that a woman has ideas. Finally, they listen to me. I have to think more about proposing things, how to say an idea, what words to use, and this means effort and tension.
>
> Men haven't restrained my career because I've done well. But my career has been more tense, less relaxed. Sometimes I propose cultural programs with excellent women journalists, but they do not accept them because they aren't a model of beauty and youth that a woman must have to appear on television.
>
> I think the major problem Chilean women face is a false representation of women in the news media. There are a lot of women in the media, but they do not make decisions. Instead, they obey the guidelines of a male and conservative power.[14]

Patricia Escalona. In the fall of 1994, Patricia Escalona became the first woman to head the news agency ORBE.[15] Her route to the top began with graduating in journalism from the University of Chile in 1965, working for *El Sur* in Concepción, teaching journalism, and serving as editor of the newspaper *La Tercera*. Today, she says that women write on all topics without restriction and are treated equally because of their dominance. The biggest problem is low wages for both men and women. Escalona does not advise a young woman to study journalism because so many students are graduated in journalism in Chile. Women need training, she stresses, to perform their roles as journalists better and to be better informed. Her aspiration as a journalist is "to provide better information every day."

María Jimena Duzán in Colombia. Wanting to explain the turmoil that her country has been through in recent years, María Jimena Duzán courageously went into the jungles of Colombia's drug trafficking even after her sister, also an investigative reporter, was killed by right-wing vigilantes in the drug wars and after her editor was gunned down outside the newspaper office.[16] Duzán followed in the footsteps of her late father, the well-known *El Espectador* journalist Lucio Duzán, by becoming a columnist at age sixteen. By the time Colombia's "decade of bloodshed" began, she had a following as well as hard-news experience. She traveled and talked to guerrillas, government officials, and ordinary people, discovering what she calls the "disarticulation," or collapse, of her country. "One piece of the country didn't have anything to do with another. I wanted to really understand. [Colombia's trouble] wasn't only due to the guerrillas, paramilitary squads, narco trafficking. . . . The violence was much more complex. I wasn't a drug reporter. I am just a journalist who wanted to put into context what was going on in Colombia."[17]

Journalists hold a special place in Colombia, a place so important that they became pawns in the drug wars. They can be more important than cabinet ministers, Duzán says, because they become "poles of orientation" to help readers understand the news. In the mid-1990s she spent part of each morning at the Center for Journalists at the University of the Andes in Bogotá. "We were training people to be journalists," she stresses, "not training journalists." She had twenty-seven students, half of them women, from backgrounds in economics, political science, and sociology. She has a political science degree from the University, but she notes that her training as a journalist was on the job.

Duzán's reporting won one of four 1990 Courage in Journalism Awards from the International Women's Media Foundation and formed the basis for her book on the cocaine wars.[18] Being a woman was irrelevant in her work as a journalist, she says. In Colombia, almost all television news programs are headed by women, and many of them work in print journalism. "My generation made a big revolution of having women participate in the society, especially in journalism. So I didn't have any problems because women still aren't a threat. I talk with a lot of international women journalists, and my experience was very different from their struggle. For me, it was my decision to get into all these topics. Without that, I wouldn't have the place I have now." While maintaining that gender has been irrelevant in her success, Duzán claims that women are more sensitive and more sensible, and she has a special approach to violence. "That could have helped," she states, "but that's the only way gender wasn't irrelevant."

Colombians have become accustomed to female bosses, she says, with women heading seven of the eight national television channels and many female journalists in management positions in the countryside. But Duzán cautions that they have not achieved the level they deserve. "It doesn't mean the situation for women is good in Colombia. It means some women have been lucky, went to the University, and had a chance to find a job in journalism. There were a lot of jobs. . . . I wouldn't say it's going to be the same in fifteen years when the demand is less and the number of journalists is greater."

Elena Poniatowska in Mexico. The role of women journalists has improved in recent years, French-born Elena Poniatowska believes, because the situation of women generally has improved around the world.[19] Poniatowska, a reporter for *La Jornada*, a liberal newspaper in Mexico City begun within the last fifteen years, was the first woman to win Mexico's National Journalism Award, although she did not win it by catering to the establishment. Quite the contrary happened. Her book about the 1968 government massacre of three hundred citizens in Tlatelolco, a plaza in Mexico City, came out in 1971; in the mid-1990s it was in its forty-fifth edition.[20] When the government tried to give her a prize for the book when it was published, she declined, asking: "Who's going to give a prize to the dead?"[21]

Now in her sixties and the widowed mother of three, Poniatowska became the kind of journalist that her time and place demanded. At age nine, she and her Mexican mother left Europe for Mexico; her Polish father stayed behind to fight in World War II. She studied in Philadelphia and at Manhattanville College in New York before gradually beginning a writing career. Events in Mexico pushed her toward serious journalism. "In Mexico, there is so much to write about, so much to document."[22]

Poniatowska began her career in journalism in the 1950s, at a time when women journalists were not sent on many trips and few could be war correspondents. Mexican women journalists may have had a harder time getting good positions, she says, because fewer women studied at universities than in some other countries. "This is a very traditional society. The weight of the Catholic Church is very heavy, so it's harder for women to advance. Traditionalism, machismo, is heavy. Women should be at home!" However, Poniatowska sees younger female journalists doing much better. For example, Avila Salinas, a young journalist with *Reforma*, the new, respected daily newspaper in Mexico City, is gaining an excellent reputation. Several women at *La Jornada* write about politics and cover wars. And Mexico's *El Financiero* newspaper maintains a correspondent, Dolia Estévez, in Washington, DC. A highly regarded journalist, she says that she has faced no hurdles because she is a woman.[23] In Mexico, Estévez asserts, "women have great opportunities to develop in this great profession." Even so, Poniatowska notes, "the best jobs are in the hands of men, and the power is still in the hands of men."

Nila Velázquez in Ecuador. Vice rector of the Catholic University of Santiago in Guayaquil, Nila Velázquez has worked in newspaper and television journalism for about three decades and is a columnist for *Hoy*, a national newspaper. "I've never had problems from being a woman," she says. "I did my work and I was promoted, without discrimination."[24] Problems that stem from machismo or traditionalist thinking that might limit women, she argues, can be solved through professionalism and training. Velázquez studied at the Centro Internacional de Estudios Superiores de Periodismo para América Latina (CIESPAL).

In Venezuela, journalist Pedro López says that he worked at *El Siglo*, a politically powerful regional newspaper, from 1984 to 1991 under Norys Sarmiento Aponte, the first female editor at a newspaper in his country.[25] His view is that women are not necessarily discriminated against, despite their delayed access to management positions in national newspapers. Only in the late 1980s did a woman, Alba Sánchez, become political news editor and then editor-in-chief of *El Naciónal*, one of the largest and most influential national newspapers. Another woman, Lucy Gómez, has held top positions at *El Diario* (Caracas), a newspaper of growing influence with labor.

According to López, more important than gender considerations are political considerations. Political party alliances with newspapers and publishers have more to do with who succeeds in newspapers than does talent or skill, he contends, and journalists' groups do not protect journalists from politics because the National Journalism Association (*colegio*) is controlled by men affiliated with government. Women have little influence in the group, he says, so they formed their own fempress (as in Chile), but it has little influence. Feminist journalists have a poorly defined image, and their material, even when published in the mainstream press, is read by few people. In López's experience, "discrimination in Venezuelan journalism based on gender isn't so accentuated as that based on political discrimination or the control of the journalists' unions."

In Cuba, women's role in journalism has deteriorated because "at this moment, we have problems," says Nancy Gómez, a graduate of the

University of Oriente, who responded to an electronic mail message broadcast throughout the region.[26] Women in Cuba, she says, have the same opportunities as men. One question in the survey was: "Would you advise your little sister or daughter to become a journalist? If not, why?" Gómez responded, "No, I wouldn't."

Although it is impossible to speak of Latin America as one entity, groups such as Freedom House—dedicated to furthering human and civil rights around the world—paint the region with broad brushstrokes when assessing human rights. Doug Payne, a journalist who has covered Latin America for Freedom House for more than a decade, points to two signs of hope for the region, despite some lapses: independent, probing media and women's contributions to democratic institutions, including the media. "Women are breaking the bonds of Latin America's rigidly male-dominated society," he writes, "and that puts them at the forefront in the struggle to keep democracy in Latin America from failing yet again."[27]

Real progress has been made by women seeking jobs in journalism in Latin America. Although they have less power than men, and their salaries are lower, many women journalists are enjoying their work and realizing satisfaction from it. Their fate rests with that of their sisters throughout the society. Not even the richest elites can be unaffected by the plight of the poorest women. Latin American women have created their own brand of feminism, ranging from the radical to the working wife or homemaker, which allows them to choose the intensity level they desire. And, finally, Latin American women, including journalists, cannot be free to pursue careers and home lives as long as men are tied to a paternalistic, macho ideology that limits both them and women.

Notes

1. Virginia W. Leonard, review of *Women and Education in Latin America: Knowledge, Power, and Change*, ed. Nelly P. Stromquist, *Journal of Developing Areas* 28, no. 2 (January 1994): 281–83.

2. Ann Varley, review of *Women's Employment and Pay in Latin America*, by George Psacharopoulos, *Journal of Latin American Studies* 16 (February 1994): 14–15.

3. Leonard, review of *Women and Education in Latin America*.

4. "Latin American Women: The Gendering of Politics and Culture," in *North American Congress on Latin America Report on the Americas* 27, no. 1 (July/August 1993): 16.

5. *Guía de medios centroamericanos de comunicación* (North Miami: Latin American Journalism Program, Florida International University, 1994).

6. Sofía Montenegro, "Who Was Going to Trust a Montenegro?" in *Sandino's Daughters Revisited: Feminism in Nicaragua*, ed. Margaret Randall (New Brunswick, NJ: Rutgers University Press, 1994), 286–311. Material has been

edited, and only those remarks inside quotation marks are presented exactly as in the original.

7. Ibid.

8. Lucía Castellón and Alejandro Guillier, "Chile: The Emerging Influence of Women in Journalism," *Media Studies Journal* 7, nos. 1–2 (1993): 231–39.

9. Ibid., 231.

10. Ibid., 233.

11. Ibid., 238.

12. Ibid.

13. Carolina Rossetti, interview with Chilean journalist Mariela Vallejos, August 5, 1984, for this report.

14. Ibid.

15. Patricia Escalona, survey returned September 8, 1994.

16. Maria Jimena Duzán, telephone interview with author, September 18, 1994.

17. Ibid.

18. Maria Jimena Duzán, *Death Beat: A Colombian Journalist's Life inside the Cocaine Wars* (New York: Harper Collins, 1994).

19. Elena Poniatowska, interview with the author, September 1, 1994.

20. Elena Poniatowska, *Massacre in Mexico* (New York: Viking Press, 1971).

21. Nicole Peradotto, "Latin American Author 'Writing Makes Me Feel Useful' Visits Lewiston to Discuss Her Books," *Lewiston* (Idaho) *Morning Tribune*, October 8, 1993.

22. Ibid.

23. Dolia Estévez, survey returned September 9, 1994.

24. Nila Velázquez, Ph.D., survey returned September 14, 1994.

25. Pedro López, survey returned by electronic mail, September 1994.

26. Nancy Gómez, survey returned by electronic mail, September 1994.

27. Doug Payne. Slightly different wording is used in two versions of Payne's exposition. The one used here comes primarily from a Federal Information System release dated December 16, 1993, that was based on a special transcript of a Freedom House press briefing at the National Press Club. Similar material was published in "Giving Democracy a Bad Name," *Freedom Review* 25, no. 1 (February 1994): 26–31.

3

Professional News Organizations in Latin America

Bruce Garrison and James Nelson Goodsell*

Whether journalism is a profession has been debated for years. Although journalism lacks the licensing, disbarring, and other mechanisms of medicine and law, it does possess several professional criteria, and its broad goal—educating the populace on matters of public concern fully, fairly, and accurately—is lofty indeed and worthy of any profession. In Latin America, journalists generally receive poor salaries and have relatively little professional status. Various organizations have been formed to increase their prestige and professional standing, which is desperately needed, but some of the organizations, especially colegios, have been criticized as clashing with freedom of the press. The authors of this chapter discuss this problem along with other professional issues, including education to practice journalism. They provide cogent material on the principal professional organizations, especially the Inter American Press Association, the largest and most powerful in the region, which has been criticized as a club for rich, conservative newspaper owners. Over the years, however, the IAPA also has been quite effective in fighting for press freedom.

Bruce Garrison is a professor in the Journalism and Photography Program, School of Communication, University of Miami, in Coral Gables, Florida. He is the author of seven books, including Latin American Journalism *(1991), which he cowrote with Michael B. Salwen. Professor Garrison has also written or cowritten chapters for numerous other edited books and has written articles for an array of academic journals in mass communication, journalism, and other disciplines. James Nelson Goodsell holds the Knight Chair in the Journalism and Photography Program, School of Communication, University of Miami. He served for more than thirty years as a reporter, national news editor, and Latin America*

*Both authors acknowledge the important contributions of Michael B. Salwen to this chapter.

correspondent for the Christian Science Monitor *before joining the Miami faculty in 1993. He also worked as anchor for Monitor Radio and as a reporter for the Monitor's television programs and for public television.*

Professional organizations play an increasingly important role for journalists around the world. As Latin America's formerly totalitarian governments became democracies in the late 1980s, professional groups throughout Central America, South America, and the Caribbean basin assumed a growing role in setting the standard for the increasingly independent news media of the hemisphere.[1] Like those in North America, professional news organizations in Latin America and the Caribbean, regardless of their form, serve an important function for working journalists. In a region where many people expect journalists to accept bribes, confusion exists about professional standards. Latin American journalists' perceptions of their professional roles and functions influence how they practice their craft. Journalists in different societies may see their roles ranging from that of servants of power and authority, independent information transmitters, social gadflies, watchdogs over political power, soldiers for national development, or political analysts.[2]

The adjective "professional" should not be confused with the noun "profession." To perform a professional job is to perform a job that meets high standards. In this regard, even a grave digger may perform a professional job. But experts agree that a profession must meet certain criteria. While they do not agree just what these criteria are, five common ones are systematic theory, authority, community sanction, ethical codes, and a culture.[3]

In the United States, the professional status of journalism has been debated for years. U.S. journalism is not a true or undisputed profession such as law or medicine in which there are certain barriers to entry.[4] International media scholar John C. Merrill has sounded the clarion call against journalism's seeking professional status, asserting that it would be harmful to pluralism, journalistic autonomy, and press freedom. Merrill has written that "people like me, we see journalism as a profession as harmful . . . to the whole concept of openness; we see certain types of people being frozen out of journalism—eccentrics, etc. We see professionalism of this type as a danger to a free and open press where everyone can practice regardless of education, political views, etc." Although Merrill is not as bothered by the word "professional" as an adjective as he is by the word "profession" as a noun, he worries about the connotations of the word.[5]

Matters are different in Latin America. The quest of Latin American journalists to attain "professionalization," Merrill says, "implies, I think, that there is the attempt being made to achieve some kind of status for journalism in Latin America that it doesn't now have. . . . It probably means that journalism is considered weak or inefficient in some way; therefore it needs to be professionalized."[6] Mexican communication scholar Fernando Reyes Matta has criticized the trend toward professionalism in Latin American journalism, but for other reasons. Reyes Matta views the trend as a distinctly Western and particularly U.S. style of professionalism that involves objectivity and neutrality. In his view, the Latin American tradition of news involves political interpretation, not objectivity.[7]

Journalistic associations and educational institutions helped launch journalism programs in universities throughout Latin America in the late 1940s and 1950s, ostensibly as a means of promoting professionalism in journalism. What was originally meant to increase professionalism evolved into a drive to turn journalism into a true profession. Over the years, the universities and journalistic organizations were able to persuade many Latin American governments to require practicing journalists by law to obtain degrees and belong to recognized organizations. This arrangement was accepted by the journalists because it provided a means of restricting entry into the field—a method that kept their skills in demand and tended to keep salaries high. It also suited the universities, providing them with students and closer relations between universities and news media industries.[8]

Leading Organizations for Journalists

Professional organizations in Latin America operate at several levels. Internationally, a handful of organizations have evolved as the most influential and dominant in the latter half of this century. Among them are the Inter American Press Association (IAPA) and the International Broadcasting Association (IBA). Another group, the Latin American Federation of Press Workers (Federación Latinoamericana de Trabajadores de la Prensa, or FELAP), was established in 1976 and represents about two dozen different national groups from its headquarters in Buenos Aires. Members are primarily rank-and-file journalists; the organization serves as a trade union by protecting the interests of members.

The national and regional organizations include the *colegios* (which are discussed below, and which are detailed in Chapter 6), trade unions, and associations. A *colegio* is not a union, per se, although it works to enhance the lives of its members. It sets and enforces standards for entry into the "profession" and is closer to a U.S. bar association in which membership is required in order to practice law than to a trade union that simply looks out for members' welfare. Typical of the national organizations is the National Federation of Brazilian Journalists (Federação Nacional de Jornalistas Brasileiros, or FNJB) in Brasília. This group, started in 1946, strongly pushes press freedom and democratic values among journalists in Brazil through meetings, seminars, and workshops. This organization represents regional trade unions with more than thirty thousand members. On a much smaller scale, Costa Rica's National Union of Journalists (Sindicato Nacional de Periodistas, or SNP) serves that country's working journalists as a trade union based in San José.

Colegios exist throughout the region. In Venezuela, for example, journalists belong to either the National Association of Journalists (Colegio Nacional de Periodistas, or CNP) or the National Press Workers Union (Sindicato Nacional de Trabajadores de la Prensa, or SNTP). Similar groups can also be found in Costa Rica, Peru, Chile, and Honduras.

Of all organizations for journalists in Latin America, the Inter American Press Association (Sociedad Interamericana de Prensa, or SIP) stands out for its length of service and scope of concern about press freedom and professional practice. For decades, the IAPA has placed itself at the forefront of international journalism in the Western Hemisphere. The organization has many purposes, but none is more important than its role as international news media observer. While many media watchdogs speak out against press abuses in Latin America, the thirteen hundred-member IAPA, headquartered in Miami, focuses specifically on speech and press freedom issues in the Western Hemisphere, particularly in the Caribbean and Latin America. IAPA members are mainly newspaper editors and publishers, with a few magazine executives, news service correspondents and executives, broadcasters, and scholars. While there is a growing number of members from U.S. and Canadian news media, two-thirds are Latin Americans. The IAPA's active members represent thirty-four countries in the hemisphere, including U.S. territories.

As with all media watchdogs, the IAPA has no real power other than its ability to publicize the plight of journalists and speak as a single voice representing its members. But it is often viewed as a heavyweight in the arena of international public opinion. In the mid-1990s, for example, one of the IAPA's main agenda items is supporting and publicizing the Declaration of Chapultepec. This ten-point document was created in Mexico City in 1994 to reinforce free speech and free press throughout the Western Hemisphere and is seen by the IAPA's leadership as a means of strengthening democratic institutions and of increasing freedom of expression and freedom of the press as fundamental human rights. "A free press enables societies to resolve their conflicts, promote their well-being, and protect their liberty. No act or law may limit freedom of expression or the press, whatever the medium," the introduction to the statement of principles states.[9] (Most of the Declaration is reprinted in the Conclusions section of this volume).

Massive lobbying and publicity campaigns are common strategies used by the IAPA. But the organization also uses personal visits to influence public opinion and national leadership. A mission by an IAPA delegation to a country or the semiannual international meeting attracts attention at the highest levels and often results in an address by a president or his designate plus government-sponsored social events. When a media organization or an individual journalist in Latin America experiences a press freedom problem, IAPA leaders generally will launch campaigns against the offending government, and members will discuss the situation in their own publications.

In 1943 the second National and Pan American Congress in Havana established the organization under its current Spanish name, SIP. Cuban liberals exercised control over the executive committee of the Pan American Congress and, from 1943 to 1949, convinced the Cuban government to subsidize the organization's secretariat in Havana. During a New York meeting in 1950, the organization was restructured and the bylaws revised.[10] Instead of representing countries, as was done previously, member journalists attended on behalf of their media organizations.

While the IAPA may not be that visible in the news industry or to the public in the United States, it is widely recognized in important circles throughout Latin America because its membership is dominated by some of the continent's most influential journalists, who are often also leading businesspeople and occasionally political party leaders. The IAPA's defense of beleaguered journalists dates to 1953, when Demetrio Canelas, publisher and editor of *Los Tiempos* in Cochabamba, Bolivia, was sentenced to death for refusing to succumb to government demands to cease his editorial attacks on the government.[11] Within the next decade, the IAPA was praised for defending a number of Latin American journalists including Pedro Joaquín Chamorro in Nicaragua and Germán Ornes in the Dominican Republic. Probably the greatest praise came from Argentine dictator Juan Domingo Perón, who had a 437-page book published denouncing the IAPA! During the 1960s, the IAPA continued to campaign against abuses of press freedom in dictatorial nations such as Cuba, Haiti, Paraguay, Honduras, and Guatemala.

The IAPA has a history of working with other international and national press organizations. In 1952, for instance, the IAPA joined forces with its broadcast counterpart in Latin America, the Inter-American Association of Broadcasters (IAAB) (the organization has since changed its name to the International Broadcasting Association). As a result of their "Panama Agreement" in 1952, the IAPA and the IAAB stated that any act of suppression against a newspaper or broadcast station in the hemisphere would be considered an act of suppression against all newspapers and broadcast stations in the hemisphere.[12]

IAPA members convene twice a year at international locations to discuss issues such as press freedom and government relations with the press. The organization's major subgroup, the Freedom of the Press and Information Committee, dominates meetings with member reports of soured government and press relations, violent incidents, and other attempts to suppress news. This IAPA committee has been active for four decades. It first attracted attention under the leadership of Jules Dubois, the long-time Latin American correspondent for the *Chicago Tribune*. Dubois, in the course of covering the hemisphere, began speaking out on press freedom issues, writing about them for his newspaper and meeting with government officials. After Dubois's death and as the IAPA expanded efforts to boost freedom of the press throughout the hemisphere, the committee was headed—in succession—by Raúl Kraiselburd of *El Día* (La Plata, Argentina), Wilbur G. Landrey, international editor of the *St. Petersburg Times* (Florida), and Robert Cox, editorial page editor of the *Post and Courier* (Charleston, SC) and former editor of the *Buenos Aires Herald*. Currently, the committee is led by Eduardo Ulibarri, editor of *La Nación* (San José, Costa Rica). In addition, one of the most active proponents of hemispheric freedom of the press has been Edward Seaton, former IAPA president and editor of the *Manhattan Mercury* (Kansas). His efforts to secure changes in laws that restrict freedom of the press in Latin America and to win the release of jailed journalists have been quite successful. Seaton was also instrumental in organizing the Hemisphere Conference on Modernizing Journalism Education, which was cosponsored by the IAPA and held at Cantigny, Illinois, in September 1995. It drew the largest and most widespread group of Latin American journalism deans ever to assemble. Twenty attended from twenty different Latin American universities. Six U.S. mass communication deans were invited as well. The major goal was to foster a more professional orientation in journalism education in universities throughout Latin America.

High on the IAPA's international agenda has been its fight against *colegio* laws, which mandate that journalists be members of legally recognized organizations to practice their trade.[13] It also has fought efforts by governments, such as Mexico's, to restrict and control imported newsprint and other supplies and limit imported equipment.

Professor Robert N. Pierce described the IAPA, as well as several other press organizations, as taking "a rather uncomplicated view of press freedom" in which "the enemy is always the government, private investors are the only rightly owners, commerce is the best calling of the media, society can exert demands on them [the press] only through the marketplace, and any legal norms beyond the most basic defamation and pornography laws are unacceptable."[14] A number of critics see this "simplicity" borne out in IAPA reports that often describe the state of press freedom in various nations with the bold pronouncement: "There is freedom of the press in . . . ," or "There is no freedom of the press in. . . ."[15] Other critics see the IAPA as associated with conservative forces, especially with Cuban exiles.[16] This conservative predilection did result in the expulsion of *New York Times* journalist Herbert Matthews from the IAPA's board of directors during the mid-1960s for his sympathetic views of Fidel Castro.[17]

Leftist critics claim that the IAPA represents the business interests of its members, that it is an organization of rich newspaper owners. They also claim that while the IAPA criticizes government attempts to curb freedom everywhere, including the United States, it tends to be harsher on Communist and left-wing nations. Generally, though, the IAPA sees little or no role for even benign state intervention in press policies. To this end, its policies and concerns are at odds with another leading Latin American journalism association, the Latin American Federation of Press Workers, founded in 1976. This left-leaning organization comprised of journalists in the region strongly advocates New World Information and Communication Order policies as a way of improving the lot of Latin American journalists and freeing Latin American media from dependence on developed nations.[18] The IAPA, however, has a long history of condemning abuses by governments of both the left and right.[19] It also has frequently criticized the United States and Canada. According to Julio E. Muñoz, executive director and former director of the IAPA's Technical Center, the guiding philosophy behind the IAPA is that the news media should maintain independence from governments.[20]

Occasional missions to meet with governmental leaders take place under extraordinary circumstances, such as when news organizations of a country have been physically damaged by government or private groups, or when news organizations have been restricted in reporting and publishing, or have been closed by government decree. The missions usually bring pressure by meeting directly with officials. Sometimes governments that believe they have made significant human rights improvements have invited representatives of the IAPA to observe improvements firsthand. The organization also pressures governments by sending messages to national leaders, urging them to rescind decisions that have closed publications or otherwise made news reporting difficult.

The IAPA has taken a leadership role in professional development of members and their employees. The organization offers technical training through its Miami-based Technical Center. Established in 1957, the center is responsible for continuing education of members through frequent production, technical, and management seminars. According to Muñoz, the center helps Latin American media become strong financially as the best means of maintaining autonomy from government. In addition, the IAPA provides an independent circulation-auditing service and offers a series of annual awards for international reporting and photography as well as scholarships for journalists from Latin America to study in the United States and vice versa.

With the transition to democracy by most of Latin America's non-democratic states in the 1980s, Muñoz sees the IAPA's role shifting from fights against governments to dealing with nongovernmental problems. He views the rise of narco-terrorism as a major threat to 1990s Latin American journalists and has noted that nations where Latin American journalists are in greatest physical danger are the same nations where the drug trade thrives.[21]

Colegios as Professional Organizations

Legally recognized Latin American professional journalism organizations, frequently known as *colegios*, have often worked to improve the economic lot of journalists, but the issue of mandatory membership in *colegios* has developed into a heated hemispheric debate. Many U.S. journalists view *colegios* as de facto licensing of journalists and a means by which government may control the press. But the reasons for *colegio* laws are complex. Many were established not by government but by journalists. Thus, U.S. journalistic organizations out to defend their Latin American brethren sometimes find themselves at odds with rank-and-file journalists.

Early empirical studies by Professors Dario Menanteau-Horta, J. Laurence Day, and Jack M. McLeod and Ramona R. Rush reported that, overall, Latin American journalists during the 1960s expressed high professional aspirations.[22] They viewed themselves as playing potentially important roles in their societies. But the journalists raised serious doubts that they could practice their lofty ideals in societies where these roles were not valued. During the late 1980s, several studies again began to address journalistic professionalism in Latin America when the debate over the value of *colegios* emerged.[23] A. Carlos Ruofolo surveyed

108 Latin American journalists working for elite newspapers in Brazil, Colombia, and Costa Rica. He reported modest levels of professionalism. His study, however, highlighted the fact that journalists in different Latin American nations may have varying levels of professionalism but noted that Brazilian journalists had relatively high professional orientations compared to Colombian and Costa Rican journalists.[24]

In addition, Latin American universities have played a central role in promoting *colegio* laws and the establishment of *colegios*. Claiming to uphold professional standards through education, ethics, and professional meetings, *colegios* have a good deal in common with guilds and unions. But they are more than unions and coexist with unions in many nations.

Professional Organizations and Higher Education

Until the midtwentieth century, journalism education was viewed as a uniquely North American practice. Latin American journalists had educations in the more traditional arts and letters. Writing in 1931, when there was not a single journalism school in all of Latin America, Professor J. Edward Gerald reported that many Latin American journalists spent from U.S. $50 to $100 each to enroll in mail-order, quack journalism correspondence courses from sellers in the United States. For their money, the journalists received out-of-date instructions and poorly prepared materials.[25]

It is difficult to obtain a precise measure of the number and scope of educational programs for Latin American journalists, but the number is increasing rapidly. In 1954, UNESCO (United Nations Educational, Scientific, and Cultural Organization) identified 650 journalism training programs worldwide, all but 100 of them in the United States.[26] In 1950, only 7 journalism programs were in Latin America; by 1978, almost 100, and by 1985, almost 200.[27] Despite this increase, many Latin Americans continue to learn about journalistic practices abroad, particularly in the United States, Europe, and the states of the former Soviet Union. Variations of the U.S. journalism education model historically have been dominant: some journalism skills training, liberal arts courses, and conceptual courses dealing with mass media, such as journalism history and law. Some Latin American programs included a fourth component: developmental journalism. Still, even with the growth of indigenous training in Latin America, many news managers in the region claim that journalists receive insufficient education, especially in professional skills. While U.S. journalists have some of the same complaints about journalism education in their own country, the U.S. news managers continue to hire journalism graduates.

The first Latin American journalism programs were associated with the humanities, but, with the support of professional journalistic organizations, they soon incorporated professional training.[28] Professor Mary A. Gardner notes that this trend was precisely the opposite of that in the United States, where journalism schools initially stressed professional skills and later included theory and research components. She observes that the dangers of practicing journalism in the region at least partially accounted for this trend.[29]

The first program in the region, established in Argentina's Universidad de La Plata, was created by the Circle of Journalists (Círculo de Periodistas) in 1934. A month later, another developed in Buenos Aires.[30] Soon came programs in Brazil in 1935 and Mexico in 1936. Peru instituted a program in 1945, followed by Chile and Venezuela in 1947. The first Central American program was in Guatemala's Universidad de San Carlos in 1952, attached to the humanities faculty.[31] In Cuba, the First National Congress of Journalists in 1942 helped establish a professional program in Havana run by experienced journalists and limited to fifty students each year. The Cuban program sought to professionalize journalism by establishing the Guild of Journalists (Colegio de los Periodistas), which required successful completion of the program to practice journalism.[32]

During the late 1950s, UNESCO, which has advocated restructuring what it views as the unbalanced "world communication order," discussed the creation of regional centers for journalism education in Latin America. As a result, UNESCO founded the International Center of Advanced Studies in Journalism for Latin America (Centro Internacional de Estudios Superiores de Periodismo para América Latina, or CIESPAL) in Quito, Ecuador. CIESPAL has educated journalists throughout Latin America. The support of *El Comercio*, the leading daily in Quito, and the Ecuadoran government also were central in the establishment of CIESPAL. One of its major founders was Raymond B. Nixon, then a professor at the University of Minnesota and editor of *Journalism Quarterly*. Many scholars and media practitioners from the United States, Europe, and Latin America have lectured at CIESPAL, which included a scientific aspect to the study of journalism. The fact that CIESPAL's founders referred to the program as a School of Mass Communication Science instead of a School of Journalism was meant to stress the scientific foundation of journalism.[33]

Before CIESPAL, most communication research in Latin America came from a variety of disciplines and often approached communication tangentially within the larger frameworks of sociology, psychology, anthropology, or other disciplines.[34] Professors E. Lozano and J. Rota noted a trend toward a developing Latin American research tradition in communication.[35] They interviewed leading Latin American communication scholars in order to describe aspects of this emerging tradition. The scholars they interviewed suggested that Latin American communication research involves advocating social justice.

Several other international journalism organizations operate in Latin America. The Committee to Protect Journalists (CPJ), based in New York City, focuses on personal abuses to journalists, chronicling attacks and even killings of journalists by military, paramilitary, police, and other groups. CPJ issues an annual list of journalists killed in the line of duty. In Latin America in the past five years, CPJ lists have identified at least four dozen newsmen and newswomen killed as they pursued stories, a number of which had focused on drugs.

The World Press Freedom Committee, based in Washington, DC, concentrates on freedom from all government interference and supports a full and free flow of information. In 1986 it disseminated the unanimous opinion of the Inter-American Court of Human Rights, saying that licensing journalists violates human rights, an opinion that flew in the face of Costa Rica's *colegio* laws. Ironically, the Inter-American Court is based in San José, the Costa Rican capital.

In a mid-1995 development, the Costa Rican Supreme Court ruled that the obligatory licensing of journalists was unconstitutional and contrary to the Western Hemisphere Convention on Human Rights, to which Costa Rica is a signatory. But *colegio* authorities indicated that they might appeal, although the organization would in the interim abide by the ruling. The implication in the Costa Rica court's decision is clear; it opens up the journalistic profession to more qualified applicants.

In sum, in the field of journalism in Latin America and the Caribbean, organizations—which play a key role in any professional or quasi-professional environment—are taking on increasing importance for journalists, news organizations, and regional and national news media. Certainly, without these organizations, no matter what their origins, the conditions for journalists would be poorer, their voices quieter, their lives more dangerous. Groups such as the Inter American Press Association have had great impact. The IAPA's ability to focus the spotlight on abuses has forced governments to think twice before restricting press freedom. Its record is impressive. But the fact that abuses of freedom take place means that the IAPA and the other organizations cannot relent. Their presence is mandatory to protect press freedom.

Notes

1. Michael Salwen and Bruce Garrison, *Latin American Journalism* (Hillsdale, NJ: Lawrence Erlbaum Associates, 1991).

2. Leo W. Jeffres, *Mass Media: Process and Effects* (Prospect Heights, IL: Waveland Press, 1986); Marvin Alisky, *Latin American Media: Guidance and Censorship* (Ames: Iowa State University Press, 1981).

3. Ernest Greenwood, "Attributes of a Profession," *Social Work* 2 (July 1957): 45–55.

4. Bruce Garrison and Michael B. Salwen, "Newspaper Sports Journalists: A Profile of the 'Profession,' " *Journal of Sport and Social Issues* 13 (November 1989): 57–68.

5. John C. Merrill, personal correspondence with author, December 15, 1989.

6. Ibid.

7. Fernando Reyes Matta, "La evolución histórica de las agencias transnacionales de noticias hacia la dominación [The historical evolution of transnational news agencies toward domination]," in *La información y el nuevo orden mundial*, ed. Fernando Reyes Matta (Mexico City: ILET, 1977); idem, "The Information Bedazzlement of Latin America: A Study of World News in the Region," *Development Dialogue* 2 (1979): 29–42; idem, "The Latin American Concept of News," *Journal of Communication* 29 (Spring 1979): 164–71.

8. Mary A. Gardner, "*Colegiación*: Another Way to Control the Press?" in *Media in Latin America and the Caribbean: Domestic and International Perspectives*, ed. W. C. Soderlund and Stuart H. Surlin (Ontario: Ontario Cooperative Program in Latin America and Caribbean Studies, 1985), 76–94.

9. "Declaration of Chapultepec," brochure published by the Inter American Press Association, Miami, FL, 1994, p. 5.

10. James W. Carty, Jr., "Cuban Communicators," *Caribbean Quarterly* 22 (December 1976): 59–67.

11. Mary A. Gardner, "The Inter American Press Association: A Brief History," *Journalism Quarterly* 42 (Autumn 1965): 75–82; Linda C. Shanks, "Harold Hoyte: He's Living on Cloud 9 as a Prominent Caribbean Publisher," *Presstime* 10 (December 1988): 36.

12. M. F. Harvey, "The IAPA," *American Editor* 3 (1959): 5–15.

13. José Luis Valverde, "Licensing and the IAPA," *IAPA News* 335 (July 1989): 8.

14. Robert N. Pierce, *Keeping the Flame: Media and Government in Latin America* (New York: Hastings House, 1979), 218.

15. Ibid.

16. Robert U. Brown, "IAPA Attacks Communists' Infiltration of Press," *Editor & Publisher*, November 3, 1962, 62–63.

17. Jerry W. Knudson, "Herbert L. Matthews and the Cuban Story," *Journalism Monographs* 54 (February 1978): 2.

18. "FELAP and the New Information Order," *Times of the Americas*, May 17, 1989, 12.

19. Simon Hochberger, "IAPA and the Search for Freedom," *Journalism Quarterly* 34 (Winter 1957): 80–85.

20. Julio E. Muñoz, interview with author, Miami, January 26, 1990.

21. Ibid.

22. Dario Menanteau-Horta, "Professionalism of Journalists in Santiago de Chile," *Journalism Quarterly* 44 (Winter 1967): 715–24; J. Laurence Day, "How CIESPAL Seeks to Improve Latin American Journalism," *Journalism Quarterly* 43 (Autumn 1966): 525–31; Jack M. McLeod and Ramona R. Rush, "Professionalism of Latin American Journalists, Part I," *Journalism Quarterly* 46 (Autumn

1969): 583–90; idem, "Professionalism of Latin American Journalists, Part II," *Journalism Quarterly* 46 (Winter 1969): 784–89.

23. Robert A. Logan and Robert L. Kerns, "Evolving Mass and News Media Concepts: A Q-Study of Caribbean Communicators," *Mass Comm Review* 12 (1985): 2–10; A. Carlos Ruofolo, "Professional Orientation among Journalists in Three Latin American Nations," *Gazette* 40 (1987): 131–42; Garrison and Salwen, "Newspaper Sports Journalists."

24. Ruofolo, "Professional Orientation among Journalists."

25. J. Edward Gerald, "Aspects of Journalism in South America," *Journalism Quarterly* 8 (June 1931): 213–23.

26. Dennis R. Cooper, "Basic Training for Third World Journalists" (Ph.D. diss., University of Tennessee at Knoxville, 1987).

27. J. Rota, "Training for Communication in Latin America: Present State and Future Needs" (paper presented at the meeting of the International Communication Association, Honolulu, Hawaii, 1985).

28. J. Fernandez, "Problems Related to the Training of Journalists in Latin America," *Gazette* 12 (1966): 45–51. See also Jerry W. Knudson, "Journalism Education's Roots in Latin America Are Traced," *Journalism Educator* 41 (Winter 1987): 22–24, 33; and M. Cuthbert, *Evolution of Communication Training in the Caribbean* (New York: UNESCO, 1985).

29. Mary A. Gardner, "Latin American Newspapers," *Community College Journalist* 8, no. 4 (Summer 1980): 10–13.

30. Jerry W. Knudson, "Licensing Newsmen: The Bolivian Experiment," *Gazette* 25 (1979): 163–75.

31. Ibid.

32. Ibid.

33. Day, "How CIESPAL Seeks to Improve Latin American Journalism"; Fernandez, "Problems Related to the Training of Journalists"; Knudson, "Journalism Education's Roots"; Raymond B. Nixon, *Education for Journalism in Latin America* (New York: Council on Higher Education in the Americas, 1970).

34. J. M. de Melo, "Communication Theory and Research in Latin America: A Preliminary Balance of the Past Twenty-Five Years," *Media, Culture and Society* 10 (1988): 405–18.

35. E. Lozano and J. Rota, "Encounters and Dissolutions: A Critical Reflection on Latin American Communication Research" (paper presented at the meeting of the International Communication Association, Dublin, Ireland, 1990). See also Steven H. Chaffee, C. Gomez-Palacio, and Everette M. Rogers, "Mass Communication Research in Latin America: Views from Here and There" (paper presented at the meeting of the International Communication Association, Dublin, Ireland, 1990).

4

An Unusual Approach in the United States to Latin American Journalism Education

J. Arthur Heise and Charles H. Green

Of the more than four hundred journalism-mass communication schools, departments, or other entities at U.S. colleges, none has such a specialized program as the one at Florida International University in North Miami. The Latin American Journalism Program in the School of Journalism and Mass Communication there is unique in the United States. It aims at upgrading the quality of professional journalism in Central America and, more recently, in the Andean nations of South America. Most of the money to support the program has come from the U.S. Agency for International Development, and most of the credit for creating and running it goes to the authors of this chapter, who provide a telling account of what it was like to establish this creative program and of the difficulties they encountered, especially when the operation was untruthfully said to be linked to the Central Intelligence Agency.

J. Arthur Heise is founding dean of the School of Journalism and Mass Communication at Florida International University and director general of its Latin American Journalism Program. He has worked for the Associated Press in Berlin and for the Buffalo News. He has published two books and more than fifty articles, monographs, and papers. Charles H. Green is director of the Latin American Journalism Program at Florida International University. A journalism graduate of North Texas State University in Denton, he spent nearly a quarter of a century with the Associated Press as a reporter, foreign correspondent, and executive, half of that time in Latin America. Before accepting his current position, he was distinguished editor-in-residence at Michigan State University.

María Olga Paiz was young to be doing what she was doing that night in 1994. Only twenty-one, she walked onto the stage and was blinded by television lights. The president of her country stood and applauded. So, too, did members of his cabinet, diplomats, educators, and her colleagues from seven countries in Central America. Her mother watched with pride as María Olga, a reporter on the Guatemalan news magazine *Crónica*, received the grand prize of the Premios PROCEPER and a $1,000 check for the best journalistic work in Central America in 1993.* No one had heard of the award several years before, but now journalists referred to it as the Pulitzer Prize of Latin America. María Olga won for her investigative stories on death squad massacres in Guatemala and the mass graves they left behind. Rene Galdámez of Radio Venceremos in El Salvador won a radio reporting award for covering the discovery of a guerrilla arms cache in Managua. Others won radio, television, and print awards for stories ranging from prison riots to floods.

The Premios PROCEPER contest is a major component of the Latin American Journalism Program (LAJP) at the School of Journalism and Mass Communication at Florida International University (FIU) in Miami. It has become the largest international journalism program in the United States operated by a university, but LAJP was born simply. It began in the mid-1980s, when Florida International University moved to strengthen its mass communication program. A top priority in the long-term planning—which resulted in converting a small department into a freestanding, fully accredited school by 1991—was to create a strong, distinct international focus. The natural target area was Latin America.

J. Arthur Heise, then department chair, submitted an unsolicited proposal to the U.S. Agency for International Development (USAID). Its Latin American Office of Democratic Initiatives funded programs aimed at strengthening democratic institutions such as legislatures, courts, and electoral systems. The Fourth Estate, although critical to any democratic society, had been largely ignored to that time. A search of the literature quickly revealed that limited up-to-date information was available about journalism in Latin America. What systematic work had been carried out—much by Professor Raymond B. Nixon of the University of Minnesota—was too dated to help assess what needed to be done to strengthen journalism in the turbulent Latin America of the 1980s.

The literature search, plus wisdom from a small advisory committee,[1] suggested two things that needed to be changed. Both involved the International Center of Advanced Studies in Journalism for Latin America (Centro Internacional de Estudios Superiores de Periodismo para América Latina, or CIESPAL). Located in Quito, Ecuador, CIESPAL focused on

---

*PROCEPER is the Spanish acronym for Programa Centroamericano de Periodismo, the Central American Journalism Program. The project name was changed to Latin American Journalism Program in 1993. *Premios* is Spanish for prizes.

mass communication research and education throughout Latin America, from the Rio Grande to Tierra del Fuego. First, that territory was too extensive to be served effectively and efficiently by one center. Second, CIESPAL was perceived as having a strong political agenda, that of Latin America's left.

The proposal submitted to USAID in 1985 therefore centered only on the six Spanish-speaking countries of Central America: Costa Rica, El Salvador, Guatemala, Honduras, Nicaragua, and Panama. And it contained a pointed statement making its professional nature clear: "All training, education, and technical assistance activities will be based on the professional standards of the free press operating separately from and independent of the state in the democracies of the modern world."[2] The proposal called for a one-year, three-phase project: first and most important, an in-depth field assessment to obtain a fresh, firsthand idea of what journalists, media owners, educators, and others thought about journalism education, training, and research in Central America; second, an analysis of that information by knowledgeable Central American and U.S. educators and journalists; and, third, a nine-week experimental seminar for Central American journalists at FIU, designed to try different teaching approaches in several subjects. Results of the three phases would drive the decision on whether a proposal for further research, training, and education was needed.

USAID funded the 1985 proposal for $475,000. To lead the assessment, Charles H. Green, a distinguished editor-in-residence at Michigan State University's School of Journalism, joined FIU as the project's executive director. Green had spent twenty-four years as a reporter, editor, and news executive with Associated Press. More important, he covered Central America for a decade and a half, reporting on all its major social and political events. Fluent in Spanish, he covered the war between Honduras and El Salvador, the Sandinista revolution in Nicaragua, the start of the civil war in El Salvador, presidential campaigns, coups, and sports events. His excellent reputation among Central American journalists would later play a significant role in successful efforts to establish the credibility of FIU's program when opponents tried to attack its integrity.

Two others also joined the assessment team. Ana Cecilia With had been a Costa Rican television reporter and anchor and had worked in radio in Panama, and Francisco Vázquez, a former Chilean television journalist, was on the journalism faculty of Temple University. The three designed a series of open-ended questions to probe the status of journalism research, education, and training in all of the Central American countries except Nicaragua. Problems between the United States and the Sandinista government of Nicaragua caused the U.S. Congress to prohibit any foreign aid money being used there. This hole in the program would haunt Green and Heise until 1993, when they received a grant from the USAID mission in Managua for a special project to teach Nicaraguan journalists what they had missed over the years.

Six months and 150 in-depth interviews after the original assessment began, Green and Heise pulled together a workshop in Miami. They placed before participants the results of the field research culled from interviews, visits to virtually every news organization in the region, reviews of mass communication programs at every major university in Central America, and an array of related documents.[3] The workshop involved four days of discussion and sometimes argument among leading journalists and educators from Central America and the United States. The group included such well-known international communication professors as Raymond B. Nixon and Mary A. Gardner as well as journalists from large and small news organizations.[4] Participants agreed that there were no short-term solutions and that blindly imposing U.S. journalism practices on Central America was a formula for disaster. The ultimate aim, they agreed, should be to make the region self-sufficient in educating its journalists; the focus should be on professional journalism throughout.

The proposal that emerged called for a seven-year project with all activities conducted in Spanish. Whenever possible the best journalists and journalism educators from Central and South America would be involved, especially on the advisory council, which would help shape policy. By the end of the project, a training center would be established in Central America, operated by and for its own journalists. Furthermore, the proposal declared: "A key factor in the success of this project will be its acceptance by the journalism professional in and out of Central America as a project free from political influence and bias, focused purely on improving professional journalism in the region. That critical factor makes it imperative that the project be operated independently by Florida International University, free from political ideology and fully committed to professionalizing journalism and related mass communication fields in Central America."[5]

Short-term workshops and seminars—twenty-two per year, most in Central America—would be conducted on topics from basic newswriting to television news production. Writing would be emphasized because of the poor quality of writing in nearly all Central American journalism. Ethics would be stressed as well because journalistic corruption was common. The field research had found that most journalists were poorly paid and badly educated, making them easy targets for corruption, especially in the absence of an accepted professional code of conduct. Such a code was made a goal of the project.

A special three-summer master's degree program in mass communication was proposed. Journalists and journalism professors from Central America would come to FIU for intensive study, and in Spanish. A media directory and a journalism magazine were also planned, plus a prestigious series of prizes to be awarded annually for the best work by Central American journalists. These became the Premios PROCEPER.

The field research had shown that despite huge enrollments in social communication programs in universities, there were virtually no journalism textbooks directly relevant to Central America. U.S. texts that had been translated into Spanish were being used. One book illustrated the inverted pyramid using a college football game. What the editor apparently did not realize is that North American football is virtually unknown south of the Mexican border. Another old text described the impact color might have on television news. Thus, the proposal called for a series of texts to be written focusing on Central America. It also called for the creation of a Central American professional journalists' association, which would play a key role in establishing a permanent training center. Finally, the proposal asked for $12.3 million over seven years.

Before it was funded, however, the first shot was fired at it. Guillermo Martínez, a member of the committee that Heise had put together to advise him on the needs assessment, objected that many activities would be conducted not in Miami but in Central America and that all activities would eventually be moved to a training center in Central America and be run by Central American journalists. Martínez, an editorial writer for the *Miami Herald*, believed that this could lead to charges of involvement with the Central Intelligence Agency (CIA).

Martínez objected publicly by stepping down from the advisory committee. He resigned, as the *Miami Herald* put it, "because of the appearance that the program might be tied to the CIA."[6] Meanwhile, the now-defunct *Miami News* had been working on a detailed story about the project. The reporter had done a thorough job, but a public affairs officer at USAID in Washington had not. Although the public affairs officer had no direct knowledge of the project and had made no apparent effort to find out about it, he commented on it. Asked by the *Miami News* whether the project was aimed at countering Soviet activities in Central America, he said, "That's like asking whether the Pope is Catholic." The headline over the page-one story read: "U.S. Funds FIU Journalism Program to Counter Soviets, Officials Say."[7] That led to a critical lead editorial in the *Miami News*.

The heat was on, fanned by reports in the *Boston Globe*, the *New York Times*, and the *Columbia Journalism Review* about a different project, one at the College of Communication at Boston University. It was funded not by USAID but by a special appropriation funneled through the U.S. Information Agency (USIA). The project was to train Afghan rebels in journalism. Bernard Redmont, dean of the communication college at Boston, opposed it because he believed that he and the faculty would have no control over the content of the program, which was to be conducted just across the border from Afghanistan in Peshawar, Pakistan. In the end, Redmont resigned as dean. After he left Boston University, Redmont—who had extensive overseas experience as a newsman—accepted an invitation to join the advisory committee of FIU's project in Central America.[8]

Back in Miami the other members of the informal advisory committee to FIU's Central American project stood firmly behind it. Heise called a special meeting of the advisory council to FIU's Department of Communication. After hearing his story and answers to their questions, the council said that it had learned nothing to alter its confidence in the professional integrity and leadership of the program. A stronger statement still came from a member of the advisory council unable to attend the meeting, Manuel Jiménez Borbón, publisher of *La Nación* in San José, Costa Rica, one of Latin America's most respected dailies. Jiménez was joined in his statement by Julio Muñoz, director of the Inter American Press Association's Technical Center and a member of the informal advisory committee to the FIU project. They said, "We feel that linking the project with the CIA has been totally irresponsible, especially in the absence of any proof. No doubt there will be similar unfounded charges in the future because of [the project's] aims and importance, charges, which, as in this case, intend only to harm the project, the people in charge and the Central American journalists."[9]

This support lowered the heat outside FIU. Inside, the picture was less clear. A new president had come a few months before the Central American journalism program made local headlines. The dean of FIU's College of Arts and Sciences, where the Department of Communication was then housed, supported the department and its Central American journalism project, and so did FIU's new president after he had had a chance to review the situation.

Amid all this activity the participants in the experimental seminar for Central American journalists arrived in Miami. They were clearly concerned by what they had read, or been told, about a possible link with the CIA. As one of them put it, "If there is any link to the CIA, I'm going home." How, then, was this problem to be solved? The key was obviously Martínez, the *Miami Herald* editorial writer who had resigned from the project's advisory group and who had worried about CIA involvement. The Central American journalists wanted to meet with him before participating in the seminar, and he agreed to do so.

The Central Americans checked out all the video cameras and recorders that the Department of Communication had. They were treating the meeting as a press conference so that they could report the story back home. At Heise's request, Martínez and the Central Americans met alone. They questioned him for more than two hours while the video cameras ran. Did he have any evidence of a link between the project and the CIA? "I could answer that question with one word: no, absolutely not," Martínez said on videotape. None of the Central Americans filed a story. The seminar started the next day and was completed without interruption. Whatever commitment there had been to keep the project a nonpolitical, purely professional training program was redoubled.

As the proposal for funding wound its way through USAID, some thorny issues arose. Normally, final approval of participants in USAID or USIA projects rests with the U.S. embassy in the country where the participant lives. That was a potential problem for a project for journalists because of the training they needed and not because of their or their employer's political views. Indeed, the IAPA had recently complained to the secretary of state in Washington that a USAID program allowed the *colegio de periodistas* in Costa Rica to select participants for another program. (The IAPA and others are concerned that *colegios* are a threat to freedom of the press because in some countries only people licensed by the *colegio* are permitted to work as journalists.) The criteria for participant selection spelled out in the FIU proposal had been patterned after those of the Nieman Fellows program at Harvard. The school had the final word on selection of the participants, meaning that a waiver had to be sought from USAID. It was granted.

Publications were a problem as well. According to a directive from the Office of Management and Budget (OMB), all publications prepared with federal dollars were subject to prepublication review. Submitting a journalism review, for example, to federal officials for clearance was out of the question. Again, a waiver was granted by OMB to allow publications in this project to be produced without prepublication review by anyone. Eventually, USAID funded the project in 1988, but now came the real challenge of putting into action what had been proposed. As a first step, an advisory committee was assembled of journalists and educators from the United States and Latin America.[10] The main emphasis was getting the first seminars on line. Then came the tough part: to persuade Central American journalists to participate.

In 1989 parts of Central America continued to be ravaged by wars. Suspicion of U.S. programs was widespread. That was when the professional reputation of Green, who had spent years covering Central America for the Associated Press, took on vital importance. He persuaded Gerardo

Bolaños, a respected Costa Rican journalist, to join the project and to head its field office in San José. Together they traveled the length and breadth of Central America meeting with owners, editors, producers, and reporters in print and broadcasting.

Then came the first few seminars. Participants were told bluntly that their politics or those of the organization that employed them were to be left outside the seminar room. Writing, editing, layout, reporting, production, and ethics were the only topics to be discussed. That approach worked, and before long waiting lists for seminars offered by the Central American Journalism Project (CAJP) became the norm.

Finding qualified participants for the master's degree program was a different challenge. The pool from which the students were selected turned out to be much smaller than hoped. Two classes were selected, the first with fourteen students, the second with eleven. A graduate certificate program has now replaced the master's degree program. Another step was creating the journalism review, *Pulso del Periodismo*, with its four thousand quarterly copies going mainly to Central American journalists, but today, by request, also to South America and Cuba. The media guide has also proved popular.

By mid-1994, close to two-thirds (2,003) of the estimated 3,400 journalists in Central America had been in CAJP activities. In 1993, forty-two workshops, seminars, and roundtable meetings were held. The number declined later, but the number of participants increased dramatically as the project shifted to training in newsrooms of Latin America media organizations. A series of investigative reporting seminars and workshops introduced that subject to Central America and generated several investigative reporting teams watching government corruption and other national issues.

The idea of establishing a regional association of Central American journalists was abandoned. The advisory committee feared that such an organization would become politicized. Each country has one or more national organizations in mass communication, frequently competing fiercely with one another. The advisory committee suggested that an educational foundation be formed instead to carry on training activities after the project ends. That foundation, known in English as the International Foundation for Professional Journalism, has membership categories for working journalists, owners, and journalism educators.

The goal of establishing a training center within Central America— to be run by and for Central American journalists—is alive and moving toward realization by 1997. Some CAJP activities took longer than anticipated; therefore, USAID was asked to extend the project from seven to nine years without providing additional funding. The agency also approved the project's expansion into the Andean nations of Venezuela, Colombia, Peru, Ecuador, and Bolivia and approved funding an in-depth assessment of the status of journalism in those countries. The Central American Journalism Program then became the Latin American Journalism Program. Panama was selected as the site of the permanent training center, but a financial feasibility study showed that the center would need an endowment of at least $1.5 million to survive. The bulk of the endowment would have to come from Central American news organizations, which would be the main beneficiaries of the center, and from other sources.

Meanwhile, two problems troubled the project. One was the exclusion of Panama during the first few years of the project. That issue was quickly remedied after the normalization of relations with the United States following the departure of General Manuel Antonio Noriega. LAJP went into Panama only months after the demise of Noriega's regime. The more vexing problem was Nicaragua. LAJP's advisory committee and the project's leadership were anxious to include Nicaragua in the program from the outset. But U.S. foreign policy made that impossible, at least until the democratic Nicaraguan elections of 1990. The elections, however, were followed by a long struggle in Washington between the White House and the Senate. Finally, when that struggle ended in 1993, Nicaragua was included in LAJP's portfolio. Now, journalists from the Sandinistas' *Barricada* newspaper sit in LAJP seminars next to journalists from *La Prensa*, the newspaper owned by President Violeta Chamorro's family.

Overall, has LAJP strengthened journalism in Central America? Early drafts of the proposal included grand schemes for analyzing the content of news presented in newspapers and in radio and television newscasts in each country to see if there was a noticeable improvement in their content. That approach was soon abandoned. Such a content analysis conducted over a period of years would cost more than the program itself. Instead, more modest approaches were built into the project. One called for an external evaluation of its effectiveness after its third year by experts hired independently by USAID. They visited each country where the project operated, and they scrutinized what had been done. Their verdict? Keep right on doing what has been done.

Another evaluation strategy called for opinion surveys of journalists and of the public to be conducted in each country. The public surveys showed that people's trust in the news media has improved slightly since the project began. They consistently rated television as the most credible news medium. Surveys in newsrooms showed that 64 percent of journalists interviewed had attended at least one program activity. Ninety-three percent said that they still needed more training, particularly in specialized subjects.[11]

An additional indicator is the effort to raise a $1.5-million endowment for the permanent training center. When the project started in 1988, it seemed unlikely that more than one or two Central American news organizations would give a dime for such a center. But by mid-1994, these organizations had paid or pledged $700,000 toward the endowment. Finally, one more evaluation approach is anecdotal information. And no anecdote is more powerful than that which records what happened in Guatemala when that country's president, Jorge Serrano, decided in May 1993 to suspend the constitution.

As part of his auto-coup, Serrano censored the press, but, unlike previous times, Guatemalan newspapers would not go along. The daily *Siglo Veintiuno* (Twenty-first century) changed its name to *Siglo Catorce* (Fourteenth century). If a story was touched by a censor, the newspaper ran blank space instead. Other media did likewise. The news magazine *Crónica* was allowed to print, but not distribute, its press run. Reporters and editors stuffed copies of the magazine in their underwear and smuggled them out of the building.

When Serrano fled the country and was replaced by a constitutional president, Ramiro de León Carpio, the former human rights attorney general, LAJP heard directly from the new president about the role he thought the project had played in Guatemala. He wrote:

> Some skeptics commented, in the beginning of my tenure, that there was an inconvenient closeness between the president and the press, which would mean a loss of journalistic objectivity and professionalism. This did not happen. Now, six months after being sworn in as president, I can say that the press has again given proof of its professionalism, precisely by criticizing the government and the president.
>
> During the crisis, the press abandoned its role as observer to become an actor in the political drama. Now, having fulfilled this historical duty, the press has returned to its task of informing, criticizing, and orienting. It publishes articles, caricatures, and critical reports, some of them with great depth, some with a measured style, others with an aggressive style. As president, I am the object of journalistic criticism, which I consider a stimulus to improve, not as proof of a conspiracy against me. I accept criticism for what it is: a valid form of delivering an account of society's feelings to the president.
>
> I am convinced that these journalistic attitudes are in great part the result of the excellent work done by CAJP. As a Guatemalan citizen, I thank Florida International University for its enthusiastic support of this program, which I have known about for several years.[12]

Notes

1. The original committee members were Julio E. Muñoz, then director of the Technical Center of the Inter American Press Association; Mark B. Rosenberg, then director of FIU's Latin American and Caribbean Center; Arturo Villar, publisher and writer; and Guillermo Martínez, then an editorial writer for the *Miami Herald*.

2. J. Arthur Heise and Charles H. Green, "Central American Journalism Project Proposal: Strengthening Mass Communication Education, Training, and Research in Central America" (Department of Communication, Florida International University, Miami, August 1987), 2.

3. J. Arthur Heise, Charles H. Green, Ana Cecilia With, and Francisco Vázquez, "Journalism Education, Research and Training in Central America: An Assessment Report" (Department of Communication, Florida International University, Miami, March 1987), 28–34.

4. Workshop participants, in addition to Heise, Green, With, and Vázquez, and the positions they held in 1987: Mary A. Gardner, professor of journalism, Michigan State University; Raymond B. Nixon, professor emeritus of international communication, University of Minnesota; George Krimsky, executive director, Center for Foreign Journalists, Reston, VA; Gerardo Bolaños, writer, editor, diplomat and educator, San José, Costa Rica; Mario Antonio Sandoval, editor and assistant to the publisher, *Prensa Libre*, Guatemala City, Guatemala; Gonzalo Marroquín, director and owner, *Siete Días* television news program, Guatemala City, Guatemala; Peter Habermann, Ph.D., associate professor of communication, FIU; Mark Rosenberg, Ph.D., director, Latin American and Caribbean Center, FIU; Julio Muñoz, director, Technical Center, Inter American Press Association; and Roma Knee, U.S. Agency for International Development, Washington, DC.

5. Heise and Green, "Central American Journalism Project Proposal," 7.

6. *Miami Herald*, April 18, 1987.

7. "U.S. Funds FIU Journalism Program to Counter Soviets, Officials Say," *Miami News*, May 14, 1987.

8. Bernard S. Redmont, *Risks Worth Taking: The Odyssey of a Foreign Correspondent* (Lanham, MD: University Press of America, 1992), 211–12. In this autobiography Redmont recounted his experience at Boston University. He ended his account of the incident by noting: "Events provided another postscript to my encounter with [Boston University president John] Silber over the Afghan Media Project. At the time of the controversy, Florida International University in Miami was engaging in discussions with the USAID over a project to train Central American journalists." Redmont continued:

> Building on the principles we had fought for in Boston, and openly confronting suspicions of possible CIA manipulation of the project printed in the Miami press, the university's journalism faculty persuaded AID to agree to unprecedented conditions. The agreement provided that all activities should be "based on the professional standards of the free press operating separately from and independent of the state in the democracies of the modern world." It stipulated that it would be operated "free from political influence and bias, free from political ideology, and fully committed to professionalism." The project director, head of the journalism faculty, received full and independent authority to

defend the integrity of the program, and if he found that its integrity was ever compromised, he had the right to terminate it. All meetings and documents were to be open to anyone.

Because of these provisions, the plan won the enthusiastic support of the professional journalism community. The Florida International University team directors, citing their support for my position in the Afghan Media controversy, invited me to join the Advisory Committee of the new Central American Journalism Program. One of them said with a smile, "You'll help to keep us honest."

9. Joint statement issued May 6, 1987, by Manuel Jiménez Borbón, 2d vice president, Inter American Press Association, and Julio Muñoz, manager, IAPA Technical Center.

10. Those who have served on the advisory committee since its start include Jiménez; Muñoz; Rosario Arias de Galindo, president, *Panamá América*, Panama City; Juan José Borja, president, *El Mundo*, San Salvador; Jorge Canahuati, president, *La Prensa*, San Pedro Sula; Pilar Cisneros, former television news executive, San José; Eduardo Díaz Reyna, columnist, Guatemala City; José Alfredo Dutriz, general manager, *La Prensa Gráfica*, San Salvador; I. Roberto Eisenmann, Jr., president, *La Prensa*, Panama City; Juan Luis Correa, general manager, *La Prensa*, Panama City; Peter Eisner, formerly of *Newsday*, United States; Fernando Eleta Casanovas, manager, information services, Panamanian Broadcasting Corp. (RPC), Panama City; Tom Fenton, The Freedom Forum, United States; Rafael Ferrari, general manager, *Telesistema Hondureño*, Tegucigalpa; Mary A. Gardner, professor emeritus, Michigan State University, United States; Roma Knee, retired USAID officer, United States; Ramiro MacDonald, general director, *Guatemala Flash*, Guatemala City; Bernard Redmont, retired educator, foreign correspondent, United States; Mark B. Rosenberg, former director, Latin American and Caribbean Center, FIU, United States; Morris W. Rosenberg, retired news executive and foreign correspondent, Associated Press, United States; Rolando Santos, senior producer, CNN Spanish, United States; Fernán Vargas, president, *La Nación*, San José; Arturo Villar, president, *Latin American Business Reports*, United States; Andrés García Levin , a television and newspaper owner, Merida, Mexico; and Jorge Zedan, owner, Channel 12, San Salvador.

11. The sample of 682 journalists represents 20 percent of the estimated 3,400 journalists in the region. The newsroom surveys were conducted from July through December 1993.

12. Letter from Ramiro de León Carpio to J. Arthur Heise, December 4, 1993.

5

Effects of International Propaganda on U.S.-Cuban Relations*

John Spicer Nichols

The United States broke off diplomatic relations with Cuba in January 1961 and imposed a strict economic embargo in 1962. The embargo has existed to punish Fidel Castro for confiscating U.S.-owned property in Cuba without compensation, for becoming a staunch ally of the Soviets, for trying to spread Communist revolution throughout Latin America and other areas of the world, and for providing the Soviet Union with military bases close to the border of the United States. At the same time, the United States has maintained its military base at Guantanamo in Cuba since 1903—American servicemen refer to it as Gitmo. Each year Washington sends a rent check to Castro for Gitmo, and each year Castro has not cashed the check.

The embargo against Cuba is unlike the international economic embargo that was in place against South Africa, which was maintained by many different nations. The United States is acting alone, and the embargo—the Cubans call it the blockade—has existed for more than thirty years. For four consecutive years, from 1992 to 1995, the United Nations General Assembly has voted overwhelmingly for Washington to end it. By the mid-1990s more and more U.S. newspapers were calling on the government to do away with it as a needless remnant of the Cold War because the Soviet threat had disappeared and the embargo hurt the common people in Cuba.

Since the disintegration of the Soviet Union and the resultant loss of economic aid that kept the Havana economy going, the Cuban people have suffered. In 1994 thousands fled their country to Florida on rafts. Television coverage in the United States was intense. Although many

*This chapter was researched and written in collaboration with Alicia M. Torres, Ph.D., executive director of the Cuban American Committee Research and Education Fund. The author gratefully acknowledges the research assistance of Michele T. Carlson and Christopher J. Wethman, graduate students in the Pennsylvania State University School of Communications.

*Cubans died attempting to cross the Straits of Florida, the rafting contin-
ued until both countries worked out an immigration agreement; the Castro
administration then shut the rafters down.*

*In 1995, Cuba's economy was in free-fall. The peso was virtually
worthless, and Castro had earlier allowed the circulation of the U.S. dollar. Nearly everything was rationed. Many people went without adequate
food, health care deteriorated because of a lack of medical supplies,
shelves in stores lay almost empty, and gasoline was so precious that few
cars were in the streets. Sometimes there seemed to be more hours without electricity than with it; at night, people sat in the dark a great deal.
Beggars crowded around tourists, and a man—a tourist or foreigner—
could not walk far in downtown Havana without being approached by a
prostitute.*

*The begging and prostitution were especially ironic because in the
late 1950s when Castro was taking power he railed against such indigni-
ties under the Batista regime. Although he did get rid of most begging
and prostitution, by early 1995 the situation had come full circle. Born
on August 13, 1926, Castro, at age sixty-eight, had been at the helm of
government for three and one-half decades. During most of that time, he
waged a propaganda war with the United States.*

*The two most important mass media components of the U.S. propa-
ganda efforts have been Radio Martí, which started in 1985 during the
administration of President Ronald Reagan, and TV Martí, begun in 1990
during George Bush's presidency. Both were named for José Martí, Cuba's
national hero and the leader in the fight to throw off Spanish domination
at the end of the nineteenth century. Most criticism has focused on TV
Martí, which cost U.S. taxpayers $65 million to start up in 1990. Con-
gress has allocated at least another $14 million per year to keep it going.
TV Martí broadcasts news and propaganda at Cuba; it also has broadcast* Popeye *and* Lifestyles of the Rich and Famous. *According to critics,
it has been a colossal waste. Cuba has successfully jammed most of its
signals, and for much of its existence it was broadcast only from 3:30 to
6* A.M. *For technical reasons, its signals often have reached only owners
of satellite dishes, to which almost no Cubans have access. It has been
broadcast from a hot-air balloon off Miami, and sometimes the balloon
has fallen. TV Martí clearly violates international broadcasting regulations. Cuba appealed to the International Telecommunications Union
about it and won. Many newspapers, including the* New York Times *and*
USA Today, *have editorialized against it, but Congress continues its
funding.*

*In this chapter, John Spicer Nichols offers an interesting analysis of
the propaganda war between the two countries—with rich detail about
Radio and TV Martí—that contains new scholarly insight about propaganda generally, along with cogent commentary about the U.S. broadcast propaganda. Professor Nichols, who has participated in five meetings
with Castro, most recently in 1994, received his Ph.D. in mass communi-*

cations from the University of Minnesota and is an associate professor of communications at Pennsylvania State University. He is the coauthor of Clandestine Radio Broadcasting *(1987), which was chosen as an Outstanding Academic Book by* Choice, *journal of the Association of College and Research Libraries.* He is a member of the Task Force on Scholarly Relations with Cuba of the Latin American Studies Association and is the author of Cuban Mass Media *(1982), a volume in the* Journalism Monograph *series.*

The United States and Cuba have fought a bruising propaganda war for more than three decades.[1] The two countries—separated by only ninety miles of water but a huge ideological gulf—use high-power radio transmitters as weapons in the battle to effect changes in the domestic and international behavior of their adversary. The end of the Cold War, rather than silencing the propaganda bombardment, has resulted in a major escalation. Under the widely held belief that Western radio broadcasting contributed to the fall of communism in Eastern Europe and the Soviet Union, the U.S. government has expanded its propaganda campaign against Cuba in hope of bringing down the government of Fidel Castro, one of the few remaining Communist leaders in the world. And the Cuban leadership, although enfeebled by the demise of its economic and military patrons in the Soviet bloc, has continued its ideological counterattack over the airwaves.

Although most governments in Latin America and around the world similarly devote a great amount of money and effort to international propaganda, surprisingly little is known about the short-term and long-term effects of propaganda. But despite the many claims of success by propagandists and their sponsors, there is, in fact, no empirical evidence that broadcast propaganda can easily manipulate basic attitudes and opinions of audiences in an adversary nation, change their relationship with their own government, or communicate an alternative view of their own condition and that of the outside world. While communication research has established some marginal effects for low-involvement decision, such as which brand of laundry soap to buy, it has not found large-scale effects from persuasive campaigns dealing with high-involvement topics, such as family or cultural values, nationalism, ideology, or basic interpretations of fundamental issues.[2] Most international propaganda is predicated on the assumption that it will have the desired political effect.

The primary purpose of this chapter is to challenge that assumption. Contrary to the conventional wisdom in Washington, Havana, and other world capitals, propaganda broadcasts are not effective tools for bringing about internal changes in adversary nations or otherwise resolving international disputes. The inability of propaganda to change the opinions,

knowledge, and behavior of foreign audiences has been discussed elsewhere, and therefore will not be debated again here.[3] Instead, this chapter
will examine the negative consequences of international propaganda. The
basic thesis is that propaganda—regardless of its ability to achieve a specific foreign policy goal—is dysfunctional in the conduct of international
relations. As demonstrated by the case of U.S.-Cuban relations, propaganda tends to exacerbate existing conflict between governments and
complicate efforts to negotiate peaceful settlements of international
disputes.

In March 1960, as U.S.-Cuban relations deteriorated, President
Dwight D. Eisenhower ordered the Central Intelligence Agency (CIA) to
begin clandestine radio broadcasts to the island and to initiate plans for
the Bay of Pigs invasion, a covert operation to overthrow Castro's revolutionary government, which had come to power the previous year. The
primary purpose of the new station, named Radio Swan, was "to soften
up the Cubans' will to resist" the impending invasion by a CIA-
sponsored exile army. The clandestine station, also staffed by Cuban exiles in Miami, broadcast a steady stream of invectives against the Castro
regime from transmitters on tiny Swan Island in the Caribbean. As the
CIA invasion force landed at the Bay of Pigs on the south coast of Cuba
in spring 1961, Radio Swan reported: "The invaders are steadily advancing on every front. . . . Throughout Cuba, people are joining forces with
the underground rebels fighting Fidel Castro. . . . Castro's forces are sur-
rendering in droves." Of course, neither the invasion nor Radio Swan's
broadcasts sparked a popular uprising, and the Cuban army and civilian
militia decisively defeated the invaders.[4]

Both President Eisenhower, who had planned the Bay of Pigs operation, and President John F. Kennedy, who had implemented it, errone-
ously thought that Radio Swan and other U.S. propaganda could undercut
Castro's popular support before the invasion. Their misjudgment contributed to one of the most embarrassing U.S. foreign policy defeats, but it in
no way ended the practice of broadcasting propaganda at Cuba. For more
than three decades, the United States and Cuba have engaged in a war of
hostile propaganda that has been closely correlated to poor relations and
failed diplomatic efforts to reduce tension and solve problems of mutual
concern to the two countries.

After the failed Bay of Pigs invasion, President Kennedy greatly expanded the anti-Castro broadcasts. Radio Swan changed its name to Radio Americas and continued to broadcast to Cuba from Swan Island and
later from the Florida Keys. It was joined by numerous other clandestine
stations, some sponsored by the CIA and others operated by free-lance
paramilitary groups of Cuban exiles. During the 1962 Cuban missile cri-

sis, several commercial U.S. radio stations that could be heard in Cuba were enlisted to carry anti-Castro propaganda, and the Voice of America (VOA), the U.S. government's overseas broadcast service, greatly expanded its programming to Cuba. Additionally, as part of a CIA plot to overthrow the Castro regime (known as Operation Mongoose) after the missile crisis, the Kennedy administration placed television transmitters in military aircraft in order to beam taped television messages onto the island from just outside Cuban airspace.[5]

It was the most intense propaganda campaign in the history of the Americas. Along with it, relations between the two countries grew increasingly acrimonious. The propaganda campaign did not appear to undermine Cubans' support for Castro, however, and his revolutionary government remained in power—perhaps more firmly than before—and was even more hostile to U.S. interests in the hemisphere.

Cuba was not passive in the propaganda war. Only weeks after the Bay of Pigs invasion, the Castro government launched Radio Havana Cuba, which broadcast inflammatory propaganda, first throughout the region and later throughout the world. Utilizing more than twenty radio frequencies (mostly shortwave) to broadcast more than four hundred hours weekly in eight languages (including indigenous languages of the Caribbean region), Radio Havana quickly became one of the largest international propaganda operations in the world.[6]

The quantity and virulence of Cuba's anti-United States rhetoric grew throughout the 1960s. For example, from 1962 to 1966, the Cuban government broadcast Radio Free Dixie, a venomous English-language program directed at African Americans in the southern United States. The audience was encouraged to burn U.S. cities and commit other acts of subversion: "Black men, organize, arm and form underground and secret defense forces! The most effective anti-lynch law and force for justice is the power of one gas bomb, the switchblade, the razor, the lye-can and the bullet."[7] Although U.S. officials expressed grave concern over the content and tone of the Cuban propaganda, there is no indication that, even during the height of the civil rights movement, the broadcast had any impact on U.S. audiences.

During the late 1960s and 1970s came a correlated de-escalation in propaganda broadcasting and political tension between the United States and Cuba. As successive U.S. administrations focused their attention on the Vietnam quagmire, there was a period of U.S.-Cuban détente, and hostile propaganda nearly disappeared. In 1969, two years after the CIA ended its covert operations against Cuba, the *New York Times* reported that "the previously shrill and abrasive tone seems to have been gradually eliminated from Cuban foreign broadcasts."[8] Within the next few years,

Radio Americas ceased operations, VOA phased out its special programming for Cuba, and anti-Castro clandestine stations virtually disappeared from the airwaves. In 1974–75, Secretary of State Henry Kissinger initiated secret talks with the Castro government in hope of normalizing relations, and the United States relaxed its economic embargo against Cuba.[9]

After languishing during the administrations of Richard Nixon, Gerald Ford, and Jimmy Carter, the anti-Castro broadcasts were revived by President Ronald Reagan. In 1985 he established Radio Martí, a multimillion-dollar U.S. government station named for the nineteenth-century Cuban patriot, José Martí, to help force a change in Cuba's domestic and foreign policies. President George Bush supplemented the renewed radio propaganda with Television Martí in 1990.[10]

The demise of its Soviet patron, the subsequent collapse of the Cuban economy, and the end of Cuban military involvement elsewhere in the world have changed little. Despite these dramatically different circumstances, the administration of President Bill Clinton not only continued but also boosted the U.S. broadcasts to the island. During the 1992 presidential campaign, candidate Bill Clinton criticized President Bush for failing "to put the hammer down on Fidel Castro and Cuba" and promised that, if elected, he would use Radio and TV Martí, along with toughened economic sanctions, to bring an end to one of the few remaining Communist governments in the world. Since the election, the Clinton White House has successfully opposed congressional attempts to terminate or reduce funding for the stations, and in 1994, during an immigration dispute with the Castro government, the U.S. president ordered major increases in the broadcasts to Cuba.[11]

In sum, broadcast propaganda has long been a staple in the troubled relations between the United States and Cuba. Of the nine U.S. presidents who have struggled to deal with Castro's Cuba, most have resorted to aggressive propaganda campaigns in hope of forcing a change in Cuban domestic and international behavior, or to resolve longstanding differences between the two countries.

Dysfunctions of International Propaganda: Literature Review

Even if the stated goals of Radio and TV Martí are ingenuous,[12] a high probability exists that the stations are counterproductive. Instead of paving the way for a peaceful transition to democracy in Cuba and helping to resolve disagreements between the United States and the Castro government, Radio and TV Martí might actually be increasing the likelihood of violence, chaos, and authoritarianism on the island and expanding and complicating conflicts between the two governments.

The increasingly influential theory that "communication can exacerbate conflict as well as help resolve it" is a useful lens through which to investigate if Radio and TV Martí are, in fact, counterproductive.[13] A leader in the field of conflict research, Lewis A. Coser, argues that, notwithstanding widespread beliefs to the contrary, communication is not a panacea. In contrast to what he calls "salvation-through-communication theorists," Coser writes that "communication is *not* the universal solvent to human predicaments." Under certain circumstances, increased communication may indeed enhance human understanding and lead to the resolution of disputes; however, under other circumstances, the same type of communication may magnify existing problems or create new ones. He concludes that, "as long as there are large inequalities among human beings, as long as there exist sharp asymmetries in power and structurally induced discrepancies in access to resources, it seems unlikely that the potential for conflict will be successfully minimized, no matter what channels may be available for undistorted communication."[14]

Despite the theoretical foundation offered by Coser and others, most research in the field of international relations does not consider the dysfunctions as well as the functions of communication in resolving global conflict. For example, in *Communication and Diplomacy in a Changing World*, Tran Van Dinh writes that "communication is to diplomacy as blood is to the human body. Whenever communication ceases, the body of international politics, the process of diplomacy, is dead, and the result is violent conflict or atrophy."[15] Among the few who have recognized the dysfunctions of international communication is the eminent sociologist W. Phillips Davison, who, in *Mass Communication and Conflict Resolution*, states that "increasing the quality and quantity of communication will not solve the underlying causes of conflict; indeed, in some cases these causes may receive greater salience as a result of more accurate perceptions on both sides."[16]

In addition, Martin Patchen, who studied diplomatic communication between the United States and the Soviet Union during the Cuban missile crisis, concluded, in *Resolving Disputes between Nations*, that communication, especially coercive or provocative communication, between parties to a conflict does not necessarily lead to a resolution. As is typical of researchers in the field of international relations and global conflict, however, Patchen emphasizes diplomatic communication and does not directly examine the effect of propaganda or other mass media on the outcome of the crisis.[17] Harold Lasswell, the pioneer of political communication research, was one of the few who paid some attention to the role of propaganda. In *Power and Society*, Lasswell and his coauthor, Abraham Kaplan, hypothesize that propaganda can precipitate a crisis, even to the point of violence, when preexisting stress of high intensity is already present; however, they offered little elaboration and no empirical or anecdotal support for their proposition.[18]

C. R. Mitchell also does not directly examine propaganda or international broadcasting in *The Structure of International Conflict*, but he does examine how different types of conflict might affect the outcome of a situation. He defines conflict behavior as "actions undertaken by one party in any situation of conflict aimed at the opposing party with the intention of making that opponent abandon or modify its goals,"[19] suggesting that communication falls into that category.

The major purpose of the next section is to extend the work of these and other authors directly to international propaganda. In addition, some admittedly speculative propositions will be advanced regarding the effect of propaganda on international relations.

Propositions on Propaganda and International Relations

When two parties, such as national governments, find themselves in conflict, each side must choose from among the following potential strategies for dealing with the conflict: (1) capitulate, (2) negotiate and compromise with the adversary, (3) convert the other party to one's own position, (4) use force to compel a change by the other side, or (5) attempt to live with continuing conflict without resolution. The strategy that is selected depends, to a considerable extent, on the degree and nature of the conflict, the relationship between the parties, internal conditions of each of the parties, and conditions of the system within which the parties operate. For example, the strategy of living with unresolved conflict is unlikely to be successful except when the intensity of the conflict is very low. But the question here is: After these intervening conditions have been accounted for, which strategy will be chosen?

A government is likely to choose the strategy that will resolve the conflict at the lowest possible cost. Capitulation and compromise require giving up something to the opponent, and therefore have substantial material and political costs. The use of force could result, in addition to the other costs, in loss of lives and could bring the nation into conflict with a third party. Hence, the use of the second strategy—that is, attempting to convert the other party—will usually have the lowest initial cost to the government within both its own country and the international system. One obvious and commonly used means of attempting a conversion is international propaganda. Furthermore, using a conversion strategy tends to be a compromise position between hawks and doves within the government and may temporarily reduce domestic tensions over how best to respond to the external conflict. Establishing a radio station to broadcast propaganda to the adversary, while far short of the more aggressive strategies that the hawks prefer, is usually an acceptable response to the doves, who would have difficulty opposing a conversion strategy during a crisis.

Proposition 1: When national governments become engaged in conflict, each party initially is likely to use propaganda intended to convert the opposite side to its own position.

Propaganda campaigns are rarely successful in converting a national government's position in an international conflict. The target of the conversion strategy usually will suffer similar internal and external costs if it capitulates to or compromises with the adversary. Unwilling to give up power, prestige, or resources until all other options are exhausted, the target of the conversion strategy usually will respond with its own propaganda. In circular fashion the latter propaganda campaign will be similarly ineffective. Although no empirical research supports the notion of a large-scale conversion in public opinion in an adversary nation, Mitchell points out that, even if some individual citizens (or even individual leaders) on one side of an international dispute were converted, their national government would not automatically be restructured or replaced: "This simplistic view of a group, an organisation, a community, or a national government 'changing its mind' in the face of coercive or collaborative strategies in an analogous fashion to an individual, is so simplistic as to be dangerously misleading."[20]

The "democratic assumption" that a country's foreign and domestic policies are responsive to the opinions of the majority of its citizens certainly does not apply uniformly throughout the world. Some argue that it is largely illusory even in the United States.[21] For example, opinion polls in the United States for many years have indicated that the majority of the American people would support an effort to reach an accommodation with the Castro government.[22] Yet Democratic and Republican administrations alike have responded to special interests and have pursued policies of confrontation with Cuba. If the U.S. government is unresponsive to popular opinion on a wide range of domestic and foreign policy issues, such as gun control and the 1994 intervention in Haiti, what is the basis for believing that a hypothetical change in Cuban public opinion would somehow lead to a change in government policy?

Proposition 2: International propaganda campaigns rarely result in the conversion of a national government's position regarding a conflict with the propagandist's government.

Communication between parties to a conflict is frequently not productive. Mitchell writes that "unintended side effects from acts and statements in conflict situations appear to be the rule, rather than the exception."[23] Although one side may see its propaganda campaign as a peaceful alternative to use of force, the other side probably will see it as an intrusion into its internal affairs, and therefore as a serious escalation in the conflict. No government looks kindly on a campaign by a foreign adversary to undercut its legitimacy with its own people. Therefore, regardless of its intent, a propaganda broadcast from one party in a conflict to another is usually seen by the latter as a hostile act requiring a strong response. After hostile propaganda campaigns begin, the costs of negotiation and compromise significantly increase as does the pressure for further escalation of the conflict. If the level of conflict is already dangerously high, the parties might widen the conflict to other issues instead of risking further mutually destructive escalations.[24]

Proposition 3: Propaganda between nations in conflict tends to escalate and/or widen the conflict.

As the conflict escalates and spreads to issues other than those that originally brought the parties into dispute, the prospect of a negotiated settlement decreases and the prospect of more conflict, including the use of force, increases. Previously unrelated issues become intertwined, and negotiations become badly complicated. Therefore, an initial strategy of broadcasting propaganda may be seen as a compromise between hawks and doves, but it ultimately tends to weaken the position of the doves and strengthen that of the hawks. The strengthening of the hawks within one of the parties to an international conflict tends to strengthen the hawks on the other side, resulting in further polarization and less likelihood of a peaceful settlement.

In other words, international propaganda is akin to shouting between husband and wife in a marital squabble. The shouting is the result of an underlying conflict. Rather than resolving the disagreement, it tends to escalate the conflict and further polarize the couple. The yelling sometimes contributes to a violent outcome; it rarely is healthy for the relationship. Therefore, just as raised voices are both cause and effect of a domestic dispute, international propaganda emerges from and contributes to international conflict. While international propaganda's impact is clearly conditioned by many other factors, it tends to exacerbate existing conflict between nations, complicate negotiation of a settlement, and, therefore, reduce the prospects for a peaceful resolution.

The following case study examines whether international propaganda has helped the United States or Cuba to achieve its foreign policy objectives, or if it has been counterproductive.[25] The study draws heavily on the views of two key figures in U.S.-Cuban relations. One is Wayne S. Smith, the State Department's leading expert on Cuba, who was stationed at the U.S. embassy in Havana when Castro came to power in 1959 and who was chief of the U.S. Interests Section in Cuba when he retired from the foreign service in 1982. He also was the top American diplomat in Cuba during the 1980 Mariel boatlift crisis. The other is Ricardo Alarcón, president of the Cuban National Assembly and a former foreign minister. Widely acknowledged to be one of the most influential members of the Cuban leadership, he represented the Havana government during the majority of the negotiations with the United States on immigration.

Case Study: Radio and TV Martí and U.S.-Cuban Migration

The proposition that propaganda exacerbates existing conflict between nations and complicates efforts to negotiate a resolution to that conflict is probably best exemplified by the linkage between U.S. propaganda broadcasts and diplomatic efforts to arrange orderly migration between the United States and Cuba. Under almost any circumstances, migration would be an important bilateral issue for two countries—one poor and the other rich—separated by only ninety miles of water. The fact that Cuba and the United States have a troubled political relationship only compounds the problem. Even before Castro came to power in 1959, a steady stream of Cuban immigrants sought a better life north of the Straits of Florida. In the early 1960s, as the United States tightened its economic embargo of Cuba and Castro moved his country toward socialism, there were increasing political as well as economic pressures on Cubans to emigrate but decreasing opportunities to do so legally. Having broken diplomatic relations with Cuba, the U.S. government had no consular officials in Havana to handle normal migration matters, and, because of the embargo, there was no air service between the two countries to transport Cuban immigrants.

For those unwilling to endure the economic and political hardships in Cuba, the solution was to leave for the United States illegally (without a Cuban exit visa or U.S. entrance visa) in small boats. As the number of those making the dangerous journey increased during the summer of 1965, Voice of America hammered home the message that "Castro's Cuba was an island prison from which most of its people wished to escape."[26] The broadcasts angered Castro and helped to trigger the first in a series of migration crises. On September 28, 1965, Castro announced that, as proof that Cuba was not a prison island, as VOA had charged, any Cuban who wished to leave could do so from the port of Camarioca. Within a month, approximately five thousand Cubans were picked up by friends and family from the United States and transported to Florida on boats. Preoccupied with the Vietnam war, President Lyndon Johnson's administration quickly negotiated an agreement with the Castro government to end the crisis. Under the agreement, Cubans wishing to immigrate to the United States would be processed by the Swiss embassy in Havana and airlifted to Miami in an orderly fashion.

Such an arrangement was beneficial to both sides. The Castro government was able to purge those who were an economic or political drag on its system without the instability of a disorderly exodus. The United States regained control of its borders while maintaining a controlled flow of Cuban immigrants, mostly well-educated professionals and managers who could make a contribution to the U.S. economy and society. The crisis sparked by VOA was defused, and the so-called freedom flights continued for eight years, bringing more than 250,000 Cubans to the United States without fanfare or major incident.[27]

After a period of detente throughout the 1970s, tension between the United States and Cuba again began to rise during the 1980s. Although differences over Cuban involvement in Africa and Central America were the major source of friction, the intertwined issues of migration and propaganda broadcasts also were of central focus. With the freedom flights phased out and the U.S. government granting few visas to Cubans, migration pressures began to build once more, and the Cuban government expressed an interest in reestablishing a normal flow of immigration. Of particular urgency to the Cuban government was the problem of boat hijackings. U.S. law, namely the Cuban Refugee Adjustment Act, granted special status to Cuban immigrants who entered the country illegally. Instead of being deported, as would be the case for immigrants from other Latin American countries, Cubans who made it to U.S. shores without a visa or were picked up en route by the U.S. Coast Guard were allowed to stay, to collect government benefits, and, eventually, to apply for permanent resident status. With little prospect of emigrating legally, Cubans were stealing or hijacking boats in increasing numbers and setting sail for the United States. The Cuban government expected its U.S. counterpart to prosecute the hijackers or at least discourage the illegal migration. After all, Cuba had cooperated in ending the rash of airline hijackings that had plagued the United States in the 1960s and 1970s.[28]

The Cuban government also complained about the failure of the U.S. government to close down anti-Castro clandestine stations, which had returned to the air in large numbers after being mostly silent since the mid-1970s. Calling for the violent overthrow of the Cuban government, the stations broadcast from illegal transmitters in the United States and usually were sponsored by shadowy paramilitary groups known to have committed acts of violence on both sides of the Florida Straits.[29]

In 1980 the Carter administration, already being accused of weakness in foreign policy during an election year, did not believe that it should respond to the Cuban concerns. According to Smith, at that time the chief U.S. envoy in Havana, the Cuban leadership then decided that if the United States wanted to encourage illegal migration by small boats, it would facilitate the process. In April the Castro government opened the port of Mariel for any Cuban wishing to leave the country. By September, 125,000 Cubans, including a few thousand criminals, mental patients, and other so-called excludables, left for Florida in a disorderly boatlift. The Mariel exodus was a foreign policy nightmare for the Carter administration and probably contributed to its election defeat that year. (Another political casualty of the Mariel exodus was Bill Clinton, then the young governor of Arkansas. His handling of riots by Cuban boatpeople who were being detained at a military installation in his state was an important issue in his unsuccessful 1980 campaign for reelection.) The mass exodus also badly increased U.S.-Cuban tension after a lengthy period of détente and accordingly precipitated another spiral of hostile propaganda and conflict between the two adversaries.

The Reagan administration took a decidedly tougher line toward Cuba when it came to office in 1981. It charged the Castro government with meddling in Central America and specifically listed the broadcasts of Radio Havana Cuba and other Cuban propaganda as evidence. In response, the Reagan administration threatened military action, tightened the embargo, and countered with its own propaganda. The keystone of the entire anti-Castro campaign was establishing Radio Martí.[30] Smith, then head of the U.S. delegation, later reported that top Reagan administration officials assumed that the radio station and other measures "would force [the Cubans] to accede to all our demands." In a 1981 message to his superior in the State Department, Smith registered his dissent to the Radio Martí proposal and effectively articulated the thesis of this chapter:

> The Cubans . . . react to sheer pressure in a predictable way, either by digging their heels in, or by adopting an even more aggressive posture toward us. . . . The Cubans will *not*, as a result of our threats, moderate their behavior. On the contrary, tensions and uncertainty will beget only more tensions and uncertainty. Certainly the steps we are contemplating short of invasion, i.e., establishment of [Radio Martí], tightening the embargo, etc., will of course make the Cubans mad, and will cause them some inconvenience. They will not, however, have the slightest effect in terms of moderating Cuba's policy actions abroad. The contrary is more likely to be the case. That [Radio Martí] will be counterproductive I have not the slightest doubt.[31]

Smith's prediction was correct. Shortly after President Reagan announced his plans for Radio Martí, Castro told an audience in Havana that "you have to be quite cynical and immoral and shameless to speak of establishing a radio station on U.S. soil to campaign against the

Revolution, to try to destabilize and subvert the Revolution. You must be cynical, very cynical! There is no more vulgar and brutal form of intervention in the internal affairs of a country. . . . Of course, there will be a response."[32] With the nearly hysterical support of right-wing Cuban exiles in Miami, the Reagan administration pushed hard for congressional approval of the station.[33] Smith left the foreign service and, from the ranks of academe, became a leading critic of U.S. foreign policy toward Cuba.

Shortly after the Mariel crisis, the Carter administration sought to close the barn door after the cows were out. It held secret talks with the Cuban government with the hope of coming to a new understanding on immigration, but, as a lame-duck administration, it made no progress. In early 1984 the Reagan administration, searching for ways to prevent a new wave of Cuban immigrants and to return Cuban criminals and other excludables who had arrived during the 1980 Mariel exodus and were still in U.S. jails, quietly inquired as to whether the Castro government would be willing to resume negotiations on immigration. It was, and by December the two sides had agreed to the repatriation of the Cuban excludables and to reestablishing the normal immigration to the United States of up to twenty thousand Cubans per year, plus a total of three thousand political prisoners to be released from Cuban jails. The Cuban delegation, headed by Deputy Foreign Minister Ricardo Alarcón, hoped that the agreement represented a trend toward reduced tension, although that view probably was not shared in Washington.

The renewed flow of Cuban immigrants had barely started when, on May 20, 1985, the long-delayed Radio Martí finally went on the air. Widely heralded by the Reagan administration as a powerful force for democratic change in Cuba—and broadcasting twenty-four hours per day of specially tailored programming at an annual cost of $12 million—Radio Martí was the biggest escalation of the U.S.-Cuban broadcast war since Radio Swan. As promised, Castro responded. In the biography *Fidel*, Tad Szulc writes that Castro went into a rage over the start-up of the latest propaganda station and lashed back by suspending the new immigration agreement.[34] He also retaliated with his own propaganda campaign from high-power transmitters that could be heard throughout much of the United States and disrupted the broadcasts of radio stations as far away as Utah. The Mariel excludables remained in U.S. prisons, the political prisoners stayed in Cuban jails, and migration pressures continued to rise.

The issues of radio propaganda and migration had become closely intertwined. The rhetoric and tension between the two countries increased, and the likelihood of resurrecting the mutually beneficial migration agreement decreased. In 1986, U.S. and Cuban negotiators met in Mexico City to explore the possibility of restoring the 1984 migration agreement. At the meetings, Alarcón insisted that Radio Martí be taken off the air as a condition for reinstating the agreement or, as an alternative, that the Reagan administration grant Cuba equal access to U.S. airwaves in order to broadcast its propaganda to listeners in the United States. After all, if the U.S. government could broadcast to Cuba, the Cuban government should be able to broadcast to the United States. Under pressure from hard-line Cuban exiles in Florida, who had emerged as an important voting bloc and source of campaign contributions, and unwilling to force scores of U.S. radio stations (also a powerful constituency in politics) off the air to make room for Cuban transmissions, U.S. negotiators rejected the demands. The impasse over migration continued.[35]

Angered that the Castro government did not, as expected, give up its demands regarding radio propaganda and restore the 1984 migration agreement, the Reagan administration quickly responded by tightening the economic embargo and by imposing other tough measures against Cuba. Due in part to Radio Martí, the United States and Cuba, in the words of the *New York Times*, "traded a flurry of diplomatic jabs that have brought relations between the two mutually antagonistic countries to the lowest point in at least a decade."[36]

As the tightened embargo took its toll on the Cuban economy, the Castro government recognized the need for an immigration safety valve, and as the number of Cubans leaving the island illegally on makeshift rafts soared, the Reagan administration began to fear another uncontrolled exodus. Both sides agreed to return to the negotiating table. Cuban negotiators, again headed by Alarcón, this time presented a significantly modified position. They agreed to restore the 1984 migration agreement, which allowed for thousands of Cubans to receive immigrant visas to the United States each year, and for the deportation of Cuban criminals in U.S. jails. The Cuban government dropped its demand that Radio Martí be terminated in return for a promise by the United States "to find a mutually acceptable solution" to the radio problem and that the solution must be "in strict compliance with international law." Cuba had long argued, with considerable validity, that Radio Martí, which broadcast on AM frequencies reserved for domestic use only, violated Cuban rights under international telecommunications law. Therefore, the clear intent of the 1987 agreement was for the United States to modify its transmissions of Radio Martí to bring it into compliance with international accords or to find some other compromise with Cuba regarding radio.[37]

The agreement resulted in a warming trend in U.S.-Cuban relations, but it did not last long.[38] While it is certainly true that Cuba has not always lived up to the various agreements it has signed with the United States and other countries,[39] in the case of the intertwined migration-broadcasting issue it was the United States that did not abide by the spirit or letter of the 1987 agreement. According to the settlement, the U.S. government would grant up to 20,000 Cubans immigrant visas each year. That number was increased in 1990 to 27,875 per year as the result of a general change in U.S. immigration laws. Yet, during the eight years between 1984 and 1994 that the immigration agreement was in force, only 11,000 Cubans were issued visas—less than one half the maximum number for one year. In 1993 the United States granted only 2,700 immigrant visas to the 134,000 Cubans who applied.[40]

The United States also failed to hold up its end of the bargain regarding radio broadcasting by refusing to make any changes in Radio Martí transmissions that would bring it into compliance with international regulations or to submit the dispute to international mediation. Instead of arranging for a Cuban broadcasting quid pro quo in lieu of changes to Radio Martí, the Bush administration established TV Martí in 1990. The new U.S. station, which broadcast from a blimp floating over the Florida Keys, cost $40 million in start-up costs and an annual budget ranging from $11 million to $15 million. Zealously backed and to a large extent controlled by extremist factions of the Cuban-American community in South Florida, TV Martí aired shrill anti-Castro programming that did not meet VOA programming standards. While Radio Martí was of dubious legality, TV Martí clearly was not in compliance with international telecommunication accords. The International Telecommunication Union, an agency of the United Nations responsible for regulation of international communications, so informed the U.S. government in 1990. In short, it was not the "mutually acceptable solution . . . in strict compliance with international law" to which Cuban negotiators thought they had agreed.[41]

Castro labeled TV Martí "an act of aggression" and again promised to respond, but, with the dramatically changed conditions in the 1990s, his ability to do so was rapidly diminishing.[42] The collapse of Cuba's Soviet patron sent the island's economy into a tailspin. Within three years the Cuban national income fell nearly 50 percent. Food and other basic goods were scarce. There was not enough energy to operate the transportation system and factories, let alone to power the Cuban radio transmitters that Castro had previously used to send his own propaganda back to the United States. The shortage caused significant popular dissatisfaction and domestic political tension. Castro's popularity plummeted, and many analysts predicted the imminent fall of his government.[43]

Again concerned that Cuba's economic and political problems were paving the way for a new wave of illegal immigrants across the Straits of Florida, U.S. diplomats met in December 1991 with their Cuban counterparts seeking to bolster the 1984 immigration agreement. Cuba again sought to link the negotiations to broadcasting and to the larger issue of the U.S. economic embargo, which it argued were the causes of the immigration pressures. But neither Radio and TV Martí nor the embargo was negotiable with a U.S. presidential election less than a year away, since both candidates were vying for Cuban-American votes and contributions. Even though it was concerned about the growing potential for another Cuban exodus, the Bush administration further tightened the embargo instead of easing it. Two weeks before the 1992 election, fearing that he might be outflanked by Clinton's tough campaign rhetoric on Cuba, President Bush reversed his position and signed the Cuban Democracy Act, which included stringent new economic measures intended to, in the words of its congressional author, "wreak havoc" in Cuba.[44]

"As the Cold War has thawed, U.S.-Cuban relations paradoxically have become more frigid than at any point since the early 1960s," wrote Gillian Gunn, a leading expert on Cuba.[45] Although the original reasons cited for its conflict with Cuba were no longer valid, the U.S. government progressively hardened its policy toward the Castro government during both the Bush and Clinton administrations. Cuba was no longer an ally of and international paladin for the Soviet Union, the United States' primary Cold War adversary. The Castro government pulled its troops out of Africa, it ceased supporting revolutionary groups in Latin America, and, with its economy and political system in shambles, Cuba presented little or no threat to U.S. national interests. Conflict between the United States and Cuba took on a life of its own, however. Gunn described a process of polarization in which right-wing Cuban-Americans and congressional hawks gained greater control of U.S. policy toward Cuba and reformers within the Cuban leadership were purged. Supporters of constructive engagement on both sides were marginalized, and hard-liners were in ascent.[46]

"This is a time when we have to take the official line," Carlos Aldana, chief of ideology of the Cuban Communist Party and widely considered the third most powerful Cuban leader, told a meeting of Cuban journalists in 1992. Aldana, who previously was a prominent advocate of glasnost (openness) in Cuba, reversed course and warned the media against giving space to "enemy alternatives." But his reversal came too late. Aldana—the leading Cuban reformer, known as someone with whom the United States could do business—was purged from the Cuban leadership under ambiguous circumstances in late 1992.[47] Immediately following Aldana's demise, the Cuban government, according to the Inter American Press Association, "stepped up its repression of anyone seeking to publish free opinion." The organization published a long list of Cuban journalists and writers who had been jailed for deviating from official positions and cited numerous other examples of repression. Of particular note, a Cuban dissident, who regularly called Radio Martí to report public disturbances over shortages of food, was convicted in a show trial of "supplying enemy propaganda." The fact that the trial was open to the public, including foreign journalists and diplomats, indicates that the Cuban government was punctuating its objections to Radio Martí.[48]

Along with the hardened U.S. policy toward Cuba came a more strident tone on Radio Martí. Never the paragon of objectivity, Radio Martí increasingly was programmed to meet the political needs of hard-line Cuban exiles in Miami rather than the news and information needs of Cubans in Cuba. The former head of Radio Martí, Ernesto F. Betancourt, and many former and current members of its staff publicly or privately charged that the station's content had become badly politicized and counterproductive to long-term U.S. interests in Cuba, and independent evaluators confirmed the problem.[49]

Responding to the growing problems with the stations, Congress considered cutting off funding for TV Martí and forcing a major reform of Radio Martí. In 1993 it commissioned a federal advisory panel to investigate whether TV Martí had sufficient viewership and whether both stations were sufficiently cost effective and met government standards for quality of programming to justify their continued funding. The advisory panel's report verified that TV Martí had little or no audience in Cuba,[50] and it conceded shortcomings in Radio and TV Martí's content, political control, and cost, thereby leaving the door open for Congress to close or cut back the stations. But, in July 1994, the Clinton administration squelched congressional opposition to the stations. Claiming that Radio and TV Martí were key components to its foreign policy toward Cuba, the administration strongly reaffirmed its commitment to the stations and proposed beefing them up as a solution to the problems.[51]

The combined effects of the tightened U.S. embargo, the end of Soviet subsidies, and Cuba's own economic mismanagement had taken their toll by 1994. With their standard of living only a fraction of what it had been a few years ago, with little official tolerance for political dissent, and with virtually no chance of receiving an immigrant visa to the United States, thousands of Cubans illegally set out for Florida in makeshift rafts. During the first half of 1994 the U.S. government granted only 544 immigrant visas to Cubans, yet it accepted 4,092 so-called rafters for eventual permanent resident status. The Havana government also detained 10,975 more attempting to depart illegally.[52] Many, although the number probably will never be known, died in the treacherous waters when their rafts sank.

As the number of rafters increased in early 1994, Cuban officials and academic researchers charged that Radio Martí was badly compounding the problem. They said that the tone and context of Radio Martí's extensive coverage of the rafters encouraged Cubans to leave the island illegally in direct contradiction to official U.S. policy against immigrating illegally, particularly by such dangerous means. The Cuban officials cited what they described as Radio Martí's glorification of the rafters, including regular features about the successful lives of those who recently had made the trip and detailed coverage of U.S. Coast Guard and Cuban exile rescue operations. Preliminary results from a University of Havana survey of unsuccessful rafters who had been picked up by the Cuban coast guard indicated that their confidence in arriving safely in Florida was correlated with their listening to U.S. radio. The study, however, did not establish a causal relationship with Radio Martí broadcasts.[53]

A rash of hijackings and thefts of Cuban boats in summer 1994 was the prelude to yet another immigration crisis. Events closely resembled those leading up to the 1980 Mariel exodus. On July 13 a Cuban tugboat was hijacked and headed for Florida. It was pursued by three other Cuban tugboats, which doused it with fire hoses and rammed it. The hijacked boat capsized, and thirty-two of its sixty-three passengers, some of them women and children, drowned. The incident was reported widely in the United States, and Cuba received significant criticism for it. Although all of the facts surrounding the incident still were not fully known, U.S. officials described the deaths as a purposeful act of the Cuban government. In comments carried over Radio Martí, President Clinton called the incident "another example of the brutal nature of the Cuban regime." Within the next two weeks, three more Cuban boats, all ferries used for harbor transportation, were hijacked. In one case, the armed Cuban hijackers killed a policeman; in all three cases, some of the hijacked passengers asked to be and were returned to Cuba. Others, including the hijackers, were accepted into the United States without prosecution. The Cuban government vigorously protested the U.S. treatment of the hijackers.[54] A prominent U.S. professor of international law, in Havana doing research sponsored by the MacArthur Foundation during the year leading to the crisis, wrote that "the hijackers were always given a hero's welcome in Miami, and their feats were broadcast in Cuba over the United States-financed Radio Marti. Whenever the Cuban Government successfully interdicted such illegal emigration, the United States accused it of committing human rights violations and classified those arrested as political prisoners."[55]

On August 5 the situation bubbled over. Upon rumors of another hijacking, a few thousand Cubans gathered on the Havana waterfront. Their chants of "Down with Fidel" escalated into rock throwing, looting of tourist hotels and stores, and eventually a riot. After Cuban police quelled the extremely rare antigovernment violence, Castro toured the scene and angrily accused Radio Martí and other U.S. radio stations of inspiring the illegal departures. "Either they [the United States] take serious measures to guard their coasts, or we will stop putting obstacles in the way of people who want to leave the country," Castro said. A Clinton administration spokesperson responded, stating that "the United States. . . will not permit Fidel Castro to dictate our immigration policy or to create a replay of the Mariel boatlift, a cynical move on the part of Castro." Within days, the number of Cuban rafters increased from a dozen or so per day to hundreds—then thousands—per day.[56]

The Clinton administration's initial response to the new exodus was to reverse longstanding U.S. policy to admit Cuban rafters under the Cuban Refugee Adjustment Act. The U.S. Coast Guard was ordered to interdict the Cuban boatpeople at sea and detain them at a U.S. naval base without any rights for eventual admission into the United States. Next, under pressure from hard-line Cuban exiles and conservative legislators, President Clinton announced further tightening of the embargo, including a ban on Cuban Americans sending cash to their families on the island, even greater restrictions on travel to Cuba by U.S. citizens, and "more aggressive" use of Radio and TV Martí. The broadcasting measures included adding four frequencies to Radio Martí's shortwave transmissions, doubling the power of its AM transmissions, increasing TV Martí's hours of programming, and threatening to use military aircraft as airborne transmitters to avoid Cuban jamming of the stations. More important, Radio and TV Martí markedly changed their message to potential Cuban rafters, announcing that "the waters are unsafe. Hurricane season has started. People are dying. American policy has changed. There is no welcome for survivors. Refugees are detained. Don't go."[57]

In effect, the U.S. government stations were attempting to dissuade Cubans from doing what, according to the Cuban government, they previously were encouraging them to do. In the three days following the change of Radio and TV Martí's message, the number of Cubans picked up at sea by the U.S. Coast Guard increased from 861 to 1,293 on the first day, 2,548 on the second day, and 3,253 on the third day. U.S. officials publicly urged patience until the broadcast warnings had the desired effect of abating the illegal migration but privately acknowledged that the policy was not working. There was no evidence that Cubans were responding in rote to the new message to stay home any more than they had decided to emigrate because of the previous message. Only a Caribbean storm seemed to slow the flow.[58]

Given the long-standing linkage between U.S. broadcasts to Cuba and the immigration problem, the Clinton administration's expansion of Radio and TV Martí was throwing fuel on the fire. It also was consistent with the thesis of this chapter that parties to international conflict tend to respond with propaganda but that the propaganda also tends to exacerbate the conflict and complicate a negotiated resolution of it.

Under growing criticism for its handling of the crisis—and concluding that its new policy toward Cuba was not successfully slowing the tide of rafters—the Clinton administration finally agreed to a new round of immigration talks with the Castro government.[59] In a familiar replay of previous negotiations on the issue, Ricardo Alarcón headed the Cuban delegation, which again insisted on expanding the talks to include causes of the migration, namely the U.S. embargo and broadcasts. Under intense pressure from hard-line Cuban exiles to make no concessions to the Castro government, the Clinton administration publicly refused to consider any issue other than immigration. The Cuban delegates softened their position and, on September 9, accepted a short-term fix rather than a long-term solution to the immigration problem. Cuba agreed to "take effective measures" to stop the illegal emigration from the island in exchange for U.S. promises to "take effective measures" to end the hijackings of Cuban boats and planes and to grant immigrant visas to a minimum of twenty thousand Cubans per year. Within days, the flow of illegal Cuban immigrants stopped, and the latest crisis ended. Both sides vigorously denied that they also had entered into a secret side agreement to discuss other issues later, especially the U.S. embargo and broadcast propaganda.[60] If so, the U.S.-Cuban immigration problem and the issues with which it is intertwined will almost certainly reemerge.

The broadcasting war demonstrates that nations tend to resort to propaganda during international conflicts, although it usually proves to be counterproductive. The more than thirty years of U.S. broadcasting to Cuba, rather than improving the domestic and international behavior of the Castro government, has helped to polarize the two countries and has complicated diplomatic efforts to resolve their differences.

In the coming millennium, new communications technologies will make it easier for nations in the Americas to deliver propaganda to their neighbors. If propaganda, as this chapter argues, has the tendency to make a bad international situation worse, this enhanced technological capability could generate even greater conflict between nations of differing cultures, ideologies, and national interests. As the economies and political systems of Latin America grow more interdependent, there will be greater potential for disputes among nations, which, paradoxically, will have a much greater stake in maintaining peaceful relations. As a result, the problem of propaganda, a major contributor to inter-American conflict, will have to be addressed eventually.

Notes

1. The use of the term propaganda is in itself controversial. Most U.S. government international broadcasters vigorously deny that they are engaged in propaganda, although their work places them well within standard definitions of the term. According to *Webster's New World Dictionary of the American Language*, 2d college ed. (New York: Simon and Schuster, 1980), 1138, propaganda is "any systematic, widespread dissemination or promotion of particular ideas, doctrines, practices, etc., to further one's own cause or to damage an opposing one." See also Garth S. Jowett and Victoria O'Donnell, *Propaganda and Persuasion*, 2d ed. (Newbury Park, CA: Sage, 1992), 1–35; Bruce L. Smith, "Propaganda," in *Encyclopedia of the Social Sciences*, ed. D. L. Sills (New York: Macmillan, 1968), 579; Philo C. Washburn, *Broadcasting Propaganda: International Radio Broadcasting and the Construction of Political Reality* (Westport, CT: Greenwood Press, 1992), 82.

2. Irving L. Janis and M. Brewster Smith, "Effects of Education and Persuasion on National and International Images," in *International Behavior: A Social-Psychological Analysis*, ed. Herbert C. Kelman (New York: Holt, Rinehart and Winston, 1966), 195–96; Ralph K. White, "The New Resistance to International Propaganda," *Public Opinion Quarterly* 16, no. 3 (Winter 1952): 539–51; Howard H. Frederick, *Global Communication & International Relations* (Belmont, CA: Wadsworth, 1993), 230–31; Donald R. Browne, *International Radio Broadcasting: The Limits of the Limitless Medium* (New York: Praeger, 1982); L. John Martin, "Effectiveness of International Propaganda," *The Annals of the American Academy of Political and Social Sciences* 398 (November 1971): 61–70; Melvin L. DeFleur and Everette E. Dennis, *Understanding Mass Communication* (Boston: Houghton Mifflin Company, 1991), chap. 17; Shearon A. Lowery and Melvin L. Defleur, *Milestones in Mass Communication Research* (New York: Longman, 1988); Leo W. Jeffres, *Mass Media Processes and Effects* (Prospect Heights, IL: Waveland Press, Inc., 1986); William J. McGuire, "The Myth of Massive Media Impact: Savagings and Salvagings," *Public Communication and Behavior* 1 (1986): 173–275; K. Kyoon Hur, "International Mass Communication Research: A Critical Review of Theory and Methods," in *Communication Yearbook*, no. 6, ed. Michael Burgoon (Beverly Hills: Sage Publications, 1982): 531–54; Maxwell E. McCombs, "Mass Communication in Political Campaigns: Information, Gratifications, and Persuasion," in *Current Perspectives in Mass Communication Research*, ed. F. Gerald Kline and Phillip J. Tichenor (Beverly Hills: Sage, 1972), 169–94.

3. John Spicer Nichols, "A Communication Perspective on Radio Martí," *Cuban Studies/Estudios Cubanos* 14 (Summer 1984): 35–46, 55–56; idem, "Wasting the Propaganda Dollar," *Foreign Policy* 56 (Fall 1984): 129–40. For the view that propaganda has powerful and positive effects on U.S. foreign policy interests, see Kevin J. McNamara, "Reaching Captive Minds with Radio," *Orbis* 36 (Winter 1992): 23–40; U.S. Department of State, *Report of the President's Task Force on U.S. Government Broadcasting*, No. 9925, December 1991, 1; "Sending Cross-Border Static: On the Fate of Radio Free Europe and the Influence of

International Broadcasting, Interview: Malcolm Forbes, Jr.," *Journal of International Affairs* 47 (Summer 1993): 76; John LeBoutillier, "How to Overthrow the Soviet Government—Without Firing a Shot," *USA Today*, January 1982.

4. Lawrence C. Soley and John S. Nichols, *Clandestine Radio Broadcasting* (New York: Praeger 1987), 181; John Spicer Nichols, "When Nobody Listens: Assessing the Political Success of Radio Martí," *Communication Research* 11 (April 1984): 281–304; Peter Wyden, *Bay of Pigs: The Untold Story* (New York: Simon & Shuster, 1979), 22.

5. John Spicer Nichols, "A Word of Caution about TV Martí," *Broadcasting*, July 25, 1988.

6. Frederick, *Cuban-American Radio Wars: Ideology in International Telecommunications* (Norwood, NJ: Ablex, 1986); Baldomero Alvarez Rios, "Nacida en los dias de Giron," *Bohemia* (Havana), April 15, 1983; "Cuban Radio Plans Increase in Latin-American Programs," *New York Times*, July 21, 1965; Jack Gould, "Havana Radio Is a Major Relay for Propaganda of Asian Reds," *New York Times*, March 24, 1968.

7. Jon D. Cozean et al., *Cuban Guerrilla Training Centers and Radio Havana* (Washington, DC: Center for Research in Social Systems, American University, 1968). Also see Tad Szulc, "Radio Free Dixie in Havana Praises Negro 'Revolt' in South," *New York Times*, October 8, 1962.

8. "Cuba Tones Down Overseas Radio," *New York Times*, August 24, 1969.

9. Nichols, "When Nobody Listens," 294.

10. Karin Edlund, Jon Elliston, and Peter Kornbluh, *U.S. Broadcasting to Cuba: Radio and TV Martí, A Historical Chronology* (Washington, DC: National Security Archive, 1994), 26; Kyu Ho Youm, "The Radio and TV Martí Controversy: A Re-examination," *Gazette* 48 (1991): 95–103; Laurien Alexandre, "Television Martí: Electronic Invasion in the Post-Cold War," *Media, Culture and Society* 14 (October 1992), 523–40. Radio and TV Martí were established as divisions of the U.S. Information Agency, the overseas propaganda arm of the federal government. Both have a studio in Washington and a transmitter in Florida.

11. Gillian Gunn, "In Search of a Modern Cuba Policy," in *Cuba and the Future*, ed. Donald E. Schulz (Westport, CT: Greenwood Press, 1994), 132; "Statement on International Broadcasting Programs," *Administration of William J. Clinton*, vol. 29, no. 27 (June 21, 1993), in *Weekly Compilation of Presidential Documents* (Washington, DC: U.S. Government Printing Office, 1993), 1088–89; "Clinton Re-Affirms Support for Torricelli Bill and TV Martí," *CubaInfo* (School of Advanced International Studies, Johns Hopkins University), August 24, 1992, 1; Harry A. Jessell, "Washington Watch: The Clinton Administration May Bring New Life to TV Martí," *Broadcasting*, November 23, 1992; Catherine S. Manegold, "U.S. Government Broadcasts to Cuba, and Wonders If Anyone Is Listening," *New York Times*, August 24, 1994.

12. There is considerable evidence that when Radio Martí was established, its real goals were not those that were publicly stated. According to Wayne S. Smith, formerly the chief U.S. diplomat in Cuba, the Reagan administration was well aware that Radio Martí could not bring any additional news or perspective to Cuban listeners that they did not already receive from Voice of America, which was widely heard on the island. Rather, the station was established as part of a policy of increasing confrontation with the Castro government. See Wayne S. Smith, *Closest of Enemies: A Personal and Diplomatic History of the Castro Years* (New York: W. W. Norton, 1987), 248. It is not known to the author if the

Clinton administration actually believes in the stated goals of Radio and TV Martí or if they are a pretext for other foreign or domestic policy goals as well.

13. Herbert S. Dordick, "New Communications Technology and Media Power," in *The News Media in National and International Conflict*, ed. Andrew Arno and Wial Dissanayake (Boulder, CO: Westview Press, 1984), 38.

14. Lewis A. Coser, "Salvation Through Communication?" in *News Media in National and International Conflict*, 20.

15. Tran Van Dinh, *Communication and Diplomacy in a Changing World* (Norwood, NJ: Ablex, 1987), 8.

16. W. Phillips Davison, *Mass Communication and Conflict Resolution: The Role of Information Media in the Advancement of International Understanding* (New York: Praeger, 1974), 38.

17. Martin Patchen, *Resolving Disputes between Nations: Coercion or Conciliation?* (Durham: Duke University Press, 1988), 52.

18. Harold D. Lasswell and Abraham Kaplan, *Power and Society: A Framework for Political Inquiry* (New Haven: Yale University Press, 1950), 114–15. The authors also hypothesize that propaganda in low-intensity situations can facilitate catharsis.

19. C. R. Mitchell, *The Structure of International Conflict* (New York: St. Martin's Press, 1981), 29.

20. Ibid., 162.

21. Bernard C. Hennessy, *Public Opinion*, 3d ed. (North Scituate, MA: Duxbury Press, 1975): 12–34.

22. William Watts, *The United States and Cuba: Changing Perceptions, New Policies?* (Washington, DC: Potomac Associates and Johns Hopkins University School of Advanced International Studies, 1989), 7–9; Christopher Marquis, "Poll: Most Back Bush's Cuba Stand," *Miami Herald*, February 11, 1992.

23. Mitchell, *Structure of International Conflict*, 156.

24. Ibid., 56–66.

25. A few analyses of U.S.-Cuban relations have noted the importance of international broadcasting in the ongoing disputes between the two countries, but none have studied it systematically. See Smith, *The Closest of Enemies*; Wayne S. Smith and Esteban Morales Dominguez, eds., *Subject to Solution: Problems in Cuban-U.S. Relations* (Boulder, CO: Lynne Rienner Publishers, 1987); Philip Brenner, *Confrontation to Negotiation: U.S. Relations with Cuba* (Boulder, CO: Westview Press, 1988); Jorge I. Domínguez and Rafael Hernandez, eds., *U.S.-Cuban Relations in the 1990s* (Boulder, CO: Westview Press, 1989); and Enrique A. Baloyra and James A. Morris, eds., *Conflict and Change in Cuba* (Albuquerque: University of New Mexico Press, 1993).

26. Smith, *Closest of Enemies*, 90.

27. Ibid.; Silvia Pedraza-Bailey, "Cuba's Exiles: Portrait of a Refugee Migration," *International Migration Review* 19 (Spring 1985): 4–34.

28. Wayne S. Smith, "U.S.-Cuban Relations: Twenty-Five Years of Hostility," in *Cuba: Twenty-Five Years of Revolution, 1959–1984*, ed. Sandor Halebsky and John M. Kirk (New York: Praeger, 1985), 347–48. The U.S.-Cuban antihijacking agreement was signed in 1973 but was abrogated by the Cubans in 1976 after one of its civilian airliners was bombed by terrorists and the Cubans accused the U.S. government of complicity. The Cuban government nevertheless continued to cooperate with the United States to prevent hijacking. See James P. Rowles, "Dia-

logue or Denial: The Uses of International Law in U.S.-Cuban Relations," in *U.S.-Cuban Relations in the 1990s*, 290.

29. Soley and Nichols, *Clandestine Radio Broadcasting*, 184–89.

30. U.S. Department of State, *Cuba's Renewed Support for Violence in Latin America*, Special Report No. 90, December 14, 1981, 4; William M. LeoGrande, "Cuba Policy Recycled," *Foreign Policy* 46 (Spring 1982): 105–19; Wayne S. Smith, "Dateline Havana: Myopic Diplomacy," *Foreign Policy* 48 (Fall 1982): 157–174.

31. Smith, *Closest of Enemies*, 245.

32. Nichols, "The U.S. View of Radio Interference," in *Subject to Solution*, 151–52.

33. John Nichols, "Radio Martí: An Electronic Bay of Pigs," *Broadcasting*, May 27, 1985.

34. Tad Szulc, *Fidel: A Critical Portrait* (New York: Avon Books, 1987), 29.

35. Ricardo Alarcón, interview with author and collaborator, March 4, 1994, Havana; Juan Jesus Aznarez, "Official Links Radio Martí, U.S. Immigration Ties," EFE newswire, reprinted *Foreign Broadcast Information Service* 4, June 18, 1986, Q1; Kenneth N. Skoug, *The U.S.-Cuba Migration Agreement: Resolving Mariel*, U.S. Department of State, Current Policy No. 1050, March 1988; John M. Goshko, "U.S. May Concede Cuba Radio Propaganda Right," *Washington Post*, July 10, 1986; Bernard Gwertzman, "Cuba, in Immigration Concession, Said to Drop American Radio Ban," *New York Times*, July 9, 1986; "Talks with Havana Collapse over Its Radio Rights in U.S.," *New York Times*, July 11, 1986.

36. Joseph B. Treaster, "Downward Spiral for U.S.-Cuba Ties," *New York Times*, May 2, 1987.

37. Alarcón interview; Jon Nordheimer, "Some See Seeds of New Exodus in Cubans Floating to Florida," *New York Times*, April 20, 1987; Neil A. Lewis, "U.S. and Havana Agree to Restore Immigration Pact," *New York Times*, November 21, 1987; "Migration Agreement between Cuba and United States to Be Resumed," *Granma* (Havana), November 29, 1987; Juan Marrero, "Ricardo Alarcón Speaks about Migration and Radio Broadcasting Agreements," *Granma*, December 6, 1987.

38. Joseph B. Treaster, "U.S.-Cuba Enmity May Be Relaxing," *New York Times*, January 6, 1989; Tad Szulc, "A Thaw in Cuban Relations?" *New York Times*, December 8, 1987; Alfonso Chardy, "Havana, Washington Edge Closer," *Miami Herald*, May 1, 1988.

39. Jorge I. Domínguez, "The Obstacles and Prospects for Improved U.S.-Cuban Relations: A U.S. Perspective," in *U.S.-Cuban Relations in the 1990s*, 22.

40. Steven Greenhouse, "U.S. Will Propose Reducing Barriers to Cuba Migrants," *New York Times*, August 30, 1994.

41. *TV Martí: Costs and Compliance with Broadcast Standards and International Agreements*, U.S. General Accounting Office, No. B-248284, May 6, 1992; Douglas A. Boyd et al., "Independent Study of the Effectiveness of Radio and TV Martí," unpublished, March 31, 1994; Kyu Ho Youm, "Radio and TV Martí Controversy," 98–99; Alexandre, "Television Marti," passim.

42. "Press Conference Given by President Fidel Castro," *Granma*, April 22, 1990; *Granma*, August 5, 1990; *Granma*, November 29, 1987.

43. Edward Gonzalez and David Ronfeldt, *Storm Warning for Cuba*, MR-452-OSD, Rand Corporation, 1994; Andrew Zimbalist, "Dateline Cuba: Hanging On

in Havana," *Foreign Policy* 92 (Fall 1993): 151–67; Carmelo Mesa-Lago, ed., *Cuba after the Cold War* (Pittsburgh: University of Pittsburgh Press, 1993); Gillian Gunn, *Cuba in Transition: Options for U.S. Policy* (Washington, DC: Twentieth-Century Fund Press, 1993).

44. A month later, the UN General Assembly approved a nonbinding resolution calling for an end of the U.S. embargo on Cuba. Only Israel and Rumania voted with the United States in opposition to the resolution. See Michael Krinsky and David Golove, *United States Economic Measures against Cuba* (Northampton, MA: Aletheia Press, 1993); Gunn, "In Search of a Modern Cuba Policy," in *Cuba and the Future*, 132–33; W. Raymond Duncan, "Cuba-U.S. Relations and Political Contradictions in Cuba," in *Conflict and Change in Cuba*, 224; Clifford Krauss, "U.S. Taking Steps to Bar New Wave of Cuban Emigres," *New York Times*, August 4, 1991.

45. Gunn, "In Search of a Modern Cuba Policy," in *Cuba and the Future*, 135.

46. Ibid., 129–41.

47. Ibid., 133–34; *Foreign Broadcasting Information Service—Latin America*, January 6, 1992, 1–10.

48. Inter American Press Association, "Cuba," in *Report of the Committee on Freedom of the Press and Information*, 49th General Assembly, November 18, 1993, 1; "Cuba Publicizes Dissident's Trial," *CubaInfo*, May 18, 1994, 11; "Castro Cracking Down as the Hardships Grow," *New York Times*, January 14, 1992; "Cuba Reported to Sentence 3 Dissidents to Long Terms," *New York Times*, October 18, 1991; "When in Doubt, Crack Down: Castro Is Wielding the Police and Mobs against the Democratic Movement," *Washington Post National Weekly*, January 27– February 2, 1992.

49. Ernesto F. Betancourt, "Let Cuba Be Cuba," *New York Times*, September 6, 1991; Don Kowet, "Radio Martí Head: Tuning into Wrong Frequency?" *Washington Times*, December 19, 1991; Eugenio Rodriguez, "How I Survived Radio Martí," *New Times* (Miami), September 12–18, 1990; Churchill Roberts, "Evaluating Radio Martí," *International Communication Bulletin* 27 (Spring 1992): 7–10.

50. TV Martí does not have an audience in Cuba because it broadcasts in the predawn hours of the morning in an attempt to circumvent International Telecommunication Union regulations and because the Havana government has effectively jammed its signal. See Boyd et al., "Independent Study of the Effectiveness of Radio and TV Martí," 4.

51. "V for TV Martí, Duffey Says," *Broadcasting*, July 11, 1994; "USIA Director Recommends That Congress Maintain Radio and TV Martí Broadcasts to Cuba," U.S. Information Agency, News Release No. 087-94, July 8, 1994.

52. "The Visa Facts," *Cuba Action* (New York), Fall 1994, 3.

53. Boyd et al., "Independent Study of the Effectiveness of Radio and TV Martí," 4–5. No strong relationship between foreign media and immigration has been established in the very limited research on this issue. See Leslie Snyder, Connie Roser, and Steven Chaffee, "Foreign Media and the Desire to Emigrate from Belize," *Journal of Communication* 41 (Winter 1991): 117–32.

54. Cynthia Corzo, "Ordeal at Sea: 30 Cubans Died in Ramming," *Miami Herald*, July 16, 1994; idem, "Sinking of Tugboat Off Cuba 'Brutal,' Clinton Says," *Miami Herald*, July 19, 1994; "U.S.-Cuban Relations," *CubaInfo*, September 1, 1994, 6.

55. Debra Evenson, "Clinton Has Opportunity to Act Wisely on Cuba," *New York Times* (letter to the editor), September 7, 1994.

56. Mimi Whitefield and Susana Bellido, "Boat Rumors Spark Riots in Havana," *Miami Herald*, August 6, 1994; William Booth, "U.S. Warns Cuba against Repeat of Boatlift," *Washington Post*, August 7, 1994; Associated Press, "Castro Threatens to Let Refugees Flood Out," *Centre Daily Times*, August 6, 1994.

57. Manegold, "U.S. Government Broadcasts to Cuba."

58. Ibid.; *CubaInfo*, September 1, 1994, 3–4; "Radio Martí Pleads with Cubans to Stay Home," *New York Times*, August 22, 1994; "TV Martí and Radio Martí Were Turning Up the Volume Last Week," *Broadcasting*, August 29, 1994; Joe O'Connell, "U.S. Broadcasts Keep Cubans Posted in Crisis," *New York Times*, September 4, 1994.

59. Steven Greenhouse, "Clinton Will Open Talks with Cuba on Refugee Crisis," *New York Times*, August 28, 1994.

60. Paul Lewis, "Cuba Vows to End Exodus in Return for a Rise in Visas," *New York Times*, September 10, 1994; Tim Golden, "A Dubious Pact," *New York Times*, September 10, 1994; Steven Greenhouse, "Critics Warn That Immigration Pact Leaves Many Cuban Issues Unresolved," *New York Times*, September 10, 1994; Tim Golden, "Castro, as Promised, Turns Off the Spigot," *New York Times*, September 18, 1994; Robert S. Greenberger, "U.S.-Cuban Agreement on Immigration May Point to Discussions on Other Issues," *Wall Street Journal*, September 12, 1994.

6

Should Journalists Be Required to Belong to *Colegios* and Have University Degrees?

Ricardo Trotti and Bill Williamson

The first journalism colegio in Latin America was formed more than fifty years ago, and the debate over such organizations has existed all of that time. A colegio is a collegial association of journalists; it aims at increasing the prestige and status of the profession and its practitioners. The same phenomenon does not exist in the United States. The nub of the debate is whether membership in a colegio *should be voluntary or mandatory. If membership is required by government, then critics of colegios assail them as a form of licensing and as antithetical to press freedom.*

The authors of this chapter are well versed in both sides of the argument and definitely do not favor colegios. They also do not approve of a federal requirement that a journalist have a university degree; they see that as a potential government control over who could become a journalist, possibly weeding out critics of a national or political regime. They take the view of the Inter American Press Association, which they have served for years.

Ricardo Trotti has been coordinator of press freedom activities for the Miami-based Inter American Press Association since 1993. He was managing editor of El Liberal *of Santiago del Estero, Argentina, for six years. He has won awards for his writings on press freedom and is the author of* La dolorosa libertad de prensa, *published by Editorial Atlántida in Buenos Aires in 1993. Bill Williamson retired as executive director of the IAPA on July 1, 1994, after serving more than thirteen years in the post. Previously, he was active for nearly twenty years in the Association representing the English-language daily* Brazil Herald *of Rio de Janeiro, for which he was the editor and managing partner.*

The year 1994 was a paradox for press freedom in Latin America. Freedom of expression advanced in some countries, but serious threats loomed in others. Three Latin American countries contemplated legislation requiring membership in an obligatory collegial organization—a *colegio*—or a university degree in journalism in order to be a journalist. In Nicaragua, legislation concerning a *colegio*, introduced in the National Assembly on June 9, 1994, required a university degree and mandated a three percent tax on advertising in the media. Legislation in Chile was introduced in the Congress on July 9, 1993, establishing an academic requirement as well as a controversial clause of conscience. In 1994, President Eduardo Frei announced that he would modify some of the controversial clause's articles. In that same year, a number of journalism associations reached an agreement with the Chilean *colegio* that applicants with journalism degrees be given preference in hiring for media positions, leaving open the possibility of hiring nonjournalism graduates. And, in Venezuela, the reform project of the Law of the Exercise of Journalism was signed into law by President Rafael Calderas in December 1994, following nine months of deliberation by the Congress. The new law strengthened even more the requirement of a university degree and the obligation of journalists to be in a *colegio*, adding penalties of up to six months in prison and suspension from the profession for noncompliance. The original *colegio* requirement was imposed on August 23, 1972.

Colegios are promoted by their supporters as an appropriate means for professionalizing and dignifying journalism. But while they can be worthy, there is no evidence that obligatory membership has brought more benefits or better working conditions to journalists. In addition, recent history is replete with examples where *colegios* manipulated their memberships politically. In Nicaragua, an obligatory *colegiatura* was introduced by the Sandinista government of Daniel Ortega in 1982. Yet, during his entire administration, there was no free, independent journalism. Ortega rescinded the *colegiatura* law a few days before his term ended in 1990, so his successors would not have available that same means by which to attack freedom of journalistic expression.

The first *colegios* were formed in Cuba in 1942 and are part of journalism history in Latin America. But it is the collegium created in 1956 in Chile that has served as the model for a number of countries. Until 1978 the Chilean collegium did not require a university degree to be a journalist. In February 1981 it was dissolved by the government of President Augusto Pinochet through decree law 3,621.

Nine Latin American countries have obligatory *colegiatura* or the requirement of a university degree: Bolivia, Brazil, Colombia, Ecuador, Haiti, Honduras, Panama, Peru, and Venezuela. In most of these nations, however, membership is either ignored or not enforced. Costa Rica and Venezuela had the most rigorous requirement of *colegio* membership until May 1995, when a court decision in Costa Rica dramatically changed the status of mandatory licensing in that country. Here is a country-by-country summary:

In **Costa Rica**, in May 1995, the Supreme Court declared unconstitutional Article 22 of Law 4,420, in effect since September 22, 1969. The unanimous verdict by the seven justices responded to a 1990 appeal by Costa Rican broadcaster Roger Ajun, who had been accused of illegally practicing journalism because he was not a member of the journalists' union. The court's decision ruled in favor of Ajun and annulled Article 22, which specified that only members of the journalists' union could act as journalists. The 1995 decision affirms an advisory opinion by the Inter-American Court of Human Rights rendered in 1985, which opposed mandatory licensing as a restriction to freedom of the press and expression.

In the **Dominican Republic**, the law of obligatory collegium membership was declared unconstitutional by the Supreme Court in September 1989. In 1992, another measure was instituted, which includes voluntary collegial membership.

In **Brazil**, although Article 4 of decree law 972/69 makes it obligatory to have a journalism diploma to practice journalism, some lawmakers believe that this provision will not be included in the new constitution. In the opinion of Jayme Sirotsky, former president of the National Newspaper Association (Associacão Nacional de Jornais, or ANJ), journalists will be able to practice their profession without a diploma. In 1994 more than forty journalists appealed to federal courts.

In **Ecuador**, obligatory *colegio* membership is required by Article 27 of decree law 799-B of September 18, 1975, but the law is often ignored.

The case in **Colombia** is similar. Although a law requires a university degree in communications or journalism, it is generally ignored by many private news media. It is observed mostly by state-run news organizations.

In **Peru**, the second article of law 23,221 of October 1, 1980, which created the Journalists Collegium, requires *colegio* membership. But the collegium has never required membership for a newsperson to practice journalism.

In **Honduras**, an obligatory collegium was set out in the organic law of the Collegium of Journalists in decree 759 of December 6, 1972. The *colegio* born in Honduras in 1979 requires membership, but until 1983 there was no requirement for a university degree to practice journalism. Curiously, sports journalists are not regulated by the collegium and can be contracted freely. Students who have passed 60 percent of their classes may obtain provisional licenses to work until they receive their degrees. Many receive their licenses and work, however, and do not complete their degrees.

In **Panama**, a certificate and university degree are required, but the requirement is not enforced. The organization in charge of issuing licenses to journalists is the Technical Board, composed of members of the Journalists Collegium, the Journalists Guild, and a representative of the Justice Ministry. There are journalists working in the media who do not have a degree in social communication.

In **Bolivia**, no *colegio* exists, but a recent provision obliges journalists who are members of the National Federation of Press Guilds to have a university degree. The requirement is not enforced, however.

Proponents of national professional associations for journalists can mount an impressive list of arguments for *colegios*. Such organizations can provide a means toward professionalizing the field and enhancing the status of journalists. After all, true professions such as medicine and law are overseen by powerful, respected national associations that formulate requirements for entering the profession and set codes of ethics and standards of behavior. Such legal and medical associations carry great prestige in countries around the world. Because of their collegial and professional nature, *colegios* also can provide a measure of stability and self-esteem for journalists, and they can be a forum for discussion of current issues in mass communication and a center of continuing education in the field. Professional seminars can be held on any number of subjects in order to keep journalists up to date. Furthermore, *colegios* can be a pressure group for journalists' rights against abuses by employers because they can campaign for higher salaries and better working conditions.

The situation, however, is not that simple. *Colegios* have been debated for years. In 1994 two important international declarations—the Declaration of Chapultepec and the Declaration of Santiago—decried *colegios* as violations of fundamental principles of freedom of expression. The Declaration of Chapultepec was proclaimed on March 11, 1994, in Mexico City at a conference organized by the Inter American Press Association (IAPA). It declared that "membership of journalists in guilds, their affiliation to professional and trade associations, and the affiliation of the media with business groups must be strictly voluntary." (Most of the declaration is reprinted in the Conclusions section of this book.)

Virtually no one objects to *colegios* if membership is voluntary. But when membership is required by government in law, then libertarian proponents of press freedom see that as an artificial, unfair restriction on press freedom. It limits who can have his or her say in newspapers, magazines, radio and television stations, and other media to *colegio* members—in other words, to people who have been approved by a body created by government. So just anyone cannot have his or her say. Opponents of *colegio* laws see them as prior restraints imposed by government on freedom of expression.

The Declaration of Santiago was proclaimed on May 6, 1994, in Santiago, Chile, at a regional UNESCO (United Nations Educational, Scientific, and Cultural Organization) seminar. It declares that "in accordance with the fundamental rights of expression and association as stated in the Universal Declaration of Human Rights, the access to and the practice of journalism must be free and not limited by any means." At the seminar, considerable discussion took place over whether journalists must be required to have degrees from universities (nearly always from schools of social communication) and whether journalists must be members of *colegios*. Most delegates opposed required membership in *colegios*.

Many organizations of professional journalists have gone on record as opposing any licensing of journalists, including the International Federation of Journalists, World Association of Community Radio Broadcasters, Latin American Federation of Journalists, International Association of Broadcasting, International Press Institute, International Federation of Newspaper Publishers, and the Inter American Press Association. The Inter-American Court of Human Rights, a body of the Organization of American States (OAS), has come out against any licensing or membership requirements for journalists. On November 13, 1985, it issued an advisory opinion "that the compulsory licensing of journalists is incompatible with Article 13 of the American Convention on Human Rights insofar as it denies some persons access to the full use of the news media as a means of expressing themselves or imparting information." This article states that "everyone has the right to freedom of thought and expression. This right includes freedom to seek, receive, and impart information and ideas of all kinds, regardless of frontiers, either orally, in writing, in print, in the form of art, or through any other medium of one's choice."

The court's opinion emerged in relation to the case of North American journalist Stephen Schmidt of the *Tico Times* and *La Nación* of San José, who was charged by the Costa Rican Journalists Collegium with practicing journalism illegally. The case eventually reached the Costa Rica Supreme Court, which ruled against Schmidt and upheld a six-month jail sentence (suspended on the condition he not "repeat the crime"). The Inter-American Human Rights Commission of the OAS agreed with the Costa Rican high court, although the U.S. member of the commission wrote a strong dissent. Thereafter, the government of Costa Rica sought an advisory opinion from the Inter-American Court of Human Rights, the highest such authority in the hemisphere. The government's request was prompted by the Inter American Press Association, which has always campaigned in favor of a libertarian and unlicensed press or, at the most, voluntary affiliation in *colegios.*

Article 13 of the Human Rights Court opinion stipulated that freedom of expression cannot be coerced or restricted "by direct or indirect means." In other words, collegial association cannot be a method wherein only *colegio* members may seek, receive, and divulge information. In point 77 of their considerations, the judges said that "it would be a contradiction to invoke a restriction to freedom of expression as a means of guaranteeing it. A system of control of the right of expression on behalf of a supposed guarantee of the correctness and truthfulness of the information that society receives can be a source of great abuse and, in short, violates the right to information that this same society has."

In this tone, *La Nación* of Argentina, in its editorial "*Colegiación, no*" on October 7, 1991, declared that "as long as the professional matriculation is managed by organs of the State, by a professional *colegio*, or by labor unions, the obligation to inscribe oneself in the association will inevitably create the possibility of someone being deprived of the right of qualification. Independent journalism purely and simply will not have the possibility to exist."

What of the arguments that obligatory collegial association will lead to a more skilled newsroom staff and that journalism must be given the same status as medicine or law? Guido Fernández, former chairman of the IAPA's Committee on Freedom of the Press and Information and former editor of the daily *La Nación* of Costa Rica, has written: "The lawyer, the doctor, the chemist, and the engineer do not exercise a profession in which there is a basic human right, such as freedom of expression or information. The public faith, health, and security are individual or social values worthy of tutelage, but to inform and express opinion are duties intimately associated with all human beings, for which any restriction or limitation can endanger that which is vital to democracy: the right to dissent." In other words, doctors need a professional organization to provide control over the possibility of their harming a third party. On the other hand, allowing freedom of expression to only a few harms everyone else. It is as though the author of a book or the painter of a picture would have to seek permission beforehand.

While it seems clear that mandatory *colegio* membership is inimical to press freedom and the professional activities of journalists, state-mandated requirements that journalists possess a college degree may seem only to enhance the practice of journalism. After all, one can easily argue that the more education a journalist has, the better at the profession he or she might be. Indeed, studying mass communication—its history and philosophy, its role in developed and developing countries or in free and totalitarian states—can be enlightening for anyone, and especially for would-be journalists and communicators, no matter what communication specialization they enter. Along with the theory, philosophy, law, and other substantive material that students can learn, instruction in professional skills such as newswriting, reporting, public opinion polling, camera techniques, film editing—and on and on—can be integral parts of the curriculum.

In journalism-mass communication schools in the United States, undergraduate students usually take about three-quarters of their four-year curriculum in liberal arts and sciences and general university studies in order to receive a broad education. The philosophy behind this idea is that journalists and other mass communicators must understand the political, social, economic, and cultural forces that operate within society in order to report about them. In journalism-mass communication courses, which constitute the other one-fourth of the undergraduate's program, both substantive and skills courses are usually taught. Substantive areas include the philosophy that journalism is a public trust and the role of mass communication in society, along with mass communication law, ethics, and history. Skills courses vary with a student's chosen specialization. A typical curriculum for an aspiring reporter, for example, would include courses in newswriting, reporting, editing, and gathering information by computer. In the United States, about 85 percent of the new people hired on newspapers each year have university degrees in journalism-mass communication.

In Latin America, journalism-mass communication education has evolved somewhat differently. Most university programs, which often are called social communication, tend to emphasize theory and philosophy over professional skills. In Chile, for example, the law clearly declares that journalists must have "a professional university degree legally valid in Chile." On June 4, 1992, *La Nación* in Santiago published a declaration in support of the law by Lydia Baltra, general secretary of Chile's Collegium of Journalists, who wrote: "Only a university-trained journalist is able to select and transmit the multiplicity of information generated each day. Those who are not journalists can have space in the media through letters to the editor." But Baltra's position is questioned by many others. It would seem clear that depriving "any person" from seeking, receiving, and disseminating information and ideas, thus reserving the communicative act to an exclusive group, as in Chile, discriminates against the many to the benefit of the few.

In conclusion, the controversy over compulsory membership in *colegios* and the requirement for a college degree constitutes an ongoing debate in Latin American journalism circles. The authors of this chapter are against both requirements because their enforcement creates a form of licensing for journalists. A number of recent declarations by different professional and judicial bodies detailed in these pages support the authors' viewpoint. This does not mean that *colegios* will cease to exist, however. As voluntary professional associations, they can play constructive roles. So, too, can journalism-mass communication degrees: If schools produce graduates who are better educated, more knowledgeable, and skilled professional journalists, the schools will become the norm, with no need for laws to make degrees compulsory.

II

Case Studies of Mass Communication in Selected Latin American Countries

7

Mexico's Struggle for a Free Press

Murray Fromson

Mexico is a land of opposites—old and new, lush and barren, rich and poor. Ancient Aztec temples lie within sight of gleaming steel-and-glass skyscrapers in Mexico City; tropical vegetation on the east coast and sparkling beaches on the Pacific contrast with deserts in the south and mountains in the north; the wealthy loll in palaces while millions live in shacks.

Just as the nation reflects extremes, so, too, does the press. Mexico was the first country in the Western Hemisphere with a printing press (1536), the second with gazettes, and the third with a daily newspaper. Yet journalism developed slowly, in part because three centuries of Spanish domination stifled freedom of the press. In this chapter, Murray Fromson traces some early developments in Mexico's press system but rightly concentrates on the current scene, especially the watershed presidential election of 1994 and its effect on the press. He discusses important government controls on the mass media, including PIPSA (Productora e Importado de Papel, Sociedad Anónima), the organization that provided cheap newsprint to newspapers for many years; embutes *(payoffs) to reporters, editors, and others; and* gacetillas *(paid publicity in newspaper news columns). Overall, what mass communication in Mexico needs most, he argues, is increased professionalization.*

Professor Fromson teaches journalism in the School of Journalism at the University of Southern California in Los Angeles. As director of the USC Center for International Journalism, he has sometimes lived and often traveled in Mexico since 1985, analyzing the problems of the country's media and recruiting Mexican journalists for the Center's fellowship program.

The struggle for a free press in Mexico began, it may surprise many critics to learn, more than two centuries ago. Only now, after a hiatus of nearly one hundred years and tarnished by corruption, intimidation, collusion, and a lack of independence, the struggle may be ready to resume. In 1994, in the wake of a peasant rebellion and the assassination of the leading presidential candidate, which stunned all of Mexico, candidates from left to right talked about replacing the old authoritarian style of government with a more democratic one. Inevitably, that openness brought the role of journalism under greater scrutiny than at any time in recent history. The reason, quite simply, was that if any single institution helped to perpetuate the power of the velvet dictatorship over more than six decades, it was the government-managed mass media. And if any single institution can help to propel Mexico toward a more open society, it is a free mass media.

Much, however, will hinge on the months and years following the 1994 presidential election, which was the most open and intensely debated in Mexico's contemporary history. The unanswered question is whether the Institutional Revolutionary Party (Partido Revolucionario Institucional, or PRI), again the victor in 1994, will tolerate tenacious journalists who criticize a system that has been brought into such disrepute. The PRI has had a virtual choke hold on the nation's politics and press for more than sixty-five years. It has never lost a presidential election and has won nearly all of the state gubernatorial elections in all that time. But it has a history of election fraud and abuse of power, rarely exposed to journalistic oversight.

For too long, reporters and editors have been accused of allowing themselves to be manipulated and corrupted by the government. They have demonstrated repeated lapses of ethical conduct, absent rules to guide them, and they have worked in an environment where access to information is considered a privilege and not a right, where speculation and rumor substitute for facts. Furthermore, they have been targets of assassins hired by government agencies, thugs, and political malcontents and have been undertrained and, until recently, undereducated. Perhaps the principal fault, however, lies in the fact that Mexico's reporters and editors have worked for entrepreneurs who are more interested in making money than in good journalism. These businesspeople have demonstrated no shame for paying their hired hands minimum wages in the expectation that government or corporate bribes will more than compensate for the abysmally low salaries. Many editors coming from another generation are willing to err on the side of caution rather than encourage enterprise reporting. They see nothing ethically wrong about publishing "news" that is paid for by special interests or the government. Because of their real and suspected complicities with government and business, few Mexican journalists command the respect of their readers, viewers, or listeners. In a society where a large percentage of the people mistrust their government and much of what it says, journalists are too often viewed as handmaidens of the establishment, which means the rich, powerful, and privileged segment of the population.

For close to seven decades, the PRI and the government for which it speaks have ensured favorable news through threats or temptation. The threats exert considerable influence over the press because they are often followed by actions. The lives or well-being of reporters or editors who do not cooperate with the status quo are frequently in jeopardy. So, too, are the subsidies that most newspapers and magazines have received from the government since 1935 when it created a special agency (PIPSA, or Productora e Importado de Papel, Sociedad Anónima) to provide publishers with inexpensive newsprint. This government-provided cheap paper was a powerful control on the press for many years. An equally powerful source of control has been the government's inducement to corruption.

While dozens of Mexican journalists have been murdered in recent years, it was not always because of their enterprise reporting. Some people in the media have been linked to drugs, prostitution, and other criminal activity. But bribery, more than any other tactic, is the favored method that government bureaucrats and others have used to sway journalists. The *embute*, an outright payment of cash in an envelope mysteriously placed in a reporter's mailbox each week by a functionary of the government or personally handed to the reporter by a government public relations employee, is the most common form of payoff. It is described as "the bite" (*la mordida*).

Over the years bribery has taken many forms: free meals, transportation, hotel accommodations, junkets to Mexican beach resorts that are disguised as reporting assignments, overseas telephone calls, the right to import duty-free automobiles and other luxury items, and even the company of females for male reporters. Sometimes the office of the Mexican president is the source of the largesse. In other instances, it is the PRI. On a trip to Germany in 1991, for example, journalists assigned to cover President Carlos Salinas de Gortari received favored treatment. According to Raimundo Riva Palacio, one of Mexico's most careful and forthright journalists, who was on the trip, most of his male colleagues focused their energy on luxury shopping for wives and girlfriends in Bonn's department stores while staff members of the Presidencia press office actually wrote their stories for them. In 1992, when Salinas decided that his office would no longer subsidize reporters on overseas trips, the PRI did not hesitate to take up the slack. During the 1994 presidential campaign of Ernesto Zedillo, Salinas's choice as a successor after the first PRI candidate, Luis Donaldo Colosio, was assassinated in Tijuana, Mexican reporters covering Zedillo received royal treatment. Each received a bill and a wink later, with no assurance the PRI ever expected to be compensated. U.S. reporters paid their own way.

Some journalists unwillingly accept *embutes* because turning them down can cause trouble with colleagues. Some years ago, a journalist working for *Excélsior*, the well-known Mexico City newspaper, refused to take the weekly envelope. It so angered her fellow reporters that they gossiped about her, spread rumors about her sex life, and even fed her inaccurate information to use in stories. As she confidentially and somewhat tearfully explained to me, she finally surrendered and accepted the envelopes.

A senior executive of another Mexico City newspaper, *Novedades*, described how a representative of the PRI visited the editorial offices each week during the 1988 presidential campaign to drop an envelope containing 1 million pesos (then about $300,000) on the desk of the editor to ensure favorable coverage for Salinas. Sometimes these gifts made no sense whatsoever. *Novedades* is a property of the wealthy and influential O'Farrill family, whose loyalty to the government and the PRI has not wavered for half a century. But in an election that Salinas barely won, the PRI apparently was taking no chances. The situation was not always that way, however, especially in the previous century.

Mexico once enjoyed a golden age of journalism. Its reporters, essayists, and political cartoonists summoned incredible courage to persevere throughout much of the nineteenth century in defense of a free press. The reading audiences were tiny and newspapers reached only an elite portion of the population, but a small group of journalists refused to knuckle under to government intimidation and persisted in defense of a free press and free expression. U.S. journalists may find this situation difficult to understand because they have never had to experience life under an authoritarian regime or military dictatorship. In the United States, freedom of expression has been ensured by the Constitution's First Amendment since it was ratified in 1791. Mexican journalists have had no such protection.

The newspaper tradition began in Mexico 150 years before the country won its independence from Spain, starting with the publication of the newspaper *Gaceta de México* in 1666. In February 1826, five years after the break with Spain, *El Iris*, the first newspaper with political cartoons, was published. Appropriately, it demanded freedom of the press for all of Mexico. One of the first cartoons was drawn by an Italian lithographer, Claudio Linati, the newspaper's founder and editor. In two lengthy interviews at his home in June 1994, Rafael Barajas Durán, a widely respected political cartoonist for the Mexico City newspaper *La Jornada* as well as a historian of nineteenth-century journalism, noted that Linati's cartoons were provocative because "the political cartoon was in the middle of the battle between tyranny and freedom of the press in Mexico."[1]

The political instability that engulfed Mexico in the first years after Independence caused the birth and death of many newspapers. Laws regulating the press changed according to the government and president in power. The political newspaper *El Toro* appeared irregularly (1826–1832), depending on whether its editor was in prison. Humberto Musacchio, author of the *Grand Encyclopedic Dictionary of Mexico*, cites the history of *El Fénix de la Libertad*, first published in 1831, as an example of a vigorous press. In its first issue the editors employed language rarely seen in Mexico, denouncing the government's dictatorial attitude and the "palace intrigues, selfishness, greed, individual insecurity, and the absence of punishment for wrongdoers." They also accused the military and church authorities of being dedicated to the extermination of their enemies "and of brutally suppressing opposition newspapers." *El Fénix* declared that "the separation of the clergy from the public business is the most important issue dominant in our century."[2]

In 1841, Ignacio Cumplido left the editorship of *El Fénix* in order to start a new newspaper called *El Siglo XIX*. Musacchio describes it as "the most important newspaper of the century." *El Siglo* defended a free and universal vote, the establishment of a Federal Republic, and freedom of the press. It declared:

> It is necessary that Mexico cease to be a nation of military people and employees. . . . It is necessary that the public treasury be organized, to consolidate the nation's debt, reduce spending in order to do away with our eternally bankrupt system and the interminable series of corrupt contracts which have ruined the country, destroyed morals and made it impossible to obtain credit.
>
> It is necessary to educate the people . . . that the people be true to the government and that once the national guard is trained, we stop being as we are now, arbiters of undisciplined troops.[3]

General Antonio López de Santa Anna, five times the president of Mexico, never seemed to understand the role of a free press. In 1824–25 he banned newspapers that carried "anything of an alarming and seditious nature." In 1836 he reversed himself and included a provision in the Mexican Constitution, guaranteeing the "right of newspapers to be able to print and circulate their political ideas without the need for prior censorship." Three years later, he referred to reporters as "a race of delinquents" and urged state governors to "take the most energetic measures available . . . to pursue and apprehend" those responsible for all "seditious" printing.[4] In 1842 freedom of the press was restored, but criticism of the government resulted in widespread persecution and imprisonment of journalists. According to Barajas, the political cartoonists of the midnineteenth century "used metaphors, allusions, and elements of absurdity . . . for effectively avoiding censorship."[5]

In the rarefied air of liberty that the satirical press breathed in 1850, Francisco Zarco observed that "everyone felt as if they were journalists and that they had the right to be censors."[6] *El Demócrata*, a political, literary, and commercial newspaper founded and directed by Zarco, on March 12, 1850, noted that "we are aware of and deplore everything bad concerning our country, but we can never blame democratic institutions for having caused them. . . . We need to continue on in the real spirit of democracy. We must reform everything that is the opposite of democracy."[7] A few months later, *El Demócrata* deplored the plight of the Indian population and, in what was truly revolutionary for its time, proposed that "depending on the situation, wages for the laborer should be established and workers should be permitted to form societies [presumably unions] to defend themselves against abuse."[8]

In 1852, Santa Anna proposed a draconian law that was considered the most repressive in the history of Mexican journalism. It imposed complete censorship on all printed material, required the registration of all news vendors and places where newspapers were sold, and applied to "anything published, sold, or shown in public whether it be drawings, lithographs, engravings, cartoons, and posters."[9]

Three newspapers, including *El Demócrata*, suspended publication, but several others merely went underground and were instrumental in hastening Santa Anna's downfall in 1855. The subsequent emergence of Benito Juárez and other liberals in Mexican politics permitted the passage of a law that sanctified the freedom "to write and publish articles on any subject" and that established that "freedom of the press does not have any limits except with respect for privacy, morals and peace."[10] Juárez was president in 1858–1862 and 1867–1872. Zarco was one of Juárez's principal advisers and was instrumental in writing the free-press legislation.

"It was a strange moment," according to Barajas, "when the journalists who had suffered persecution and punishment became the same individuals who would establish the legal foundations for freedom of expression."[11] The law facilitated the inauguration of the major newspaper *La Orquesta*, the first with political cartoons that managed to survive for more than one year. It lasted sixteen years, although not consecutively. The newspaper was founded by an important liberal figure of the time, Vicente Riva Palacio, whose great-grandson is now a senior editor for *Reforma*, a lively and greatly respected Mexico City daily newspaper that started in November 1993.

Constantino Escalante, a prominent cartoonist of the era, was unsparing in his attacks, even on as revered a figure as Benito Juárez. During Emperor Maximilian's reign (1864–1867), Escalante signed his cartoons with the name of an Italian artist said to be visiting Mexico, presumably to avoid reprisals. Shortly thereafter, when the Republic was restored, first under Juárez and later under Don Sebastián Lerdo de Tejada, *La Orquesta* reappeared with many other newspapers, and Mexico enjoyed a greater period of freedom of expression than at any time in its history, before or since. While *La Orquesta* was a shining example of journalistic independence, it had one competitor of equal fervor and principle that managed to outlive it: *El Ahuizote*, which was owned by the same Rivapalacio who had helped to launch *La Orquesta*. The ridicule leveled at the government of Lerdo de Tejada by *El Ahuizote*'s chief cartoonist, José María Villasana, forced the government to resign and flee Mexico City.

Several years after the demise of *El Ahuizote*, a journalist, Daniel Cabrera, asked Rivapalacio for permission to start a new newspaper that would be named *El Hijo del* [the son of] *Ahuizote*. Cabrera often is cited as one of the bravest and most honest journalists in Mexican history. The first issue of his newspaper contained a cartoon decrying censorship. The lithograph depicted dictator Porfirio Díaz standing astride the press-freedom article of the constitution, punching down the independent press so that it drowns in turbulent waters. During seventeen years of its existence, *El Hijo del Ahuizote* was closed several times for three to six months, and it suffered countless examples of persecution. According to Barajas, few journalists were beaten in prison as often as Cabrera. The administrator of *El Hijo* said that after paying a visit to Cabrera's cell on one occasion, the prison guards "spilled a thimbleful of bedbugs on top of his body, probably hoping to induce typhus."[12]

The emergence of the thirty-year reign of Porfirio Díaz in 1877 marked the prelude to the dark years of Mexican journalism. Díaz ruled the press with an iron hand. His hatred of *El Hijo del Ahuizote* was unparalleled, and he censured the newspaper often. In 1890 he ordered Cabrera to be locked up in a hospital in Juárez and surrounded by armed guards. Cabrera's doctor was not allowed to treat him. In 1902, after having left journalism for health reasons, Cabrera was arrested once again, this time for "psychological matters." The absence of crusading journalists such as Cabrera resulted in a weakened press that did Díaz's bidding and shut off all expressions of opposition to one-party government. Despite the flourishes of independence evident during most of the nineteenth century, it is far from certain that the Mexican press had much of an impact on the people. Eighty percent of the population was illiterate, and only the elite read newspapers.

As the twentieth century opened, a young Oxacan lawyer, Ricardo Flores Magón, joined his brother and a lawyer friend to found the periodical *Regeneración*. They called it "a newspaper for an independent judiciary." In a front-page article published one month after its founding in 1900, the newspaper discussed the restrictions and hostile attitude of government officials toward the press, and it examined the legal rights of the press in Mexico. Flores Magón proved to be more than a journalist, however. He was a politician, radical, and revolutionary who ultimately turned to anarchy as the only solution for Mexico's pervasive social needs. He spearheaded the growth of the opposition Liberal Party, repeatedly attacking Díaz without any concern for his own safety, even daring at one party convention to refer to the administration of the dictator as "a den of thieves." From prison, he demanded Díaz's resignation.

Some but not all historians have described Flores Magón as the precursor of the Mexican Revolution of 1910. He was arrested frequently and in 1904 crossed the border into the United States, never again returning to his native country. From his self-imposed exile, he attempted to rally support for his cause through his newspaper. But authorities in San Antonio forced him to close *Regeneración* and leave town. In St. Louis, he was arrested again, and the offices of *Regeneración* were destroyed. He fled to Canada, where he was harassed in much the same fashion. After being arrested once more and then released from prison, he moved to Los Angeles, where he published another edition of the paper.

Flores Magón advocated the expropriation and socialization of all wealth in Mexico. In dozens of articles, he expressed the view that in order to overthrow tyranny, the people had no choice but to seize the land, mines, factories, mills, and transportation and work them themselves. Following Díaz's ouster, Flores Magón forged an alliance with Emiliano Zapata that was a precursor to the famous movement that came to be known as "Tierra y Libertad" (Land and liberty). In the United States he was arrested often because of his alleged violation of its neutrality laws. In 1918, Flores Magón was arrested for the last time and sent to Leavenworth Penitentiary in Kansas, where he was murdered in his cell on the evening of November 20–21, 1922.

After Díaz's downfall, journalism suddenly flourished. President Francisco Madero (1911–1913) tolerated a highly political and polemical press, and daily newspapers, periodicals, magazines, and broadsheets appeared on the streets of Mexico City. Cartoonists were no longer afraid to sign their names on their caricatures of the political elite. In his two-volume study of the Mexican Revolution, Alan Knight notes that Madero's enemies used newspapers to criticize him "often in bitter, scurrilous, and obscene terms; for the first time in Mexican history, the literate public enjoyed the spectacle not only of a free press but also of a press mercilessly lampooning the head of state."[13] Knight states that opposition newspapers such as *El Mañana* poked fun at Madero's short stature, his youth, his taste for dancing, his beliefs in spiritualism and homeopathic medicine, and his lack of machismo. The Mexico City press in particular took great delight in poking fun at the new political elites from the north. For example, the women identified with the Madero entourage were described as "unsophisticated and prudish" compared to Mexico City's high society of "liberally powdered women of social prominence." Madero, however, dismissed the press and resisted the urging of some followers that he place controls on it. He thought that most of the reporting and commentary were exaggerated. But during the revolt that erupted in the state of Chihuahua in 1912, when the press seemed to abound in divergent and often unfounded reports, a chagrined Madero summoned Mexico City editors and warned them that the official penal code forbade actions that caused public alarm.

Anti-Madero newspapers, such as *Multicolor* and *El Mañana*, were the targets of ongoing demonstrations. The Catholic editor of *El País* was attacked, and an alleged attempt was made to torch the offices of *El Imparcial*. The press grew more reckless and rambunctious between 1915 and 1920. But the cost of running the newspapers became so prohibitive that a daily such as *El Demócrata* was losing 70,000 pesos per week, and its willingness to accept largesse from the government made its coverage suspect.

Two important Mexico City newspapers were founded in this period. Félix F. Palavicini, a minister of public instruction and sometimes referred to as the godfather of Mexican journalism, established *El Universal* in 1916. A year later its chief rival, *Excélsior*, was founded by Rafael Alducin.

The evolution of Mexico's print journalism during the twentieth century cannot be fully understood without first grasping the importance of broadcasting. Since the 1930s, first radio and then television have exercised the greatest influence on the country's people. Furthermore, nothing symbolizes the government's influence over what the people see and hear as much as its relationship with television and radio.

The state may not exercise the same strict control over broadcasting in Mexico that it does in some other countries. Nonetheless, the claim that Televisa, a broadcasting octopus whose tentacles reach the entire hemisphere, is fully independent is a corporate myth. Televisa has government licenses to operate a network of three major national channels, an additional one in Mexico City, and dozens of repeater stations around the country. Collectively, these stations attract a viewing audience that may constitute three-fourths of the country's ninety million people. Televisa receives an enormous tax advantage from the government and provides free advertisements to state agencies. Technically, it is answerable to broadcast regulations set forth by the Federal Law of Radio and Televison, but that is only a technicality. Furthermore, there is nothing subtle about the way Televisa shows its gratitude. Emilio Azcárraga Milmo, the corporate giant's principal shareholder and the first or second richest man in Mexico, with an estimated net worth of $5 billion, has proudly proclaimed on a number of occasions: "I am a loyal soldier of the PRI."

During national or regional elections, PRI candidates have almost exclusive use of Televisa's airwaves, while the opposition is virtually shut out. In the 1988 presidential election, for instance, Televisa's main anchorman, Jacobo Zabludovsky, ignored the opposition except for one occasion, when the image of the late Italian dictator Benito Mussolini was superimposed next to the image of right-of-center candidate Manuel Clouthier delivering a campaign speech. Another segment portrayed left-of-center candidate Cuauhtémoc Cárdenas alongside photographs of Fidel Castro, Salvador Allende, and Nikita Khrushchev as the announcer asked rhetorically which historical figures Cárdenas admired most. The two opposition candidates demanded equal time on the network as compensation for slanted coverage. Neither action was acknowledged by Televisa, and the print media ignored the story after one day. Less than one week before the vote, two of Cárdenas's principal aides were assassinated outside their campaign office in Mexico City. Televisa virtually ignored the story, and the print media covered it for only two days and then lost interest. The murderers were never found.

On the night of that election and in the days that followed, the government and the PRI allegedly tampered with the election results, allowing Carlos Salinas, the PRI candidate, to win a narrow, suspect victory. Televisa acted as if there was no election. Television networks in the United States, Japan, and Western Europe usually preempt normal programming in favor of continuous live election coverage. Televisa carried on with its regular schedule of *telenovelas* (soap operas) and variety programs, as if election night were like any other night of the year. It never mentioned the controversy over the delayed count of votes.

Remarkably, stories such as the uprising in Chiapas on January 1, 1994, were treated as minor annoyances by Televisa's Zabludovsky, once he reached the studio and personally assumed the anchorman's position.

Five months later, mounting pressure from the opposition parties and public interest groups such as the Civic Alliance pressured President Salinas to call upon the broadcast industry, and in particular Televisa, to take a more evenhanded approach to coverage of the 1994 presidential election. Televisa then grudgingly offered each of the candidates fifteen minutes of free airtime during which a self-produced videotape would be broadcast several times during the final month of the campaign. But that did not compare with the time the network devoted to the PRI candidate, Ernesto Zedillo.

Televisa's monopolistic grip on the Mexican viewing audience weakened only slightly in 1994. Its impact is felt far and wide, in what Gabriel Gonzales Molina, president of the Gallup Organization in Latin America, describes as a "state within a state that has conquered the hearts and minds of audiences throughout Latin America as well as the Latino population in the United States." Gonzales Molina says, "It has become the single most important producer of Spanish-language television and perhaps the biggest television outlet in emerging regional markets worldwide."[14]

In addition to its television network interests, Televisa also owns a national *TV Guide*, a cable company, and a radio network; one of the most successful soccer clubs in Latin America; the largest soccer stadium in the country; a major stake in the recording industry; one of the most profitable restaurant chains in Mexico; a nightclub; a major commercial theater; and a rapidly expanding chain of video rental stores. Azcárraga is particularly successful in a monopolistic environment such as Mexico's. When he invested in the competitive markets of the United States in the early 1990s, he suffered colossal losses from the failure of *The National*, a daily sports newspaper, and an elegant yacht pier in Manhattan. His major U.S. stake now is as a partner in the Spanish television network, initially known as SIN and renamed Univisión in 1986.

Azcárraga and his faithful television anchorman Zabludovsky are often as silent as sphinxes when approached for interviews by other media. Their employees also refuse to talk about the network's philosophy or their own role in producing news programming for the organization. Anybody who does venture an opinion is subject to immediate dismissal. Zabludovsky reportedly has been rewarded for his loyalty to Azcárraga by becoming one of the wealthiest men in the country's broadcast industry.

Many Mexicans and foreigners consider Televisa's news coverage, particularly of Mexico, so biased that it is an embarrassment to the professional principles of broadcast journalism. A survey conducted by the independent Citizens Movement for Democracy of *24 Hours*, the major news show anchored by Zabludovsky every night at 10 P.M., dramatized the show's lopsided nature: in the first four months of the year, when politics dominated each news program, 91 percent of the stories were about the PRI presidential candidates Luis Donaldo Colosio and, after his assassination, Ernesto Zedillo.

Pressure to reduce the impact of Televisa forced the government to place two of its own television channels, 7 and 13, on the open market in 1993. The action mistakenly raised the hopes of independent broadcasters, opposition political parties, public interest groups, and others who traditionally had been denied access to Televisa. The eventual sale of the two channels betrayed the naïveté of those who hoped for change in Mexico's broadcasting climate and further demonstrated the government's byzantine maneuvering to maintain the status quo and prevent the entrance of an independent-minded owner into the market. For nearly thirteen months, bids were entertained from a variety of investors. As the bidding entered its final stages, five groups remained in contention. The most promising and qualified was thought to be Multivisión, a cable television operator, and its sister radio station, Stereo Rey. The partners were Joaquín Vargas, a veteran investor in broadcasting and restaurants, and Adrián Sada, the owner of the largest glass manufacturer in Mexico, Vitro, S.A., in the city of Monterrey.

Approximately ten days before the supposedly sealed bids were to be opened, however, officials of Hacienda, Mexico's equivalent of the U.S. Treasury Department and supervisors of the sale, made telephone calls to some of the bidders. It was an action that in the United States would have resulted in charges of impropriety and probably a congressional investigation. The Multivisión group was among those contacted and advised that its offer was too low. Vargas did not have sufficient capital to increase his bid, and his offer collapsed when he rejected Sada's offer to boost his investment in exchange for majority control of the station in the event the group won the award.

Ultimately, the stations and a theater chain were awarded to the unlikeliest bidder of all, Ricardo Salinas (no relation to the Mexican president). The government declared him the best qualified entrant because of his knowledge of the television business, a claim that prompted outrage or laughter from some quarters throughout the country. Salinas's only familiarity with television was his ownership of a chain of 226 stores that sells sets. After receiving the license, he gave reporters a sampling of his personal philosophy by proclaiming that he did not believe in democracy. He also said that a woman's place is in the home.

Salinas apparently was unable to raise all of the required $645 million in his bid, or an additional $200 million needed for new equipment and advertising. The new group, known as Azteca, had to find ways to sustain itself for the next year because Televisa had the nation's leading television advertisers under exclusive contract. Enter Raúl Salinas, the president's brother. A businessman who lives in the United States most of the year, he reportedly arranged for Ricardo Salinas to obtain a loan from the family of a wealthy executive who had once been the beneficiary of a lucrative import decision by the Mexican government.

In the hands of a complete amateur in broadcasting, Azteca took steps a year after it went on the air to secure fresh capital for its troubled investment by negotiating a joint venture with NBC. The deal included an option for NBC to buy up to 20 percent of TV Azteca in three years, stock worth an estimated $120 to $320 million. To what extent NBC was willing to exercise programming influence on its Mexican partners was unclear, but it did not involve Azteca's local news coverage. While the network was expected to toe the party line, it nonetheless provided extensive and balanced election night coverage in 1994, compared to its chief competitor, Televisa, which broadcast entertainment programming as the people waited for election results.

In the Mexican media, official censorship is unnecessary. The operators or owners of television, radio, and newspaper properties understand how far they can venture from the prevailing orthodoxy. By exercising self-censorship, they can usually stay out of trouble, but Big Brother is always watching. The Ministry of the Interior, which is roughly equivalent to the U.S. Department of Justice, has the Radio, Television, and Film Office under its wing.

Bruno López, a Mexican broadcaster who works for the Miami-based television network Univisión, recalls a meeting with the Radio, Television, and Film Office's director, Manuel Villa. The pseudocensor for the Interior Ministry, Villa showed López a special list that had been compiled, noting the "positive" and "negative" references to President Carlos Salinas, his party, the government, and the opposition.[15] This activity is a good example of the media-watching that is a cottage industry within every government ministry. Each agency designates a team of bureaucrats to clip, copy, and distribute any references about their offices in daily newspapers, magazines, and foreign publications as well as on television and radio. This costly paper flow enables government officials to be better prepared to respond to questions from their bosses, the media, or other callers.

Individual radio stations have far smaller audiences than big television stations, of course, but radio is nonetheless a popular medium that is observed carefully by the government. Mexico City has fifty-eight radio stations across the AM and FM bands, with AM reserved for news on the hour and talk shows and FM for music. Station owners allow news to be broadcast as long as it causes them no trouble. When it does, the response is quick. In 1993, José Luis Samaniega, the news director of Radio MIL, a popular station in Mexico City, resigned after having had enough of self-censorship. Then, one of the capital's most notable newspaper columnists, Miguel Angel Granados Chapa, was hired as host of a daily four-hour talk show. But one morning, after inviting Cuauhtémoc Cárdenas, the leading left-of-center presidential candidate in 1994, to be his guest for the duration of the broadcast, the red light went on. Villa threatened to shut down Radio MIL. In fact, he said he would pull the station's license within ninety days. Chapa was asked by the station to give up his popular talk show for a brief, daily commentary. He refused and resigned.

Determining the size of radio audiences is nearly impossible. An accurate gauge such as Arbitron does not exist in Mexico, nor is there an Audit Bureau of Circulation to verify the circulation claims of the country's newspapers, which are highly exaggerated. Several independent sources, including media scholar Raul Trejo Delarbre and *Reforma*'s editor Raimundo Riva Palacio, have gathered figures that dramatize the discrepancies between claims and reality.

In 1994, *Excélsior*, for many years the most prominent morning newspaper in Mexico City, claimed a daily circulation of 200,000; in fact, it appeared to be closer to 86,000. *El Universal*, another prominent morning newspaper, claimed that its daily readership was 181,000, but a more reliable figure was half that number. *La Jornada,* the only daily with a left-of-center political perspective, boasted 75,000 readers; under normal circumstances, a more accurate figure was 40,000. During periods of political crisis, however, *La Jornada* has attracted far more readers. On the day after the 1988 presidential election, which stirred up so much controversy, it was impossible to purchase a copy of *La Jornada* on the streets after 7 A.M. Circulation that day was said to have exceeded 200,000. During the Chiapas uprising in January 1994, *La Jornada*'s circulation soared from a claimed 75,000 to 230,000. According to sources inside the newspaper, the figure then leveled off at 90,000 daily.[16]

The Mexican press is faced with many critical problems, including (1) a lack of imagination; (2) an unwillingness to cover news that is relevant to a large percentage of the population; (3) undercapitalization, which prevents it from modernizing its equipment; (4) a shortage of well-trained editors and reporters; and (5) slavishness to an outworn political system that precludes it from exercising the kind of independence required of good journalism. One reason these obstacles are difficult to overcome is the inadequacy of the educational system for journalists. Many editors and reporters learn on the job. The existing journalism schools at

Mexican universities do not teach students how to be critical thinkers. Hence, many reporters are more like stenographers who can record the facts given by an official or taken from a news release, but they cannot tell readers what those facts mean.

The unprecedented violence that took place in a little more than a year (1993–94)—the Zapatista uprising in Chiapas, the assassination of Colosio, the murder of a Roman Catholic cardinal in Guadalajara, and the slaying of Tijuana's police chief—caused such confusion in Mexico City that the press suddenly found itself liberated to a degree never before imagined. Instead of exercising their independence, however, many journalists fell back on old habits. They substituted for their slavishness to the PRI with romanticization of the Zapatistas. The rebel leader, a mysterious figure always obscured by a ski mask, usually with a pipe in his mouth, and calling himself Subcomandante Marcos, was described in the kind of rhapsodic language found only in the tales of Robin Hood. Most astonishing of all, on the eve of the 1994 election, not one newspaper in Mexico appeared able or willing to investigate, discover, or publish the real identity of the guerrilla leader, seven months after he burst upon the scene in Chiapas on New Year's Day.

As if insurrection and assassination were not enough for one year, the financial crisis triggered by the decline of the peso shocked the country at the end of 1994 and dramatized the inadequacies of Mexico's press. Evidence of the pending disaster should have been detected by financial reporters months before it struck. Instead, everyone in the journalistic establishment was caught by surprise. According to one journalist, who requested anonymity: "I'm ashamed. It was embarrassing. But it showed how distracted we had become by the political events that overtook us throughout the year."[17]

The shortcomings of Mexican journalism can also be partially explained by the hiring practices of many news organizations, which recruit reporters and editors fresh off university campuses or hire journalists who never completed their high-school educations. In addition, morale at most newspapers is low because of the abysmal starting salaries that have averaged about $600 per month. But it is a policy that proves costly in the long run because skilled journalists are forced to move from job to job in search of better wages. Mexican journalists tend to marry and have children at a younger age than their U.S. counterparts, thereby placing a greater strain on their pocketbooks earlier in their careers. An example is Emilio R. Fernández, a reporter-editor for thirteen years with a master's degree in journalism from the University of Southern California. He earns $2,000 per month, half the salary paid to many other professionals in

Mexico City. He supports a wife and two children and for years he has wanted to buy a three-bedroom apartment. But he cannot qualify for a loan without a salary of at least $4,500 monthly. Moreover, he cannot afford to make payments of $1,500 per month or a required $50,000 cash down payment on an apartment costing $150,000. Many reporters either work at two jobs to support a family, rely on parents to help, or fall prey to the temptation of accepting *embutes* from their sources. A handful of newspapers—*El Norte* in Monterrey and *Reforma* and *El Financiero* in Mexico City, as well as the magazine *Proceso*—pay higher salaries and forbid their journalists to accept bribes or government "gifts." But these are the exceptions.

The current bribes and other controls date to the 1930s, when the press lost its innocence and independence as President Lázaro Cárdenas increased the government's subsidies to the media. The policy intensified under President Miguel Alemán (1946–1952). The press quickly grew accustomed to using information spoon-fed to it by government officials or commercial sources that, to this day, dominates the front pages of almost all newspapers. The stories are usually devoted to the government, the president, political parties, and corporate developments, which are usually irrelevant or boring. Some articles, however, are disguised to seem like news when in fact they are nothing more than paid political, business, or social announcements that only a sophisticated reader would recognize for what they are. These *gacetillas* are an accepted practice in an environment that does not have a recognized code of journalistic ethics, and they have existed for many years in Mexican journalism. Newspapers charge two or three times their commercial advertising rate for them, thus providing lucrative income that enables many marginal publications to survive. The *gacetillas* also subsidize underpaid journalists. A reporter who can solicit one from his or her beat can receive as much as a 15 percent commission from the newspaper. Some newspaper unions insist that the reporters take 5 percent off the top to be contributed to a common fund for all employees.

Of the estimated thirty or more daily newspapers in Mexico City, all but a handful might fail if they were denied the right to use *gacetillas* or to have access to government-sponsored advertisements or to obtain subsidized newsprint. No real justification exists for having nearly three dozen daily newspapers in a metropolis that, for the most part, lacks sufficient readership and suffers from widespread functional illiteracy. But it suits a cynical government strategy to use advertising dollars to sustain a large number of weak newspapers, thereby preventing a handful of stronger ones from dominating the official advertising market.

Many publishers who collaborate with the policy have little interest in journalism. They have broad commercial investments in sports franchises, theater chains, video stores, shopping malls, fast food franchises, automobile agencies, and banking. Some are involved in businesses closely allied to the government. But the picture is beginning to change. Although such old Mexico City warhorses as *Excélsior*, *El Universal*, and *Novedades* are unlikely to alter their way of doing business, now there is an exciting challenger from northern Mexico.

In 1971, Alejandro Junco de la Vega was working at *El Norte*, his family's newspaper in Monterrey in the northern state of Nuevo León, having just completed his bachelor's degree in journalism at the University of Texas at Austin. Unexpectedly, his elderly grandparents transferred all of *El Norte*'s stock to him. He was just twenty-four years old and overnight had become the heir to a newspaper that, in his words, was a shell of a company: "We had twenty-four to twenty-eight pages daily, with a circulation of under 30,000, but we shared the kind of commitment that people can develop with an institution."[18]

Junco de la Vega's first major lesson in dealing with the political machine came in the summer of 1973, when one of Monterrey's most prominent businessmen, Eugene Garza Sada, was kidnapped and subsequently murdered by a group of urban guerrillas known as the League of Communists. In editorials and news columns, *El Norte* demanded to know why President Luis Echeverría had not done more to solve the crime. The president responded by trying to kill *El Norte*. Through PIPSA, he cut Junco de la Vega's newsprint supply by 83 percent so he could not publish the following day, forcing the newspaper to reduce circulation, cut advertising, and omit entire sections. To tighten the screws even further, Echeverría used government funds to help a competing Monterrey publisher print his newspaper in full color.

Junco de la Vega stubbornly refused to knuckle under, and Echeverría's attempted sabotage finally collapsed. The experience was a valuable warning to the *El Norte* publisher. To survive, he knew he had to divorce himself from relying on government subsidies and find private newsprint sources across the border in the United States. It took fifteen years before the government invited Mexican publishers to seek newsprint outside of PIPSA and outside of the country. Most publishers protested, so accustomed had they become to the cheaper, government-subsidized paper products. Junco de la Vega, on the other hand, was elated. Shortly after taking charge of *El Norte*, he decided to establish a summer training program for prospective employees. For more than twenty years the program was under the supervision of Mary A. Gardner, a journalism professor at

Michigan State University. She had been a professor of Junco de la Vega's when he was an undergraduate student at the University of Texas, and he has repeatedly cited her as an inspirational counselor.

Junco de la Vega also decided to modernize El Norte's facilities and to convert to offset printing. The newsroom was overhauled, computers for reporters were installed, and state-of-the-art graphics equipment was purchased. In all, he invested $25 million to upgrade the newspaper, realizing that the business of newspapers was more than the printed product. The gathering and analysis of information, he reasoned, would be the cornerstone of his success. That thinking led to the creation of Infosel, a real-time on-line database that provided information-related services. Junco de la Vega invested in excess of $10 million to buy a satellite uplink, high-frequency radio, and telephone lines. The database ultimately provided not only financial information but also legal and medical data to two thousand clients, one hundred of them in the United States.

Still in his forties, the successful newspaper tycoon had turned Monterrey's El Norte from a marginalized daily of 30,000 into the most important newspaper in northern Mexico, with a circulation of 145,000. Junco de la Vega decided that an aggressive new newspaper was needed in the sprawling capital of more than twenty million people. Therefore, in November 1993, he tested the largest potential market in the country by launching a daily newspaper, Reforma, in Mexico City.

Originally, Reforma was to be a joint venture involving the Wall Street Journal. Junco de la Vega envisioned a newspaper with a strong business orientation, partnered with the most successful financial newspaper in the world, as having a major impact not only on Mexico but also on all of Latin America. But when the Journal and its parent company, Dow Jones Inc., insisted on a strong editorial hand as well as a guarantee of majority equity in Reforma should Junco de la Vega die or withdraw from the newspaper, the deal collapsed. Instead, he invested more than $50 million of his own money to ensure the success of the new venture. It was "like jumping off a cliff without a safety net," he told reporters from the Dallas Morning News at the time. "But really, there are no obstacles to what we want to do."[19] The failure of the potential marriage with the Wall Street Journal taught him that "when you hesitate in a business decision, you do yourself in. So we never hesitated. What I could not imagine was the bureaucracy we would encounter in initiating such a venture. Getting a building permit, a soil-use permit, coping with neighbors' complaints about the new building, problems of circulation."[20]

Junco de la Vega and Ramón Garza, his chief deputy, quickly realized that the original idea of having a thirty-two-page product in four sections would not work. In time, during the planning stages for what was to become *Reforma*, they increased the model to ninety-six pages in eight sections. Garza and his associates shrewdly undertook market surveys. They initiated a Mexico City edition of *El Norte* and began to circulate it to test reaction to a newspaper of similar appearance and size.

Reforma's headquarters in Mexico City is state of the art. The presses are mounted on suspension rods that keep them off the floor and enable them to sway back and forth to avoid major damage in the event of an earthquake as severe as the one that struck the city in 1985. Garza, the director general for both *El Norte* and *Reforma*, displays an infectious enthusiasm for all he touches, and oversees 420 editors and reporters in Monterrey and 240 in Mexico City. "We established a database for all our subscribers," he says. "We created a corps of entrepreneurs by establishing delivery franchises, offering assistance to potential employees. We also control complaints and accounts receivable."[21] *Reforma* costs one-third more than other newspapers, but from the outset it targeted upscale readers with discretionary income in neighborhoods of the more well-to-do in the southern and western parts of the city. Home delivery was essential and a key to *Reforma*'s success. Seven months after the first issue rolled off the presses, circulation was at about 45,000 and growing.

Garza says that twenty months after *Reforma* published its first edition (November 20, 1993), estimated circulation had risen to nearly 100,000 daily, a startling figure considering the newspaper's brief history. Some success stems from Junco de la Vega's decision to challenge Mexico City's newstand monopoly, controlled by the Unión de Vocedadores, which more closely resembles a cartel than a union. It controls all of the newsstand kiosks in the capital, thereby dictating which newspapers and magazines are available for street sales. The union reflects one aspect of the informal censorship that exists in Mexico. Its leader, Manuel Ramos, has close ties to the government and was invited to meet with former president Carlos Salinas de Gortari on a number of occasions.

For the second year in succession, Ramos refused to distribute *Reforma* on November 20, the anniversary of the Mexican Revolution, which traditionally is a national holiday throughout the country when all kiosks are closed. He also vetoed *Reforma*'s request to make the newspaper available for newsstand distribution on Sundays and other holidays when the kiosks normally do not operate. Junco de la Vega argued that newspapers have an obligation to publish and be distributed every day of the year and that the union had no right to prevent *Reforma* from doing so. When Ramos held his ground, Junco de la Vega declared war. He and Garza organized a rump distribution force that briefly included *Reforma* officeworkers, editors, and reporters. They hawked the newspaper in the streets on those days that the Unión de Vocedadores refused to do so. The

initial strategy proved so successful that *Reforma* created its own independent distribution system of "mini-empresarios," consisting of small
businessmen who earned more money than if they had worked through
the Unión de Vocedadores. Other independent newspapers and magazines
have expressed an interest in aligning themselves with *Reforma* distribu-
tors. In effect, Junco de la Vega's daring action broke the back of a monopoly that had existed in Mexico City since 1921.

In the wake of the latest economic crisis, which erupted in January
1994, newspapers throughout the country, including *Reforma* and its sister newspaper, *El Norte* of Monterrey, were saddled with enormous and
unanticipated financial burdens. Dozens of journalists at both newspapers lost their jobs, and at other newspapers the cutbacks were far more
severe. But Junco de la Vega remains heavily committed to *Reforma*, and
while the paper has reduced sections and the number of its pages, it is
still the most talked-about daily in Mexico City.

Newsprint costs have soared, and many of the more than thirty newspapers in the capital are faced with declining advertising revenues from
the government. The latter fact could be a hidden blessing for Mexican
journalism. There is no justification for more than a half-dozen good newspapers in Mexico City, which has a low readership base to begin with. A
historic tactic of the government and the PRI over the years has been to
perpetuate the survival of so many newspapers, most of them bad, by
subsidizing them with official advertising and under-the-table stipends to
compliant journalists. It results in a shadowy form of censorship of news
coverage because the indebted newspapers and magazines rarely criticize
the government. Slowly, that is beginning to change. The curtailment of
official subsidies will lead inevitably to the demise of the capital's worst
newspapers. The survivors will be those with an aggressive campaign to
tap the commercial advertising market where *Reforma* already has laid a
strong foundation.

Ninety percent of the financial worth of Junco de la Vega is devoted
to his newspapers. As to the assertion by other media experts that he is
changing the landscape of Mexican journalism, he replies modestly:
"Maybe I would choose other words. What I do know is that we need a
new paradigm for viewing the world of information. How to treat news
sources, how to live our personal lives and swim with sharks without
being eaten by them. We want a group of people with certain values, with
a belief in teamwork. It is too early to tell whether our system will work."[22]
Unlike *El Norte*, which was given to Junco de la Vega by his grandparents, *Reforma* was his own creation. If he succeeds—and he has no doubt
that he will—it would establish him as perhaps the most important figure
in a new era of Mexican journalism. Junco de la Vega has proven that he

is a different kind of media tycoon, one who is interested in raising professional standards.

Others are also challenging Mexican journalism. In 1989, Alfonso Dau, a wealthy land investor and former politician who earned a fortune as a real estate developer in Puerto Vallarta, was so fed up with the stodgy newspapers in his hometown of Guadalajara that he decided that the city needed a new, quality newspaper. He explained his dream to an old acquaintance, Jorge Cepeda, a sociology professor, and asked him to be the proposed newspaper's first editor. Cepeda was stunned; he knew nothing about journalism, but Dau said that he would learn and sent him to Madrid for six months to observe the daily operations of *El País*, one of Europe's outstanding newspapers. Then Cepeda went to Paris to study graphic design. By the time he returned to Guadalajara, Dau was ready to invest up to $4 million to launch *Siglo 21*.

The two men decided that the new newspaper should be a tabloid modeled on the image of *El País*. Cepeda hired a staff that, for the most part, had had little prior journalistic experience. He focused on energetic young people with writing skills and curiosity; it was the *El Norte* model. At 7 A.M. on April 22, 1992, *Siglo 21* was on the streets of Guadalajara, three hours ahead of its competition, with a startling front-page story by Alejandra Xanic warning of a probable gas explosion in one of the city's underground pipelines. Three hours later an explosion actually devastated large sections of a working-class neighborhood, killing two hundred people and injuring nearly one thousand more. Before his competitors could recover, Cepeda ordered a special edition, an eight-page supplement that included graphic photos and eyewitness accounts from the disaster scene.

Ms. Xanic, a twenty-three-year-old college graduate who had never been in a newsroom until Cepeda hired her, was later named Mexico's journalist of the year for her coverage of this event. Two months later, another investigative team from *Siglo 21* followed a paper trail that uncovered a lawsuit filed by the national telephone company against the city of Puerto Vallarta. The suit charged that the city had allowed a dangerous underground buildup of water and kerosene to jeopardize the company's telephone cables. As a result of this type of reporting, the newspaper, which had an initial run of 14,000, saw its circulation rise to 35,000 by the fall of 1994, thereby enabling Dau to cover his operating costs. *Siglo 21*'s readership would increase even more but for the lack of press capacity.

The successes of *El Norte*, *Reforma*, and *Siglo 21* augur well for the future of Mexican journalism. A decade ago the pessimists were prepared to write it off. That is no longer true. Just as the collapse of the Berlin Wall contributed to the eventual liberation of journalism in Eastern

Europe, global communications and the information superhighway may have a similar impact on Mexico. The world of computers, satellites, and fiber optics is putting its journalists in closer proximity to the rest of the globe. A new generation of reporters and editors is becoming more sophisticated and competent, more skeptical, and less willing to be surprised or kept in ignorance by the government. In the wake of the continuing economic and political crises that are having a profound impact on most Mexicans who are considered regular newspaper readers, the press has become far more aggressive in its reporting and more willing to give space to stories and commentaries that are critical of the government. It is turning out to be an unprecedented but welcome trans i on, even with some of the glaring factual, grammatical, and stylistic mis.akes that appear in every publication. These mistakes are a direct resul. of having too small a pool of well-trained or skilled journalists from which to draw.

Many important positive signs now exist. In addition to Junco de la Vega and Garza at *Reforma*, and Dau and Cepeda at *Siglo 21*, some outstanding publishers and editors are emerging, including José Santiago Healy and Martín Holguin at *El Imparcial* in Hermosillo. Mexican journalists are also becoming more professional, and some who have studied in the United States are trying to draft a Freedom of Information Act. Rosanna Fuentes, a veteran business and investigative reporter working for *Reforma*, is spearheading a drive to win support for such legislation among her colleagues. "Being a journalist in Mexico is not easy; sometimes it is not even safe," she told a women's financial group. "Our society must come to terms with the importance of openness and accountability if we are to have a modern economic and political system." In a letter to American friends, she said: "As we have discussed in the past, the problems of a truly free press in Mexico are just beginning to emerge. Free access to public records remains a core element. In any society, the lack of such access weakens the democratic process and also fosters rumors and unaccountability."[23]

Finally, another important sign is that, for the first time in years, encouraging, optimistic voices are being heard from within Mexican journalism. "There is less cynicism in the press today than ever before," says Raimundo Riva Palacio. "The political cost of being corrupt is higher than it used to be. In the past 10 or 15 years, more journalists are coming from universities than we could ever have hoped for. . . . They're better educated and informed. A totally different rapport with the power structure is developing. Moreover, journalists do not have the inferiority complex they once had. They are more professional."[24] And that is the goal— truly professional mass media.

Notes

1. Rafael Barajas Durán, interview with author, June 15, 1994, Mexico City.

2. Humberto Musacchio, *Diccionario enciclopédico de México* (Mexico City: Sector de Orientación Pedagógica, S.A. de C.V., 1989), 1540–62, author's translation.

3. Ibid.

4. Ibid.

5. Barajas interview.

6. Musacchio, *Diccionario enciclopédico*, 1540–62.

7. Ibid.

8. Ibid.

9. Ibid.

10. Ibid.

11. Barajas interview.

12. Ibid.

13. Alan Knight, *The Mexican Revolution*, vol. 2, *Counterrevolution and Reconstruction* (New York: Cambridge University Press, 1986).

14. Gabriel Gonzales Molina, "The Production of Mexican Television News: The Supremacy of Corporate Rationale" (Ph.D. diss., Center for Mass Communications Research, University of Leicester, England, 1990), 62–85, 187–92.

15. Enrique Quintana López and Janine Rodiles, "Free Trade without a Free Press? Mexican Media and the Culture of Collusion" (New York: Committee to Protect Journalists, 1994), 79–80.

16. Figures gathered by author from a range of sources.

17. Author's interview with prominent journalist who requested anonymity.

18. Alejandro Junco de la Vega, interview with author, July 1994, Mexico City.

19. Tracey Eaton and Enrique Rangel, "New Headliner in Mexico City," *Dallas Morning News*, November 28, 1993.

20. Ibid.

21. Ramón Garza, interview with author, July 1994.

22. Eaton and Rangel, "New Headliner."

23. Rosanna Fuentes, letter to author and other friends, August 1994.

24. Raimundo Riva Palacio, interview with author, July 1994.

8

The Dark Side of Cuban Journalism: Press Freedom and Corruption before Castro

Michael B. Salwen

Cuba—the largest island in the West Indies, lying less than one hundred miles off Florida—is about the size of Pennsylvania and has close to eleven million people. About two million live in Havana. Some 70 percent of the people are urban; roughly 60 percent are less than thirty-five years old. The last major colony to gain independence from Spain, in 1898, Cuba has been intertwined with the United States politically ever since. In recent years, it has been a major issue in U.S. presidential politics.

Two years after Fidel Castro took power in 1959, Cuba became a Communist, totalitarian state. Officially, Castro is president of the Council of State and the Council of Ministers, first secretary of the Communist Party, and commander-in-chief of the armed forces. Cuba is one of the most highly militarized societies in the world, and the only legal political party has been the Communist Party. Cubans do not possess such rights as equal protection under the law or the right to choose government representatives freely and openly. The cherished U.S. First Amendment rights—of religion, speech, press, and peaceful assembly—do not exist. It can be a repressive and frightening society. But Castro took over after the corrupt and brutal rule of Fulgencio Batista (1952–1959), when the elite lived in luxury and the masses suffered in squalor. He improved the life of the lower classes enormously. Education was made available to all, literacy rose to close to 100 percent of the population, and health care was made virtually free for everyone.

After Castro became closely aligned with the Soviet Union, that giant came to subsidize tiny Cuba more and more. In the late 1980s about 85 percent of the island's international trade was with the Soviet Union and Eastern Europe. The Soviets were subsidizing Cuba to the tune of some $5 billion per year. Then, in 1989, the Soviet Union fell. Soon the Cuban economy collapsed. Food became scarce; everything ran short. Castro's socialist dream turned into a nightmare.

*What of mass communication under Castro? The government and
Party have owned and controlled all print and electronic media, and traditionally the top journalists have been ideologically aligned with the
Party, often holding top government or Party posts. The media have followed the Leninist model, including its tenets of collective propagan-
dization, agitation, and organization, but there always has been some
Latin flavor as well. Broadcasting at home and abroad has been emphasized, and Castro has been characterized as having government by television because of his famous, long-winded televised speeches. Until recent
years, Cuba boasted more television sets per capita than any other Latin
American country. Most Cuban newsprint was imported from the Soviet
Union; therefore, since the Soviet collapse, newspapers and magazines
have been crippled.*

*This volume devotes two chapters to Cuba because its politics and
mass communication system are so enmeshed with the United States. In
this chapter, Michael Salwen discusses mass communication before Castro.
He demonstrates that the system was corrupt, and that bribes and subsidies were widespread as a means of reducing government criticism. This
essay is based on sections from the book* Radio and Television in Cuba:
The Pre-Castro Era *(1994) and on a paper presented to the International
and Intercultural Communication Conference in Miami in 1993. An associate professor in the School of Communication at the University of Miami in Coral Gables, Florida, Salwen has conducted extensive research
on international journalism, mass media effects, and public opinion.*

To this day, Cubans—whether they be those who remain loyal to Fidel
Castro or those committed to communism's downfall—pay homage
to the role of journalism in the social and political development of the
nation. It is almost obligatory in discussions of Cuban journalism to laud
the journalistic contributions of José Martí, Cuba's counterpart to George
Washington, with inciting patriotism and influencing the founding of the
republic.[1]

The fact is, however, that Cubans, like people everywhere, view the
contributions of journalism in their homeland with a certain misplaced
nostalgia. Scholars of Cuban media have repeatedly stressed the "corruption" and "irresponsibility" of the pre-Castro press. John Spicer Nichols
described pre-Castro journalists as "seedy, censored, venal puppets of
government and industry," adding that "every Cuban president from the
time of independence [1902] to the [Castro] revolution either had overtly
censored or more subtly bribed editors and reporters into submission."[2]
Sociologist C. Wright Mills, in one of the earliest defenses of Castro,
described the prerevolutionary press as "part of [dictator Fulgencio]
Batista's ruling gang."[3] John A. Lent asserted that, prior to 1959, journal-

istic broadcasters were notorious for their "controversial and irresponsible natures."[4] Marvin Alisky claimed that Batista, upon taking power in 1951, "decided to employ subsidies and bribes more than censorship, and his system flourished as painless control until his ouster on December 31, 1958."[5]

It was common knowledge among Cubans in pre-Castro society that politicians could buy favorable press coverage through bribes and press subsidies. Although the extent of this abuse was unknown, the sheer number of newspapers and radio stations in Cuba, far more than the market could support, would suggest that at least many of the smaller media organizations were receiving funding from sources other than circulation or advertising.[6]

During the 1940s and 1950s, Havana was one of the most media-rich cities in the world.[7] Although the number of newspapers fluctuated, as some failed and new ones were founded, the city of five hundred thousand to seven hundred thousand residents sometimes had twenty or more newspapers during this period, including Chinese and Yiddish ones. Some newspapers claimed circulations of up to one hundred thousand, but these figures were suspect because of the lack of independent circulation audits.[8]

It is important to study the status of journalism in pre-Castro Cuba because the disreputable reputation of the island's journalism, the corruption of which predated the Batista dictatorship, contributed to the inability of the press to criticize government abuses after Castro came to power, a time when full public debate about his reforms was most needed. Castro was not hesitant in denouncing newspapers and journalists by name as enemies of the state during his marathon speeches, reminding Cubans of newspapers' associations with the Batista government. From 1959 to 1961, before Cuba became an avowed Marxist-Leninist state with all mass media under state control, the Castro government sought public support for its actions toward the press. Castro and his officials pointed to press corruption to justify confiscating privately operated mass media organizations. Evidence suggests that there was at least enough public support for the government to move against these organizations.

In 1959 celebrations filled Havana's streets when Cubans learned that Batista had fled the island for asylum in the Dominican Republic. Almost immediately, a process started to ferret out and punish his supporters. Members of Batista's military police, who systematically arrested and murdered opponents of the regime, were prosecuted by the new government. In some cases, they were executed by firing squads. Industrialists who profited by their connections to the Batista government saw their properties confiscated. These actions were immensely popular.

Attention also turned to individual journalists and to newspapers, and then later to radio and television stations, that were accused of collusion with the Batista government. Faced with evidence against them—sometimes indisputable, other times dubious or flimsy—Batistianos in the mass media were denounced as collaborators with the former dictatorship. In addition, censors during the Batista era were arrested, and the new government announced it was terminating press subsidies permanently.

In the beginning, at least, the most egregious examples of Batistiano media organizations were punished. The day after the dictator fled, several newspapers with close affiliations to his government were expropriated and converted into government organs.[9] *Alerta*, operated by Batista's minister of communications, Ramón Vasconcelos, was converted into the organ *Revolución*. *El Tiempo*, operated by Senator Rolando Masferrer, a ruthless thug who headed a private army involved in killings and tortures throughout the island, saw his newspaper confiscated.[10] Radio outlets associated with Batista were also confiscated, including the Circuito Nacional network, operated by his son-in-law.[11] No television stations were confiscated during these early days. Since its beginnings, Cuban television, unlike newspapers and radio, has stayed out of the political fray and operated as entertainment media for profit.[12]

During the giddy days of celebration over Batista's downfall, few media voices came to the defense of pro-Batista newspapers and radio stations confiscated by the government. Cuban editors did not subscribe to the libertarian notion of freedom of the press as it was practiced in the United States. Angel Fernández Varela, an editor of the respected daily *Información*, has insisted that his newspaper and other commercial ones did protest the takeover of the Batistiano newspapers, but he added: "It's one thing to speak up, and it's another thing to speak up in a hard-hitting way. . . . Everybody thought that this was a particular problem with Batista and the people related to Batista, not the big [newspapers] that were independent."[13]

In the first weeks after Batista fled Cuba, the humor magazine *Zig Zag*, which was not regarded as a Batistiano organ, published a cartoon depicting his former cronies lining up behind Castro. An indignant Castro denounced the magazine in a speech, threatening to lead a boycott against it. The magazine then refrained from further comment about the new leader. Once again, the newspapers remained silent. Carlos Todd, a U.S.-educated columnist at the English-language *Times of Havana*, one of the earliest press critics of Castro, wrote of the incident: "The Cuban press did not understand that if such coercion and intimidation could be applied to any one of its members, the others were also open to similar attacks by Castro and the government."[14]

During this early stage of the revolution, the mainstream press generally supported Castro's policies. Still, the press would occasionally engage in tempered criticisms, such as questioning excessive zeal on the part of government agencies instituting reforms. The government responded to these criticisms by reminding Cubans how the media under Batista were compromised. In most cases, that reminder alone was enough to quell the criticism.

Shortly after Batista's flight from Cuba, *Revolución*, the semiofficial government newspaper, caused a stir by publishing a list of what it claimed were magazines, newspapers, and journalists (identified by name) who received monthly government payments, ranging from $500 to $16,000.[15] According to the list, only three news organizations refused to accept subsidies: the *Times of Havana*, *Prensa Libre*, and the magazine *Bohemia*. *Revolución* claimed that the list was "found" in the presidential palace after Batista fled the island. It was not clear from the list whether the sums associated with the newspapers indicated bribes or money for government advertising, which was a perfectly legal practice. The list was damning, nonetheless.

In April 1959, *El Mundo*'s respected columnist Juan Luis Martín, a fervent anti-Communist, had been arrested and held incommunicado. He was not charged with any offense and was released two weeks later without explanation. Cuba's journalistic community remained silent about the incident. Only the *Times of Havana*, which confirmed rumors from *El Mundo* staff members, carried a one-column description of the arrest.[16]

By late 1959 several episodes of press harassment had occurred, although there was no evidence that Castro was behind them. They might have been the work of overzealous officials, but they constituted a prelude to eventual government confiscations of the print and broadcast media. In late 1959 and early 1960 foreign correspondents who wrote critical stories about Cuba were harassed. *Miami Herald* correspondent James Buchanan was imprisoned for allegedly helping a Cuban fugitive escape the island. He served thirteen days in jail before being released with a fourteen-year suspended sentence.[17] Other foreign reporters were briefly detained or harassed.[18] *Chicago Tribune* correspondent Jules Dubois, regarded as an early supporter of Castro, started criticizing the disintegration of personal freedoms. In a speech in late October 1959, Castro denounced him as an enemy of Cuba. After the speech, Dubois had to be rescued from a mob.[19]

For Havana's newspapers, being assailed by Castro, or by the unofficial voice of Castro through government organs, portended danger. Ritual public burnings of magazines and newspapers accused of anti-revolutionary inclinations were becoming commonplace. Todd, of the *Times of Havana*, frequently wrote about freedom of the press issues and claimed that the new government had effectively manipulated the issue of press bribery to paint all journalists as corrupt:

> The method of discrediting the press . . . was subtly carried to a fine art. It is true that newspapers accepted subsidies [during the Batista regime]. They had been doing so under every single government in years past. They had to in order to exist. . . . The subsidies that these newspapers accepted were partly paid by the government in ministerial advertisements. Newsmen also received money for covering and giving prominence to government news in their particular sector. Certainly some newspapers were sold out to Batista & Co. That is irrefutable. All of them? That is something else again.[20]

In the summer of 1959 the Castro government laid the legal foundation for expropriations of industries, including newspapers and radio and television stations, that had illegally profited under Batista's rule. Article 24 of the Fundamental Law permitted the Ministry of Recovery of Stolen Property to confiscate the belongings of industries and individuals who had accepted gifts, favors, and subsidies from the Batista government.[21] After several newspapers were expropriated by the government during September and October 1959, the privately operated newspapers left in Cuba feared that their properties, too, would be confiscated. They turned for assistance to the Inter American Press Association (IAPA), the main media watchdog in the Western Hemisphere.[22] While investigating, the IAPA office received photocopies of canceled checks from Batista government agencies made out to the newspapers. The checks were reported to have arrived "by pure coincidence" from anonymous sources. Despite these checks, the IAPA concluded that Cuban newspapers were not compromised by Batista. In announcing its findings, the IAPA explained that it was common practice during the Batista years and those of previous Havana governments to pay newspapers to carry government advertising, edicts, and listings of public works.[23]

In 1959 and 1960 virtually all of Cuba's private newspapers and broadcast outlets were overtly or subtly accused by government officials, labor unions, and sometimes even Castro himself of having been undermined by the Batista regime. In many cases the accusations originated within the newspapers themselves, when, without management's approval, employees in Linotype rooms and newsrooms inserted messages accusing the publishers of being enemies of the state. These charges were usually followed by government confiscations. Many newspapers went out of business during these lean economic times as advertisers cut back on their expenditures.

Castro, at this time, was openly attacking what he regarded as anti-revolutionary elements of the press. Perhaps one of the most notorious incidents of his verbal attacks on the press, naming the publisher and charging him with treason, was against the daily *Avance* in January 1960. The incident started after publisher Jorge Zayás wrote an article critical of his newsroom employees who, without his permission, had attached disapproving statements to some local and foreign wire service stories in the newspaper that they regarded as critical of Castro and the Cuban government. The statement read: "The contents of this newspaper do not conform to the truth, nor to the most elemental journalistic ethics."

Zayás responded the next day with a front-page editorial, warning his readers that the appended messages reflected the views of disgruntled employees and should be ignored. In following editions, the employees responded with their own retort to their employer, saying that their messages represented their "freedom of the press." Zayás, fearing that the insubordinate employees were receiving government encouragement and that he might be in danger, found refuge in a foreign embassy and later fled the country. While Zayás was in the embassy, Castro delivered a five-hour speech, devoting two hours to an attack on Zayás and *Avance*:

> Freedom of the press is not what he [Zayás] thinks it is. Freedom of the press is not freedom to sell oneself to the highest bidder, as he has done with his newspaper.
> For this reason, what the journalistic class needs is a total revamping. To bring to light the malfeasance [in society], as he has not done. And let journalists have the assurance that when they face the wrath of the corrupters, they can count on the firm support of the revolutionary government.
> The journalistic class needs to purify itself, and [only] then will it see itself as worthy of the benefits and longings it has been demanding. The professional class of the press needs to get rid of the shameful burden of the criminals and the embezzlers of public funds, and then it can count on the backing of all [Cubans].[24]

When Castro came to power, Havana had seventeen daily newspapers. By April 1960, only four independent daily newspapers remained. Two of them, *El Crisol* and *Información*, were not known for taking political stands. *El Crisol* consisted largely of sports and crime news. *Información*, which prided itself on its "objectivity," refrained from political commentary.[25] Only the conservative *Diario de la Marina* and the liberal *Prensa Libre* took strong editorial stands on political issues.

Before it was confiscated, *Diario de la Marina* publisher José Ignacio Rivero anticipated that disgruntled employees would denounce *La Marina*. To counter that, Rivero planned to publish a full-page endorsement of the paper's policies signed by 318 of the 450 employees. But the newspaper was "intervened" (the term used by the government) early on the morning that the letter was to be published.[26] The day after the intervention, a crowd chanting anti-American slogans held a symbolic funeral celebrating the death of *La Marina*.[27] Rivero fled for safety to a foreign embassy. Later, in exile, he received the IAPA's Hero of Freedom medal.[28]

At this time, the government sought public support for its confiscations. The takeover of the archconservative *La Marina*, which appealed to an elitist upper class, probably enjoyed wide support.[29] But *Prensa Libre* had no known connections with the Batista government. Its owner, Sergio Carbó, a hero of the 1933 revolution, was often highly critical of Batista, and the paper steadfastly refused to accept subsidies during the Batista regime.[30] *Prensa Libre*'s strong defense of *Diario de la Marina* after that paper was confiscated almost assured the government takeover of *Prensa Libre* itself, which occurred on May 16.[31]

It is not necessary to detail every incident in the well-chronicled history of the Castro government's takeover of the press. Suffice it to say that newspapers' connections to the Batista regime provided Castro with the moral justification and popular support to take over the private press. But in what follows, it will become evident that the subsidies did not suddenly emerge during the Batista years. They date to the founding of the republic. Ironically, press subsidies were perhaps most prevalent during the administrations of democratically elected governments preceding Batista's March 10, 1952, coup—a period described by one expert on Latin American media as "a high point in [Cuban] press freedom."[32]

The Cuban press grew rapidly after the establishment of the republic on May 20, 1902.[33] A Washington report, prepared in 1919 for U.S. manufacturers considering expanding into Cuba, noted that Havana had a population of four hundred thousand and supported thirteen daily newspapers. It added that "it's a poor month in Havana when at least one paper isn't born and when another doesn't die."[34] The report encouraged U.S. investors to exploit this competitive situation to their advantage: "It may be a matter of interest to advertisers to know that the explanatory word 'advertisement' required by law and appearing at the bottom of reading notices in American newspapers is not required nor used in Cuba. Neither is a distinctive face of type used, and, as a consequence, many of the papers run riot with paid propaganda and publicity of all sorts disguised as news. Those advertisers who insist that paid advertising entitles them to free publicity will find that the Cuban dailies will lend a helping hand."[35]

During the early years of his administration, President Gerardo Machado y Morales (1925–1933) implemented a system of newspaper "subsidies" to blunt press criticism of his rule. Machado, however, did not use subsidies systematically. When the subsidies failed to silence the criticisms, he turned to censorship.[36] The notorious legacy of his censorship made it difficult for future governments to be so blatant. After a period of national chaos following Machado's overthrow, the popularly elected but corrupt governments of Fulgencio Batista y Zaldívar (1940–1944), Ramón Grau San Martín (1944–1948), and Carlos Prió Socarrás (1948–1952) instituted effective systems of press subsidies coupled with outright bribes.[37]

The highly competitive newspaper environment made it almost impossible for any newspaper to survive on circulation and advertising alone. At first, the subsidy system seemed innocent enough. Many well-meaning Cuban intellectuals and politicians argued that government subsidies were needed to promote a free press because newspapers provided an important public service.[38]

Those who opposed subsidies called for the adoption of "professional" journalistic standards. To this end, Cuba's journalists lobbied for the first journalism *colegio*, the Colegio Nacional de Periodistas (National Collegium of Journalists), in Latin America. It was established in early 1942. *Colegios* are professional organizations that set professional standards.[39] At about the same time the Manuel Márquez Sterling School of Journalism was established; it operated on government funding through the Ministry of Education.[40] It is questionable whether the *colegio* was effective in improving the state of Cuban journalism. As Lent has written: "Although these actions seem laudable on paper, it is doubtful that they did much to change media-government relationships, since they came about through presidential decree and received government funding."[41]

During the 1940s one of the island's most prestigious dailies, the liberal *El Mundo*, instituted a series of policies, including raising salaries, to ensure that its reporters were not compromised.[42] *El Mundo*'s policies might have garnered it respect, but they did not translate into profit. The financially troubled newspaper was sold in 1949 to a group of buyers led by the wealthy Amadeo Barletta, a man of dubious character of whom more will be mentioned.[43]

To this point, we have presented a broadbrush portrait of questionable journalistic practices in pre-Castro Cuba. But the portrait raises questions: Who were these people accused of corrupting Cuban journalism? What were they doing that gave them such reputations? Two cases illustrate the corruption and irresponsibility in the pre-Castro press. While the examples are not necessarily typical, they were well known in Cuba at the time and typify the image of the pre-Castro press. The first example profiles an individual, Amadeo Barletta, a leading media entrepreneur with a shady reputation. The second describes a journalistic practice: news sources buying favorable coverage in newspapers' social sections.

Barletta, a Batista supporter, was reputed to be one of the wealthiest men in Cuba. His assets, which included a television network as well as *El Mundo*, were valued at more than $40 million. His fortune rested on his exclusive General Motors franchise in the island.[44] Mills, writing in 1960, before Castro became an avowed Communist, claimed that Barletta epitomized the iniquity in the pre-Castro press. Mills applauded the Castro government's decision to expropriate Barletta's properties:

> There was a man [Barletta] who was a friend of Mussolini. When Italian fascism was defeated he came to the Americas. In the Santo Domingo republic he was in business with [dictator Rafael] Trujillo. He left there, he came to Cuba, he set up a business here. . . . Then he bought a big newspaper, *El Mundo*, and also radio and TV channels. He established some 43 businesses in Cuba—from selling Cadillacs to rich Cubans to the smuggling of drugs. . . . Now, of course, his whole illegal world has been discovered and exposed by the revolution. The files of all these businesses are somewhere in the Office for the Recuperation of Stolen Property. But that is the kind of man who was running one of our biggest newspapers.[45]

Barletta's ties to Mussolini and Fascist Italy, which haunted him throughout his life, and especially after Castro came to power, dated to his tenure as the Italian consul to the Dominican Republic in 1930–1935. While in Santo Domingo, he also held the exclusive right to distribute General Motors automobiles. Barletta was arrested by Dominican police in April 1935 and charged with tax evasion and with leading an assassination plot against Generalísimo Trujillo. Mussolini dispatched a warship to Santo Domingo, to attack if Italy's consul were not released. The U.S. Department of State sent word to Dominican officials that it would not defend the Dominican Republic from an Italian attack. Barletta was released six weeks later. A *New York Times* report speculated that Trujillo might have arrested Barletta because his holdings in the Dominican Tobacco Company threatened the government's tobacco monopoly.[46]

After the Dominican incident, Barletta was appointed Italian consul representative in Havana. Once again, he obtained exclusive rights to distribute General Motors automobiles in his Ambar (Amadeo Barletta) Motors dealership. U.S-Italian relations worsened in 1941, and Barletta's name appeared on a Washington blacklist of wartime Fascist sympathizers. The Cuban government, at the request of the Department of State, declared Barletta and other alleged Fascist sympathizers persona non grata.[47] He went into exile in Argentina.

After the war, Barletta returned to Cuba. He petitioned the Department of State to remove his name from the blacklist so he could regain his lucrative General Motors franchise. An arrangement was reached for his son, an American citizen who had served with the U.S. Army during the war, to operate the dealership. But the elder Barletta continued to run the company's daily operations.[48] In 1949, Barletta and the Mestre brothers—Goar, Abel, and Luis Augusto, all of whom operated the CMQ radio network—were competing to purchase the financially troubled *El Mundo* newspaper. In publication since 1901, *El Mundo* was considered a liberal counterweight to the conservative *Diario de la Marina*.[49] For both Barletta and the Mestre brothers, being associated with *El Mundo* meant being associated with prestige.

Goar Mestre was well known in Cuba for his entrepreneurial skills and escapist, salacious *radionovelas*.[50] He was blunt about his reasons for wanting to acquire *El Mundo*: "I always wanted to own a newspaper, especially one with the prestige of *El Mundo*. We might have made money with it. I can't say for certain. But that was not our main goal in acquiring this newspaper. Some things you do for the reputation of the organization."[51] He did not have the financial resources of Barletta and therefore could not meet his offer for *El Mundo*. After Barletta acquired *El Mundo*, Goar Mestre made several overtures to him to purchase the newspaper, but Barletta always refused.[52] "The amazing thing is that I don't think that [Barletta] made money with [*El Mundo*]," Mestre said. "I'm sure he held onto it because it was his ticket to power and respect."[53]

The editorial quality of *El Mundo* rapidly deteriorated under Barletta. In January 1954 the newspaper's editor-in-chief, Luis J. Botifoll, planned to publish a signed, front-page editorial calling for unity against the Batista government. Barletta, accompanied by Batista's security agents and police, entered the newsroom and had the editorial removed before it could be published.[54] News of the incident appeared in other Cuban newspapers.[55] Botifoll's statements after the incident, accusing Barletta of collusion with the Batista dictatorship, further damaged his reputation.

When the Castro government seized Barletta's properties in March 1960 and placed him under house arrest, he became a pariah, even within segments of the business community.[56] According to a doctoral student who interviewed a number of anti-Castro exiles during the early 1970s, many Cuban businesspeople believed that Barletta "deserved his fate."[57] Todd, of the *Times of Havana*, described the government campaign against him that accompanied the seizure of his properties: "Overnight, Barletta became a public enemy. The government-controlled press published photographs of the publisher at the palace being greeted by a cordial Batista. . . . It must be understood that *El Mundo* had not criticized the regime, and had maintained a discreet silence about all the repressive measures taken by the government against the independent press."[58]

After taking refuge in the Italian embassy (Barletta was an Italian citizen) and fleeing Cuba, he reestablished his General Motors franchise in the Dominican Republic and continued to identify himself as president of *El Mundo* in exile, even though that was just one of his many businesses. The IAPA elected Barletta, as owner of *El Mundo*, to its board of directors.[59]

Not all press corruption in pre-Castro Cuba originated with the government. Private individuals who wanted to advance their political or business careers or simply to climb the social ladder paid journalists for favorable coverage in the society pages of leading newspapers. The *crónicas* were avidly read by class-conscious Cubans interested in keeping abreast of the upper crust. These pages featured private clubs, parties, and nightclubs. It was no secret that the *cronistas*, as the writers of these pages were known, would insert names in their stories for the right price. As one observer wrote about the significance of the *crónicas*, "It was not sufficient that one had successfully assaulted the ramparts of high society, attended a certain party, joined a certain club. What was important was that the whole world should know about it. The social chroniclers' daily battle reports decorated virtually every Cuban newspaper, and were avidly followed by the whole bourgeoisie."[60]

A young Sergeant Batista, like many other aspiring Cuban leaders, paid the *cronistas* for favorable publicity to further his career. He had attracted wide attention in 1933, after he had led a revolt of enlisted men and sided with student revolutionaries to topple the provisional government of Carlos Manuel de Céspedes. Batista was determined to remain in the public spotlight and advance his political career. However, he had several obstacles to overcome if he was to ascend in Havana society. Orphaned at thirteen, he was taken into a U.S.-run school and raised by Quakers. Before joining the military, he worked as a canefield laborer, store clerk, and railroad fireman. Because of his dark complexion, Batista, who was of Spanish, Indian, African, and Chinese descent, was disparagingly referred to as *El Negro* by the class-conscious and race-conscious upper crust. During the latter days of Batista's rule, many wealthy Cubans supported Castro, who was of Spanish descent, over Batista simply because of the race factor: Castro was of "good blood" and from "a good family."[61]

Batista believed that favorable reports in the *crónicas* about his hobnobbing with Cuba's upper classes at Havana's best nightclubs would help him overcome his social handicaps. He dutifully donated money to charities, which was noted in the *crónicas*. It was speculated that he might have divorced his first wife, from peasant stock, and married the refined Marta Fernández de Miranda to climb the social ladder.[62]

Some *cronistas*, such as Enrique Fontanilla of the *Diario de la Marina*, and his successor, Luis de Posada, were reported to have earned a "banker's living" in their positions. As *New York Times* Cuban correspondent Ruby Hart Phillips wrote of the late Fontanilla: "One mention of a name by him was sufficient to put a person into Cuban society. Grateful *Habaneros* [upper-class Havanans] rewarded him with thousands of dollars."[63]

Although it was always known that favorable news in the *crónicas* could be had for a price, after Castro came to power the practice seemed like a bourgeois holdover from the Batista era. In May 1959 the Ministry of the Treasury proposed legislation to tax people whose names appeared in newspaper social pages. According to the proposed tax, people whose names appeared in the *crónicas* would be assessed $1 for each adjective used to describe them, $5 per column inch for individual photographs, and $10 per inch for group photographs.[64] But the tax was never enacted. On June 5 the treasury minister withdrew the proposal following a barrage of complaints from Cuban and U.S. news organizations.[65] This rare instance of a federal agency's backing off indicated that the government was sensitive to such criticisms.

As these incidents demonstrate, Cuban governments, including the democratically elected administrations that preceded Castro, had created and institutionalized a system of bribes and subsidies to keep the press on a leash and minimize government criticisms. Democratic administrations considered this sort of press control much more palatable than outright censorship because it gave the appearance of freedom of the press.

The bribes and subsidies were widespread and well known among the public. Indeed, Cuba is far from unique in having such a situation. Payoffs to reporters and other such professional shortcomings—as viewed from the U.S. perspective—had been ingrained in most Latin American mass media systems for years. In fact, such payoffs for favors had existed in many aspects of the broad culture in Latin America, not just in mass communication. But the payoffs in the Cuban press were not salient public concerns requiring policy action until after Castro came to power and made them major issues. Riding on a crest of moral authority, he challenged press criticism against him by pointing to the institutionalized system of press subsidies and reminding the public of how the press had helped to maintain the Batista dictatorship.

Exactly how widespread were journalistic abuses? Journalism in pre-Castro Cuba frequently failed to meet even minimal professional standards and, as a result, suffered a credibility crisis among the public that helped Castro muffle press criticism and eventually take over the media.

That is a lesson for news media in Latin American republics today that are shifting from despotism to democracy.

Notes

1. Luis A. Baralt, *Martí on the U.S.A.* (Carbondale: Southern Illinois University Press, 1966); Ramón Becali, "Martí y la prensa en los campos de Cuba libre," *Bohemia*, January 29, 1971; Emilio Roig de Leuchsening, "Los dos primeros periódicos de Martí y los unicos publicados en la Habana," *Carteles*, January 25, 1953.

2. John Spicer Nichols, "Cuba," in *World Press Encyclopedia*, ed. George T. Kurian (New York: Facts on File, 1984), 258.

3. C. Wright Mills, *Listen, Yankee: The Revolution in Cuba* (New York: McGraw-Hill, 1960), 139.

4. John A. Lent, "Cuba," in *International Handbook of Broadcasting Systems*, ed. Philip T. Rosen (New York: Greenwood Press, 1988), 79.

5. Marvin Alisky, *Latin American Media: Guidance and Censorship* (Ames: Iowa State University Press, 1981), 157.

6. Television came to Cuba in 1950. Although there is some evidence that press subsidies existed in Cuba's television industries, such practices were probably less frequent because television owners usually had significant financial resources and were not as dependent on bribes and subsidies as small newspapers and radio stations. Michael B. Salwen, "Three Pioneers of Cuban Television," *World Communication* 20, no. 1 (1991): 11–22.

7. Marvin Alisky, "Havana Havoc: Too Many Dailies," *Nieman Reports*, April 10, 1956, 16–18.

8. Michael B. Salwen, *Radio and Television in Cuba: The Pre-Castro Era* (Ames: Iowa State University Press, 1994).

9. Daniel James, *Cuba: The First Soviet Satellite in the Americas* (New York: Avon, 1961), 203.

10. Guillermo Martínez Marques, "Cuba's Free Press: A Target of Coercion," *Miami Herald*, May 15, 1960.

11. Jerry Redding, "'Castro-ating' the Media," *Educational Broadcasting Review* 5 (June 1971): 35–42.

12. Salwen, "Three Pioneers of Cuban Television."

13. Angel Fernández Varela, personal interview, Miami, March 7, 1991. Fernández Varela served as editor at *Información* from 1951 to 1960.

14. Carlos Todd, "Communist Penetration and Exploitation of the Free Press," study prepared for the Subcommittee to Investigate the Administration of the Internal Security Act and Other Internal Security Laws, Committee on the Judiciary, 87th Cong., 2d sess. (Washington, DC: GPO, 1962), 30.

15. Wyatt MacGaffey and Clifford R. Barnett, *Twentieth-Century Cuba: The Background of the Castro Revolution* (Garden City, NY: Anchor Books, 1962), 266.

16. Bertram B. Johannson, "Anxiety Cloaks Press in Cuba," *Christian Science Monitor*, May 8, 1959; Carlos Todd, "Let's Look at Today," *Times of Havana*, April 16, 1959.

17. "Buchanan Flying Home after P. del Rio Trial," *Havana Post*, December 23, 1959.

18. Jay Mallin, "Castro Soon Forgets, Chastises U.S. Press," *Editor & Publisher*, August 22, 1959, 59; idem, "2 AP Men Released by Castro Agents," *Editor & Publisher*, May 14, 1960, 92; idem, "Fidel's Kind of Freedom," *Time*, January 11, 1960, 45; idem, "Castro Press Raps Dubois," *Editor & Publisher*, August 15, 1959, 52.

19. "Dubois Replaced in Havana," *New York Times*, October 29, 1959.

20. Carlos Todd, "Let's Look at Today," *Times of Havana*, June 8, 1959.

21. "Illegal Deals During Batista Regime to Backfire in Property Seizure," *Times of Havana*, July 9, 1959.

22. Michael B. Salwen and Bruce Garrison, *Latin American Journalism* (Hillsdale, NJ: Lawrence Erlbaum Associates, 1991), 30–33.

23. P. D. Eldred, "IAPA Clears Cuban Newspapers of Charges," *Havana Post*, October 6, 1959.

24. "Insolente Actitud," *Revolución*, January 21, 1960, 1, 2, 6, quotation on page 6.

25. David Kraslow, "Fidel Indicted as Dictator by His Words?" *Miami Herald*, April 5, 1960.

26. "Castro Union Seizes Last Free Papers," *Editor & Publisher*, May 21, 1960, 14.

27. " 'Get Out, U.S.,' Screams Cuban Student Mob," *Miami Herald*, May 14, 1960.

28. "Cuba," *Hispanic American Report*, May 1960, 309.

29. Irving Peter Pflaum, *Tragic Island: How Communism Came to Cuba* (Englewood Cliffs, NJ: Prentice Hall, 1961), 62.

30. Samuel Faber, "Revolution and Social Structure in Cuba, 1933–1959" (Ph.D. diss., University of California, Berkeley, 1969), 440–45.

31. Boris Goldenberg, *The Cuban Revolution and Latin America* (New York: Praeger Press, 1966), 203.

32. Alisky, *Latin American Media*, 156.

33. Jorge L. Martí, "The Press in Cuba: Its 'Rebirth' Since 1939," *Journalism Quarterly* 22 (1944):124–29.

34. J. W. Sanger, *Advertising Methods in Cuba*, Special Agents series no. 178, Department of Commerce (Washington, DC: GPO, 1919), 19.

35. Ibid.

36. Lent, *Mass Communication in the Caribbean* (Ames: Iowa State University Press, 1990), 118.

37. Marvin Alisky, "Cuban Press Censorship Replaces Bribery," *Nieman Reports*, April 1957, 17–18. In historical context, the elected government of Batista was probably less corrupt than that of Grau and Prio.

38. Martí, "The Press in Cuba," 125.

39. Michael B. Salwen, Bruce Garrison, and Robert T. Buckman, "Latin America," in *Global Journalism: Survey of International Communication*, 2d ed., ed. John C. Merrill (New York: Longman, 1991), 307–8.

40. Martí, "The Press in Cuba."

41. Lent, *Mass Communication in the Caribbean*, 118.

42. Martí, "The Press in Cuba," 128–29; Herminio Portell Vilá, *Medio siglo de El Mundo: Historia de un gran periódico* (Havana: Lex, 1951).

43. "Group Purchases Havana Morning Paper *El Mundo*," *Havana Post*, August 5, 1949; Salwen, "Three Pioneers of Cuban Television."

44. James, *Cuba*, 212–13.

45. Mills, *Listen, Yankee*, 139–40.
46. "Dominicans Free Italian Ex-Consul," *New York Times*, May 22, 1935.
47. "Italian's License Canceled," *New York Times*, August 10, 1941.
48. Salwen, "Three Pioneers of Cuban Television."
49. Portell Vilá, *Medio siglo de* El Mundo, 158.
50. Michael B. Salwen, "The Origins of CMQ: Pre-Castro Cuba's Leading Radio Network," *Historical Journal of Film, Radio, and Television* 13, no. 3 (1993): 315–32.
51. Goar Mestre, personal interview, Key Biscayne, May 10, 1990.
52. Ibid.
53. Ibid.
54. "Truce Prevails in *El Mundo* Internal Feud," *Editor & Publisher*, January 16, 1954, 50.
55. "Expone Botifoll lo ocurrido en el diario *El Mundo*," *Diario de la Marina*, January 3, 1954; "Policy Fight Snarls Havana Newspaper," *New York Times*, January 4, 1954;
56. "Barletta Loses All to Gov't," *Havana Post*, March 10, 1960.
57. Alfred L. Padula, "The Fall of the Bourgeoisie: Cuba, 1959–1961" (Ph.D. diss., University of New Mexico, 1974), 269.
58. Todd, "Communist Penetration and Exploitation of the Free Press," 35.
59. "Latin Press Ends Its Meeting Resolving to Resist Despotism," *New York Times*, October 26, 1975.
60. Padula, "The Fall of the Bourgeoisie," 15.
61. Ibid., 16.
62. Ibid., 15–23.
63. Ruby Hart Phillips, "Society-News Tax? Cuban Editors Shocked," *New York Times*, June 2, 1959.
64. Ibid.
65. Ibid.

9

Birth, Death, and Resurrection of Press Freedom in Chile

Robert T. Buckman

Chile is a narrow strip of land more than 2,600 miles long but only some 265 miles across at its widest point. It is highly urban, with most of its thirteen million people living in the central valley, where the largest cities and most important mass communication enterprises are concentrated. Chile has a rich tradition of literature and journalism. It had the first regularly published newspaper in Latin America and a flourishing of press freedom during the 1800s and 1900s, yet it also was the first country in the Western Hemisphere to have a democratically elected Marxist president, Salvador Allende, in 1970. Here, Robert Buckman provides a detailed portrait of Chilean mass communication, especially the press. He sets the historical scene, particularly regarding the early newspapers, before describing events in the twentieth century, with appropriate emphasis on the Allende years. He rightly concludes that Chile is a suitable role model for other Latin American mass communication systems.

Professor Buckman teaches journalism at the University of Southwestern Louisiana in Lafayette, specializing in public affairs reporting, feature writing, and international communication with an emphasis on Latin America. He has also worked as a reporter and editor for more than twenty years, with numerous assignments in Latin America, including Chile, where he also taught under a Fulbright Fellowship in 1991. He has written and cowritten many articles and book chapters on topics related to Latin America.

The first thing one encounters when entering the Biblioteca Nacional on Avenida Bernardo O'Higgins in downtown Santiago, Chile, is a hand-powered, screw-type printing press more than 180 years old. It was on this press that Father Camilo Henríquez printed *La Aurora de Chile*, the first regularly published newspaper in Latin America, during Chile's struggle for independence. It is somehow symbolic that a printing press occupies such a hallowed spot. Of all the Latin American republics, it was Chile where freedom of expression bloomed the most brilliantly in both the nineteenth and twentieth centuries. As Hubert Herring observed in his history of Latin America, Chile "has had rather more than its share of distinguished historians and essayists, attesting to the vigor of the nation's intellectual life."[1]

Chile's proud literary tradition includes such renowned novelists as Alberto Blest Gana in the last century and Enrique LaFourcade, José Donoso, and Isabel Allende today. Among Latin American nations, Chile alone has produced two Nobel Prize laureates in literature: the poets Gabriela Mistral in 1945 and Pablo Neruda in 1971. During the nineteenth century, it provided a haven for writers and thinkers driven into exile by dictatorships in their homelands, most notably the Spaniard José Joaquín de Mora; Andrés Bello of Venezuela, who founded the University of Chile and spent the remainder of his life in his adopted land; and Domingo Faustino Sarmiento of Argentina, who returned to his homeland to become both a newspaper publisher and president of the republic.

Free thinking has been a hallmark of the Chilean experience. The occasional lapses into repression and censorship, most recently during the 1973–1990 military regime, have been aberrations. Literature has been a national passion, second perhaps only to soccer. Chile today is vigorously and enthusiastically rediscovering its roots after nearly seventeen years of banned publications, banned names, banned images, and banned ideas. The Chilean mass media operate in a climate freer than that which preceded the Marxist experiment of President Salvador Allende and the military dictatorship of General Augusto Pinochet that crushed it. Blessed with a high literacy rate, a booming economy, and a sound technological base, the country appears destined to enter the twenty-first century as a model for the rest of Latin America.

Chile's colonial history offers little hint of the rich intellectual and cultural tradition associated with the postindependence republic. Geographically and politically, the country was a backwater of Spanish America, an isolated appendage of the viceroyalty of Peru. Trade and communication with Spain were tortuous, and Chile lacked the abundant gold and silver of Mexico and Peru. As Spain began losing its grip on its colonies early in the nineteenth century, Chile still had few schools, no public libraries, and no printing press.[2] Even the importation of books was prohibited, the better to stifle the insidious ideas of the French Enlightenment or the North American experiment with republican rule.[3] Only native-born Spaniards were entrusted with authority, although the Creoles, Spaniards of American birth, formed the bulk of the educated elite.

In 1808 a popular uprising in Spain forced King Carlos IV to abdicate the throne to his more popular son, Fernando VII. Carlos sought the intervention of Napoleon, who invaded Spain, but, instead of reinstating Carlos, installed his own brother, Joseph, on the Spanish throne. When news of this usurpation drifted across the Atlantic, the colonists debated whether to recognize the new monarch or to govern themselves. An open cabildo, or governing council, was established on September 18, 1810, still observed as Chilean independence day. This first, moderate government was toppled a year later by young José Miguel Carrera, who established the first public schools and contracted with a Swiss-born American merchant in Santiago, Mateo Arnaldo Hoevel, to import from the United States a printing press and the necessary expertise to operate it. Samuel Burr Johnston, a Boston typesetter, and two assistants arrived in Valparaíso on November 21, 1811, aboard the U.S. frigate *Galloway*. Symbolically, the press was part of a shipment that also included fifty rifles and one hundred pairs of pistols.[4]

If any person were to be singled out as the father of Chilean journalism, it would be Father Camilo Henríquez, the passionate, highly literate, multilingual, forty-two-year-old prelate whom the junta chose as editor of Chile's first newspaper. Like Thomas Paine, he had written essays advocating independence, and Thomas Jefferson influenced his writings. The great Chilean historian Vicuña MacKenna later observed that "there spun around in his brain the audacious theories of the French encyclopedists, the aristocratic and authoritarian doctrines of the English politicians, and the eminently practical theories of the North American legislators."[5]

This first newspaper would have a limited audience. The population in 1812 is estimated at between five hundred thousand and one million; half of these were native Indians, all of whom were illiterate. Half of the remainder were Europeans or their progeny, the other half mestizos, or mixed blood. Only the male half of the Caucasians had received much education before independence, and even some of them considered it beneath their dignity to read or write. Wrote the typesetter Johnston: "The state of literature in Chili (*sic*) is very low, almost all the learning in the country being confined to the priests."[6]

Nonetheless, into this unpromising milieu there appeared on the streets of Santiago on the morning of February 12, 1812, the prospectus of Henríquez's government-sponsored newspaper, *La Aurora de Chile*, a four-page sheet that would be published weekly over the next fourteen months for a total of sixty issues, plus one extraordinary issue and one supplement, until the Spanish Army reoccupied Santiago. The price: six pesos per year in the capital, nine in the interior and twelve "anywhere else."[7] Henríquez's inspirational front-page commentary of that maiden issue is revered in Chilean literature:

> Now it is in our power, the great, precious instrument of universal en-
> lightenment, the Press. . . . The voice of reason, and of truth, will be
> heard among us after the sad and insufferable silence of three centuries.
> Ah! In those centuries of barbaric oppression and outrage, Socrates,
> Plato, Tullius, Seneca had been dragged to prison, and the most cel-
> ebrated writers of England, of France, of Germany had perished with-
> out pity in our midst. Centuries of infamy and weeping! Wisdom will
> remember you with horror, and humanity will weep at your memory.

The appearance of *La Aurora* was met with great public excitement.
According to a contemporary account, "men ran through the streets with
an *Aurora* in their hands, detaining as many as they met, reading and
rereading its contents, expressing congratulations for such happiness and
prophesying that, by this means, the ignorance and blindness in which
they lived would be banished, and that the resulting enlightenment and
culture would transform Chile into a kingdom of wise men."[8]

Although his newspaper was government sponsored, Henríquez had
a mind of his own, and *La Aurora* was heavily slanted against the royal-
ists. In August 1812, Carrera, still seeking to steer a moderate course,
issued a decree mandating Henríquez to be more objective. The recalcitrant cleric refused to publish it, and in his next issue he printed a treatise
by the English poet and essayist John Milton on press freedom. For two
months the junta tolerated this first example of journalistic independence
in Latin America; then it issued a harsher decree establishing a censorship tribunal and ordered Henríquez to publish it. He complied, but in the
same issue he published another treatise by Milton that had admonished
the English people to establish a republic lest they be tyrannized "by a
king like Spain's."

La Aurora published its last issue on April 1, 1813, with no hint of
the reason. Its successor, also government sponsored, *El Monitor Araucano*
(named for the fierce southern tribe that had defied Spanish conquest),
appeared a week later with Henríquez as editor. It was published a more
ambitious three times per week on the same press, although more toned
down. The feisty Henríquez began publishing anonymous letters to the
editor whose authors were referred to as *particulares*; some probably were
written by Henríquez himself. The junta issued a decree banning such
letters and requiring that *El Monitor* publish only "official articles and
interesting news."

Henríquez also became involved with Chile's—and Latin America's—
first nonofficial newspaper, *El Seminario Republicano* (established in
1813), when its founder, the Guatemalan writer José Antonio de Irisarri,
turned it over to Henríquez after operating it for a month. Both newspapers were printed on what was still the country's sole press.

Back in Spain, King Fernando was restored to his throne in 1814, and he soon sought to assert his authority over his rebellious American colonies, which only fueled the fires of rebellion further. Carrera had left the junta to lead an army in the field, and in his absence the junta concluded a treaty with Spain by which Chile received virtual autonomy but recognized the sovereignty of Fernando. Carrera led his army to Santiago, assumed dictatorial powers, renounced the treaty, and dismissed Henríquez as editor of *El Monitor*, which is puzzling considering their mutual dislike of the monarchy. Carrera named as Henríquez's successor an Argentine, Bernardo Vera y Pintado, whose style, according to historian Alfonso Valdebenito, "was more up-to-date and polished than Father Camilo's, although fiery and hot-headed like his."[9] The 183d and final issue of *El Monitor Araucano* was published on October 1, 1814, the day before the republican forces under Carrera were vanquished in a disastrous battle at Rancagua. Three days later, the Spanish army entered Santiago to begin a thirty-month period of occupation referred to in Chilean history as the Reconquest. Henríquez fled to Argentina, where he became editor of the government organ, *La Gaceta de Buenos Aires*. Meanwhile, in Santiago the Spanish authorities captured his old printing press and within a month began publishing *La Gazeta del Gobierno de Chile*, a government gazette, more commonly called *La Gazeta del Rey*. Its editor, a Dominican priest named José María de la Torre, was as devoutly and eloquently royalist as Henríquez had been republican, and he called on the country's writers and thinkers in helping "to dissipate the thick, dark ignorance that was spread by the sinister *Aurora de Chile*, the fallacious *Monitor Araucano*, the seditious *Seminario Republicano* and other papers that have defaced our printing press."[10] Initially a weekly, *La Gazeta del Rey* became semiweekly and eventually published 173 regular and 13 extra issues. Its last issue was dated February 11, 1817; the following day, the combined armies of the Chilean liberator Bernardo O'Higgins and his Argentine counterpart, José de San Martín, defeated the Spanish at the battle of Chacabuco, and Santiago changed hands for the last time.

O'Higgins, named supreme dictator, wasted no time in publishing a new weekly newspaper. He reinstated Vera y Pintado as editor, and on February 26 the first issue of *La Gaceta del Supremo Gobierno de Chile* appeared with *"Viva la Patria!"* (Long live the Fatherland!) emblazoned under the flag. Its name soon was changed to the shorter *Gazeta de Santiago de Chile*, and later to *La Gazeta Ministerial de Chile*, which was to publish 230 regular and 126 extraordinary issues.[11] A second organ appeared in 1817, *Seminario de Policía*, a police gazette printed by Mateo Hoevel for nineteen issues on a press that had been transported across the Andes and left in Santiago by San Martin's army.

Although O'Higgins governed Chile as dictator, it was during his relatively enlightened rule that the first private presses were imported and four more nonofficial newspapers began publishing in 1818. These four papers—*El Duende*, *El Argos*, *El Sol*, and *El Chileno*—were primarily opinion organs, each of which sought to outdo the others with its polemics. In terms of journalism excesses, they may be likened to the outrageous U.S. gazettes published by John Fenno and Phillip Freneau during the first decade after adoption of the U.S. Constitution. They marked a turning point in Chilean journalism, and according to journalism historian Raúl Silva Castro, "were outstanding for the causticity of their language and the richness of their authors' imaginations."[12] Their editors wisely chose not to attack O'Higgins, however; Luis Galdames has noted that the press under O'Higgins "was very much restricted in whatever touched on political comment."[13]

Although these four newspapers' impact was far-reaching, their lives were ephemeral. *El Sol*, edited by the Colombian writer Juan García del Río, survived the longest, publishing thirty-one issues. Enjoying an even longer existence was *El Telégrafo*, which García del Río launched three months after *El Sol* ceased publication; it continued for seventy-five issues. During this period, Camilo Henríquez returned to Chile and established the country's first magazine, a scientific and literary journal called *El Mercurio de Chile*. Appearing in 1820, it lasted twenty-five months.

O'Higgins was forced to resign in 1823, touching off a period of near anarchy and civil war between Conservatives (*pelucones*) and Liberals (*pipiolos*). Chile's nascent press was caught up in these turbulent events, just as it would be a century and a half later. After the fall of O'Higgins, newspapers proliferated and vanished almost overnight, like mushrooms after a thunderstorm. A total of eighteen newspapers appeared during O'Higgins' tenure, fifteen of them in his final year in power. By 1830, at the end of the anarchic period, 103 newspapers had begun publication, but in 1831, after the Conservatives had consolidated their grip on power and had moved to suppress Liberal commentary, only 3 new newspapers appeared.[14] The press during the anarchic period was characterized by vitriolic attacks of the basest sort. Deserving of special mention was the Conservative mouthpiece *El Hambriento*, an irreverent satirical sheet edited and written anonymously. It ran for ten issues in 1828 and 1829. Silva Castro called it "one of the most caustic and foul-mouthed newspapers in Chile." Its nameplate proclaimed itself "an undated public paper, without literature, impolitic, but appetizing and amusing."[15] The consensus among Chilean historians is that the guiding force behind *El Hambriento* was the iron-gloved Conservative ideologue who dominated Chilean politics from 1830 until his assassination in 1837: Diego Portales.

The brightest beacon during this otherwise tawdry journalistic period was the monthly scientific-literary journal *El Mercurio de Chile*, a revival of the like-named magazine that Henríquez had published from 1820 to 1822. Published by the Spaniard Joaquín de Mora from 1828 to 1829, it contributed greatly to the country's literary and scientific awakening and enjoyed a government subsidy. It published the first catalogue of Chilean plants and the first articles on political economy and public finance, in addition to its regular offerings of scientific articles, poetry, literary criticism, and foreign news.[16] Portales later would expel de Mora from the country.

Pedro Félix Vicuña published the first newspaper outside the capital, *El Telégrafo Mercantil y Político*, in the port city of Valparaíso, fifty miles from Santiago, for eighty issues in 1826–27. Apart from being Chile's first provincial newspaper, it was the first devoted to general news rather than to official decrees or political commentary. After *El Telégrafo Mercantil y Político* folded, Vicuña quickly established another paper. On September 12, 1827, *El Mercurio de Valparaíso* was born; two years later, it became Latin America's first daily and today claims the distinction of being the world's oldest continuously published Spanish-language daily. In 1880 the paper was purchased by Augustín Edwards, scion of an Englishman who had made a fortune building railroads in Chile. Edwards launched a Santiago edition of *El Mercurio* in 1900, and it remains Chile's newspaper of record today under the direction of the third successive Augustín Edwards. Many journalism scholars rate it as one of the world's finest newspapers.

Silva Castro dismissed these first two decades of Chilean journalism as a "squandering of human effort" and as "one of the most lamentable spectacles in our history," although conceding it had been a "trial period."[17] The historian Brian Loveman wrote of the anarchic press: "The highly partisan tabloid newspapers slandered the opposition at will. Political factions and various governments stretched freedom of the press to its limits."[18]

From 1831 to 1861, three successive Conservative presidents governed Chile for ten years each, a period labeled the Autocratic Republic. Although the climate was unsalubrious for free expression, intellectual and journalistic activity blossomed in 1842. Three literary journals appeared: *El Seminario*, founded in Santiago by a literary society; *El Museo de Ambas Américas*, edited by the resilient Colombian García del Río; and *La Revista de Valparaíso*, edited by an Argentine, Vicente Fidel López, who had come to Chile to escape the dictatorship of Juan Manuel de Rosas, as had his countryman, the future Argentine statesman and newspaper publisher Domingo Faustino Sarmiento. That same year Sarmiento joined the editorial staff of *El Mercurio de Valparaíso*, still the country's only daily. Valparaíso's second daily, *La Gaceta de Comercio*, appeared in 1842. Before the end of the year, Sarmiento established Santiago's first daily, *El Progreso*.[19]

Three decades of Conservative government gave way in 1861 to three decades of more enlightened Liberal rule. Historians have described the last third of the nineteenth century as the golden age of Chilean literature. Scientific and artistic activity also flourished, and there was an explosion of schools, libraries, and museums. According to Galdames, "Nothing, however, showed better this slow but sure development of national culture than the progress of the daily and periodical press." In 1860, the year before the beginning of the so-called Liberal Republic, only two dailies survived: *El Ferrocarril*, a Liberal organ in Santiago, and the durable *El Mercurio de Valparaíso*. By 1890 that number had risen to about twenty, seven of them in the capital, and "half a hundred periodicals in cities of lesser importance made a chorus with these."[20]

Early newspapers had been primarily partisan organs, but the new breed also began to report general news. The intercontinental telegraph whetted the public's appetite for news, as did Chile's 1879–1884 War of the Pacific with Bolivia and Peru. The war brought about a number of "extra" periodicals. "Among the educated class," wrote Galdames, "the daily was, from that time on, as necessary as food."[21] Moreover, virtually all of Chile's great men of letters of that time cut their teeth on journalism. The most prominent contributed regularly to three influential magazines: *Revista del Pacífico*, *Estrella de Chile*, and *Revista Chilena*.[22]

The Liberal Republic ended with the victory of the congressional forces in the civil war of 1891 and was followed by a thirty-four-year period of weak presidents called the Parliamentary Republic, in which the Liberals, Conservatives, and Radicals vied for power. Chile experienced one of its few lapses into military rule in 1925, out of which came a new constitution that strengthened the power of the executive and retained broad if qualified press freedom that *generally* was respected for the next forty-five years. Article 10, Section 3, loosely promised "freedom to express, without prior censorship, opinions, orally or in writing, through the medium of the press or in any other form; yet without prejudice to the liability of answering for offenses and abuses that may be committed in the exercise of this liberty in the manner and in the cases as determined by law." At least five presidents before Allende sought to exploit these constitutional qualifications to apply temporary restrictions on opposition media, but these attempts often failed and were not commonplace or egregious.

The print media grew rapidly from 1925 to 1970, spurred by near universal literacy, and the broadcast media were born. By the time of the Allende government, there were forty-six dailies, eleven of them in Santiago. There also was an abundance of magazines, some with international reputations, such as the highly respected weekly newsmagazine *Ercilla*, founded in 1933 in the style of *Time*. Also noteworthy were the satirical magazine *Topaze*, the Jesuit-owned *Mensaje*, and the women's magazine *Paula*, owned by the Edwards family, whose staff writers in the 1960s included Isabel Allende. Radio began in 1922 and expanded rapidly along U.S. commercial lines, although the government controlled a network to ensure educational and cultural programming. By 1968 there were 150 stations of diverse formats.[23] Television arrived in 1960, and in a unique model the first three franchises were granted to major universities. The government established its own station in 1969, the last year of the Christian Democratic government of Eduardo Frei.

After the 1925 constitution, the partisan press showed renewed vigor, and in the 1930s the Christian Democratic, Communist, Socialist, and Falange (fascist) Parties joined the fray. Parties also purchased radio stations, as did labor unions and the Catholic Church. The level of rhetoric between the left and right, with the Christian Democratic Party (Partido Demócratacristiano, or PDC) holding the middle ground, intensified in the 1960s. When Allende was elected in 1970, the stage was set for a political and journalistic showdown that was destined to have tragic consequences.

Because none of the three candidates in the 1970 presidential election received a majority, the constitution required the Congress to choose the president. Traditionally, Congress ratified the top vote-getter, in this case Allende, whose Marxist-oriented Popular Unity (Unidad Popular, or UP) coalition had received 36.2 percent. But the Christian Democrats, who controlled the largest number of seats, were concerned with Popular Unity's platform, which declared that "these means of communication (radio, publishing houses, television, press, movies) are fundamental for aiding the formation of a new culture and a new man. For that reason, they must be given an educational orientation, and they must be freed from their commercial character, adopting measures so that social organizations can get control of these means, eliminating them from the nefarious presence of monopolies."[24]

The Christian Democrats extracted Allende's support for a Statute of Democratic Guarantees, which passed Congress two days before it voted for president; Allende voted for it as one of his last acts as a senator. This statute prohibited the expropriation of a mass medium without congressional approval, and the UP controlled only about a third of the seats. It also precluded discrimination in the "sale or supply" to the media of "paper, ink, machinery, or elements for their operation, or with respect to the authorization or permission necessary for their acquisition within, or outside of, the country."[25] Congress confirmed Allende as president by a vote of 153 to 35, and he was sworn in on November 3.

Public opinion in Chile soon became polarized for or against the UP government, and the media chose up sides as well. Allende could count on support from five of the capital's dailies: the government-owned *La Nación*, which served as a mouthpiece for whichever party was in power; *El Siglo*, owned by the Chilean Communist Party (Partido Comunista Chileno, or PCCh); *Ultima Hora*, the organ of Allende's own Socialist Party; *Puro Chile*, a garish, sensational tabloid also controlled by the PCCh; and *Clarín*, another sensational tabloid and Chile's circulation leader, which had been pro-PDC until left-wing journalists infiltrated the staff. Left-wing magazines and reviews included *Punto Final*, *Vistazo*, *Chile Hoy*, and *Ahora*. The regime also controlled a number of radio stations as well as three of the four television stations: Channel 9 of the University of Chile, Catholic University of Chile's Channel 13, and the government-owned TV Nacional on Channel 7. The opposition later gained control of both university stations.[26]

Arrayed against the UP regime were the three Santiago dailies controlled by the Edwards family: the prestigious *El Mercurio* and its two tabloid sister papers, *Ultima Hora* and *La Segunda*, the latter an evening paper. The Edwards chain also included seven provincial dailies. Also in the opposition camp was the conservative daily *La Tribuna*. The Christian Democrats purchased *Diario Ilustrado*, the right-wing daily, and changed its name to *La Prensa*. The PDC also resurrected an old picture magazine, *Vea*. Right-wing opinion magazines included *P.E.C.*, *Impacto*, and *Sepa*. The opposition parties or their supporters also controlled numerous radio stations, and Catholic University of Valparaíso's Channel 4 remained outside government control or domination.

The only major publications drawing a reasonably neutral stance during the Allende period were the daily newspaper *La Tercera*, owned by Germán Picó; the prestigious weekly newsmagazine *Ercilla*, edited by the pro-PDC Emilio Filippi; and the newsmagazine *Qué Pasa*. Allende's first overt move against the opposition media came only a week to the day after his inauguration, when he announced that a study had been undertaken for the possible expropriation of *El Mercurio*, the nemesis of the left. The next day Augustín Edwards III resigned as board chairman, apparently to appease the government, and went into self-imposed exile.[27]

Four months later Allende said that his threat to expropriate *El Mercurio* had been misinterpreted.[28]

Government pressure, however, persisted on the daily. In January 1971, tax inspectors "raided" *El Mercurio*'s offices, alleging that the paper owed $380,000 in delinquent taxes. The subsequent investigation exonerated the paper.[29] Another incident involving *El Mercurio* was a police raid in October 1971, ostensibly to search for illegal weapons. Nothing was found.[30] The regime undertook a number of other measures within its legal purview to harass the opposition media, some of them attempts at outright closure of offending publications or stations. In fairness, however, it should be noted that at least five of Allende's predecessors likewise had withheld government advertising, withheld information from hostile media, or claimed national security as a justification for restricting reporting.

A more serious attempt by the Allende government to control the media involved the attempted nationalization of the paper industry. State control of this resource, which was a major export earner, had been a key point in the UP platform. The opposition feared, however, that nationalization of paper was a gimmick to intimidate the media, as had been the case in Mexico and in Argentina under Juan Perón. Making the issue more politically intriguing was the fact that only one privately owned firm made newsprint—the Paper and Carton Manufacturing Company, owned by none other than the conservative former President Arturo Alessandri, who had narrowly lost to Allende in 1970. When Alessandri refused to sell, the government decreed price increases for raw paper while freezing prices on finished paper products in an effort to drive the firm into bankruptcy. But Alessandri stubbornly bore the losses, forcing the government to offer seven times the market value for the company's stock in a bid to gain controlling interest. The opposition rallied around Alessandri by contributing to what was called the National Freedom Fund in order to outbid the government in purchasing shares from any stockholder who wished to sell. The takeover attempt failed, and the company remained in private hands throughout the Allende period, although the firm lost $30 million in the battle.[31]

The government was more successful in taking over the PDC-owned Zig-Zag publishing company three months after coming to power by mediating a labor dispute in favor of the workers, granting them a 67 percent wage increase that was twice the inflation rate. When the firm filed for bankruptcy, the government seized it. The name was changed to Quimantú, and the regime used it to begin publishing Marxist propaganda books and other publications. The UP also published a magazine, *Mayoría*, at Quimantú. Interestingly, the respected newsmagazine *Ercilla*, edited by the pro-PDC Filippi, also was printed at Quimantú, which may or may not help explain the magazine's moderate position throughout the Allende era.[32]

The most frequent—and heavy-handed—government tactic was invoking the national sedition law, an especially common practice during Allende's last year, as the level of journalistic rhetoric increased. Although both sides were guilty of grossly distorted and exaggerated reporting, it was the opposition media that came under the gun. The usual procedure was for the government to file *querellas*, or criminal lawsuits, against opposition media or their owners, some of whom were jailed. Among the most controversial were *querellas* against *El Mercurio*, for reporting that Chile had only enough foreign exchange dollars for another forty-five days; Mario Carneyro, editor of *La Segunda*, who was jailed for reporting that the interior minister was involved in illegal arms imports; Marcelo Maturana, editor of *P.E.C.*, who was arrested for reporting a schism in the ranks of the armed forces; and *La Tribuna*, which was the target of forty-seven *querellas*, and whose editor, Raúl González Alfaro, was jailed repeatedly. Once the paper was prevented from going to press for carrying an item "offensive to the armed forces." The government also attempted to sell the paper's building at auction for delinquent social security contributions, but a crowd physically blocked the auction, so the government agreed to a settlement. Finally, the opinion magazine *Sepa* was slapped with seventeen *querellas*, and three times publication was suspended for brief periods. In almost all cases the courts, which were generally hostile to the UP government, dismissed the suits, and they ordered Carneyro and Maturana released.[33]

The renegade left occasionally employed extralegal measures against opposition media. Extremist groups such as the Movement of the Revolutionary Left (Movimiento de Izquierda Revolucionaria, or MIR) sometimes seized opposition media. The Concepción daily *El Sur* was so seized, and its occupiers published a pirate newspaper briefly before authorities intervened. Extremists held *La Mañana* of Talca for eight months; the government took no action to expel them. The Supreme Court eventually ordered the paper returned to its rightful owners, but before vacating the premises the extremists removed ten tons of newsprint, machinery, and spare parts.[34]

Numerous power struggles arose over control of key broadcast media. Early in the UP regime, the government stacked TV Nacional's board of directors with a UP majority. The government then sought to change the format of the popular forum program, *Tres Bandas*, on which representatives of the parties of the left, right, and center would debate current issues. At first, the government changed the format to have two UP representatives against one from the right and one from the center, or PDC. After the UP representatives began making a poor showing of themselves, the board canceled the program in August 1972, explaining that it caused "tension" among viewers. TV Nacional's other programing was heavily slanted in favor of the government.[35]

An even greater power struggle occurred at both the university stations in Santiago, which had been controlled by the UP. In 1972, however, campus elections brought the opposition to power at both schools, and both stations' news staffs were purged.[36] The struggle to control the television airwaves intensified when the Catholic stations in Santiago and Valparaíso sought to extend their signals to other cities. Allende already had vetoed such a bill, but after the 1972 campus elections the Catholic universities defied him by setting up repeater stations. A showdown came in Concepción, where Catholic students gathered at the station's construction site to fend off pro-UP attackers. The state-owned power company briefly shut off the station's power, and the Interior Ministry ordered the station to cease transmitting because it lacked a license. Father Raúl Hasbún, Channel 13's director, defied the order, whereupon the state power company began jamming its signal. Three weeks later, the power company was raided and two vital parts to the jamming transmitter were stolen.[37]

The battle over radio was almost as intense. According to Robert Alexander, in its first two years the UP government had bought twenty existing stations, established five new ones, and controlled ten others through forcible takeover by extremists. The remainder of the country's 170 stations at the time were outside the government's direct control but frequently were targets of harassment and, in some cases, closure.[38] The government's primary target was the PDC's Radio Balmaceda. When the station's license came up for review, the government refused to renew it and planned to turn the station over to the University of Chile, then still under UP control. The station continued to transmit, whereupon the government "raided" its frequency by having another station transmit at the same bandwidth. A government official then removed the condenser from Radio Balmaceda, silencing it. In May 1972, through the intercession of PDC deputies in Congress, the station was granted a thirty-year license renewal, although it continued to suffer harassment.[39]

Probably the government's most effective legal tool in silencing opposition broadcasts was its prerogative to order all stations into a national network during periods of crisis. This tactic has been employed frequently in Latin America but nowhere for the durations that Allende used it. During a crippling strike by independent truckers in October 1972, Allende kept the network in force for several weeks, permitting only government-sanctioned news. After twenty-five days, Radio Santiago and Radio Minería in the capital rebelled and resumed normal programming. Authorities closed Radio Santiago in just fifteen minutes, while Radio Minería managed to stay on the air for two hours. The station director told listeners, "We prefer arbitrary silence a thousand times to being part of a network of falsehoods."[40]

The media played a key role in heightening the tension that led ultimately to the military coup. Opposition press criticism began slowly and cautiously, but it grew bolder in response to the pro-UP press attacks against the "bourgeoisie." Ultimately, government harassment of the opposition media only incited them to harsher criticism rather than intimidating them into submission. The increasingly shrill rhetoric of the media on both sides closely paralleled the growing polarization in the political arena, which reached a watershed in 1972 when the PDC abandoned its centrist position and joined the right-wing National Party in an opposition coalition.

For the first two years of the UP government, opposition media criticism was largely in keeping with the model of a free and responsible press serving as a check on the power of government, although even this traditional role offended the more militant UP officials. Over time, however, opposition media leaped at any opportunity to embarrass or discredit the government. One of the more comic examples came during Fidel Castro's visit in late 1971. Opposition papers carried on their front pages a photo that appeared to show the Cuban leader dancing cheek to cheek with Jaime Suárez, secretary-general of the government, the ultimate smear in a machista society.[41]

By late 1972 the media debate had degenerated into a no-holds-barred gutter fight, with organs on both sides exchanging sensational, often fabricated charges and countercharges. By July 1973 the situation had become so volatile that even the heretofore staid and dignified *El Mercurio* stated that "it is the categoric duty of sensible people to put an end to looting and disorder stimulated by an inept and crazy government that smothers us. . . . In order to accomplish this task of political salvation, we have to renounce all political parties, the masquerade of elections, the poisoned and deceitful propaganda, and turn over to a few select military men the task of putting an end to political anarchy."[42] Two months later, on September 11, 1973, that is precisely what happened. The three armed forces and the *carabineros* (national police), unified under the command of General Augusto Pinochet, bombed the Moneda Palace when Allende refused to surrender. They moved swiftly to seize all key installations and institutions in the country, sometimes wresting control from armed militants. Allende's body was found in the Moneda after troops stormed in, and it is still hotly debated in Chile whether he died by his own hand or the military's.

Numerous factors contributed to the coup, such as rampant inflation, chronic shortages, growing class hostility, and the real or perceived threat of an armed Marxist takeover of the country. Two years later, a U.S. Senate select committee chaired by Frank Church unveiled clandestine Central Intelligence Agency support for anti-Allende elements, including various media; *El Mercurio* alone received $1,665,000 to help it resist government economic pressures.[43] Chile now was on the brink of a new era, one in which diversity of viewpoint would be replaced by a dull monotone. But there can be little doubt that the media, both left and right, had contributed immeasurably to their own undoing. As Robert Pierce later observed of the media "orgy" of the Allende period, "No society would have tolerated a continuance of this frenzy; if the media had not lowered their own voices, the ruling power would have forced them to do so, whether that power had been a dictatorship of the left or right or even a democratically elected congress."[44]

With the coup, all communication media initially came under military censorship. Only four newspapers still appeared in the capital: the three Edwards papers—*El Mercurio, La Segunda,* and *Ultimas Noticias* —and Picó's *La Tercera.* All Marxist-oriented media were closed permanently, and many of their editors and writers were among those jailed, exiled, or "disappeared." Isabel Allende, a distant cousin of the fallen president who then was writing an innocuous, nonpolitical humor column for the Edwards-owned magazine, *Paula,* was inexplicably fired. Pinochet even closed the government-owned *La Nación* for two years.

Before long, prior censorship was lifted in favor of "self-censorship," which can best be described as press freedom under a Sword of Damocles. Editors were required to guess what was acceptable and what would bring about sanctions, usually forced closure for a specified period. Most of the surviving media were safely promilitary, though even some of them began to chafe at such uncharacteristic limitations on their freedom to report openly or to express even mild criticisms of government actions.

For the remainder of the 1970s, there were few examples of diversity of viewpoint. The Jesuits' *Mensaje* was allowed to reappear, which together with two other opinion journals, *Apsi* and *Análisis,* were the only periodicals that could be considered vociferous in their opposition to the Pinochet regime. All three were closed repeatedly during periodic crackdowns on street demonstrations and general dissent. A new weekly newsmagazine, *Hoy,* established and edited by Emilio Filippi, also was a critic of the regime, though its language was less strident. The surviving broadcast media, of course, were purged of any Marxist elements.

In 1980, Pinochet promulgated a new constitution, under which Chile still is governed. This latest magna carta was ratified overwhelmingly in a plebiscite in which the opposition was denied access to the mass media. Its language on press freedom was virtually identical to that of its 1925 predecessor. Article 19 (Section 3, Subsection 12) guarantees "freedom to impart opinion and to inform without prior censorship in any form and by any means; without prejudice to the liability for offenses and abuses that may be committed in the exercise of this freedom, in accordance with the law, which shall be determined by duly constituted quorum." Unlike his predecessors, however, Pinochet construed "offenses and abuses" as pornography, the publication of Marxist ideas, images of Allende, interviews with exiles, and reportage on the torture of dissidents or on the fate of thousands of "disappeared," any of which could result in closure.

Still, during the 1980s the government permitted a gradual *apertura*, or opening. As a result, progovernment media gradually reported on a wider variety of topics. In 1984 the Picó family, owners of *La Tercera* and reliable supporters of Pinochet, were permitted to begin publishing a lowbrow, sensational, working-class tabloid daily, *La Cuarta*. A new television station was licensed to Universidad del Norte in Antofagasta. The opposition media, meanwhile, became increasingly bolder.

The coverage of two separate news stories observed by this author, one from 1976 and one from 1987, exemplify the relative expansion of press freedom. In 1976, Orlando Letelier, who had served as ambassador to the United States, foreign minister, and finally as defense minister under Allende, was killed in a car bombing in Washington, DC, where he was living in exile. News reports soon surfaced in the United States that the federal prosecutor's office and the Federal Bureau of Investigation suspected the involvement of the National Investigations Directorate (Dirección de Investigaciones Nacional, or DINA), Chile's secret police. Tensions grew between the two governments as the investigation deepened and implicated the DINA commander, General Manuel Contreras, and a subordinate, Colonel Pedro Espinoza. In 1979 the Chilean Supreme Court, packed with Pinochet appointees, refused a U.S. request for their extradition. Throughout this legal and diplomatic wrangling, the Chilean media dutifully parroted the official government line that the DINA was blameless, that the assassination was carried out by leftist elements to discredit the regime. For good measure, the media besmirched Letelier's memory and questioned his relationship with his female private secretary, Ronni Moffitt, who also was killed in the blast.

This obsequious progovernment coverage was in sharp contrast to that of the second story. In 1987, two young people, Rodrigo Rojas and

Carmen Gloria Quintana, were caught up in a street demonstration and detained by soldiers who allegedly doused them with gasoline and set them afire. Rojas died of his burns a few days later, and Quintana was left badly scarred. The torching became an international incident, to the point that Pope John Paul II irked the Pinochet government by paying a highly publicized personal visit to Quintana during a state visit to Chile. Unlike the coverage of the Letelier assassination, however, the print media and radio were far more open, objective, and even skeptical in their coverage of the incident, to the point of questioning the official version that the two youths were armed with Molotov cocktails and accidentally had immolated themselves. If this were true, some commentators noted, why was the lieutenant in charge of the operation officially reprimanded? By the late 1980s, after a Chilean officer had surrendered voluntarily to U.S. authorities and contritely confessed his role in the Letelier assassination, the Chilean media became more objective in their ongoing coverage of that story as well.

Despite the *apertura*, the Chilean press did not enjoy even the qualified freedom promised in the 1980 constitution. Television remained firmly under the regime's control, and the opposition media continued to be subjected to raids or censorship during states of siege that followed periodic incidents of civil unrest. Each year during the Pinochet regime, the Inter American Press Association listed a host of cases of raids, arrests, exiles, or lawsuits against journalists attempting to carry out their duties. In 1987, for example, *Análisis* editor Juan Pablo Cárdenas was convicted of "offending the armed forces" and sentenced to 541 nights in jail; he was free during the day. Marcelo Contreras, editor of *Apsi*, was indicted in 1989 for alleging in an article that Pinochet owned a mansion in Paraguay. Perhaps the most notorious incident followed the September 1986 assassination attempt on Pinochet by the resurgent MIR that left five of the general's bodyguards dead. José Carrasco, foreign editor of *Análisis* and an MIR activist, was abducted from his house by plainclothesmen; his body was found the next day dumped in a park.

Probably the two highest-profile journalists who struggled against the yoke imposed on the media, but who managed to avoid jail or worse, were Emilio Filippi, editor of *Ercilla* before, during, and shortly after the Allende era, and Patricio Bañados, Chile's best-known television journalist. Because they were Gandhi-like in their resistance rather than militant leftists, and because both were held in high esteem in professional circles, they escaped the fate of other journalists and survived to play leading roles in post-Pinochet Chilean journalism.

Born in Valparaíso in 1928, Filippi was named editor of the highly respected *Ercilla* in 1968, late in the Frei administration. He kept his magazine firmly on a moderate course during the turbulent Allende years, one that Filippi called "political rationality." Although *Ercilla* was considered in opposition to Allende, it eschewed the hysterical rhetoric in which other print media were engaging. His evenhanded coverage won him Chile's National Journalism Prize in 1972.[45]

Like most centrist Chileans, Filippi initially welcomed the coup as a means of restoring order, but few expected the draconian regime that followed. Filippi soon chafed under the restrictions placed on the media by the new regime, and his objective coverage annoyed the government. When a group of pro-Pinochet investors bought *Ercilla* to turn it into a mouthpiece for the regime, Filippi resigned and took forty staff members with him. He borrowed $250,000 from friends, and on June 1, 1977, *Hoy*, a rival weekly newsmagazine, appeared on Chile's ubiquitous street corner news kiosks. The new magazine was an instant success, the only news medium that was both independent and generally objective, neither a progovernment sycophant nor an opinion organ like *Análisis* or *Mensaje*. In other words, it was what *Ercilla* used to be, and eventually it eclipsed its rival in circulation. *Hoy* first ran afoul of the regime in June 1979 when it published interviews with two exiles, Clodomiro Almeyda, leader of the Socialist Party, and Carlos Altamirano, a top official of the Communist Party. A correspondent from *Hoy* interviewed Almeyda in France while another reporter in Panama reached Altamirano by phone in Cuba. The government ordered *Hoy* suspended for two months.

With the *apertura* of the 1980s, Filippi decided to establish something still lacking in Santiago—a truly independent daily newspaper. In 1984 he submitted the necessary request through channels but received no response. His attorneys then took on the government in its own court system, citing Pinochet's 1980 constitution. "First, the constitution guarantees the right of petition," Filippi explained to this author in 1989. "If someone has the right of petition, they have the right to a reply. Second, we demanded that when they did answer us they would have to say why. For two years they had us tied up in court. In 1986 the Supreme Court ruled that the government had to answer us and give its reasons. So they gave us the authorization effective March 11, 1987."

To finance his new newspaper, Filippi sold his interest in *Hoy*, although he remained on the board of directors, and raised another $2 million by selling 1.5 million shares to forty investors. To tweak Pinochet's nose a bit, Filippi timed the first issue of *La Epoca* for March 18, 1987, six years to the day after the constitution went into effect. It was and is a respectable tabloid, much like Spain's *El País* in format. The first issue sold out immediately, although public enthusiasm eventually tapered off. Another opposition daily also appeared later that year, *Fortín Mapocho*.

Although *La Epoca* never has matched *Hoy* in economic success, it too incurred the wrath of the Pinochet government. In the October 1988 plebiscite that would have extended Pinochet's rule until 1997, *La Epoca* editorially endorsed the "No" forces, which triumphed 54 percent to 43 percent. The newspaper was placed under prior censorship during states of siege, and Filippi was twice brought up on charges, once for running an advertisement paid for by the Communist Party, the other for the nebulous offense of insulting the armed forces. Moreover, Filippi had been hauled into court five times while editor of *Hoy*, but none of the charges had stuck. Although he never was physically harmed, he was accustomed to receiving death threats. On one occasion the head of a pig was thrown over his garden wall with a note that said, "Así caerá su cabeza, cerdo comunista" (This is how your head will fall, Communist pig).

Asked later how he survived the Pinochet experience virtually unscathed, Filippi replied: "Because I was pretty well-known, so for that reason I was never touched, and they knew that I really wasn't a leftist or a Communist, that I was a Christian Democrat. But to them, a Christian Democrat was the same as a Communist. Quite the contrary. If I had to be called antisomething, I would be anti-Communist, but I don't want to kill them just because I'm against them." Filippi's international reputation for courage during the Pinochet era earned him the IAPA's Pedro Joaquín Chamorro Prize in 1980, the King of Spain's International Journalism Prize and Columbia University's Maria Moors Cabot Award in 1983, and the *World Press Review*'s Editor of the Year distinction in 1984.

As eminent a figure in broadcasting as Filippi was in print, Patricio Bañados, born in Santiago in 1935, is literally a pioneer of Chilean television, joining the Catholic University of Valparaíso's station when it was licensed in 1959. From 1960 to 1962 he was with the University of Chile channel in Santiago and then spent nine years working abroad, capitalizing on his fluency in English. His wanderlust satiated, he returned to Chile for good in 1975 and went to work for the government-owned TV Nacional, but he quickly learned how much Chile had changed in his absence. "I clashed head-on against the regime," he recalled.[46] He was relegated to reporting on mundane features, which at least spared him the ignominy of reporting slanted news as an anchor. In 1979 he went to work for the University of Chile station again, this time as an anchor, and his ad-libbed editorial comments created sparks. He was briefly dismissed in 1982 when, during former President Eduardo Frei's funeral, he refused to read prepared news copy that blamed Frei for leading the country to communism. In 1983, after dutifully reading news copy extolling the government for obtaining credits from the United States, Bañados added: "Chile has a foreign debt that will have, one day, to be paid, and paid in interest." He was promptly fired.[47] Blacklisted from television for seven years, he supported himself with low-paying radio and advertising jobs.

During the 1988 plebiscite on Pinochet's continued rule, Bañados agreed to produce and host the fifteen-minute campaign segments allowed the "No" campaign. The Bañados segments may well have provided the necessary margin of victory for the "No" campaign. "I thought I could risk it," Bañados said. "I don't [believe in] life at any price. There are lives I would not like to live. So if you have to risk your life for something, you risk it and that's it." Like Filippi, Bañados became inured to the occasional death threats. "I was followed by those idiots of his [Pinochet's] secret police. A man tried to run over me one time. A couple of guys followed me and said, 'We'll get you.' Another couple of times they called my home and said they would put a bomb in my house. Unfortunately, [once] I wasn't on the phone and my daughter, who was fourteen, was and she got scared." He added somewhat cavalierly, "Nothing serious."[48]

After the plebiscite, Bañados was ostracized even more. Pinochet was then a lame duck, and, in accordance with the constitution, he called free presidential and congressional elections for December 1989; but he still wielded unchecked authority for a year and a half. Bañados was bitter that he found so little appreciation from the democratic forces after he had risked his career—and possibly his life—for them. Nonetheless, in 1989 he agreed to do television spots for Patricio Aylwin, a Christian Democrat who ran as candidate of a coalition of several centrist and left-wing parties. Aylwin received 55 percent of the vote.

After Aylwin was sworn in, the blacklist was lifted, and Bañados began receiving offers for appearances on TV Nacional; the other, more conservative stations still shunned him. For a time, Bañados was lukewarm about returning to television because of what he had experienced. "I didn't want to be 'The Face' again, not anymore," he explained. "I had done more than enough, but I didn't want to be again 'The Face' antagonizing a large part of the country, and for what? It took me quite some time, and finally I decided that this is my profession, so I took a very regular job here as a sort of journalist-announcer-coordinator of programs."[49] He again is a regular fixture on television.

Thus, the twenty-year-long political and journalistic nightmare extending from 1970 to 1990 came to an end. Pinochet was out of power, although he was allowed to remain army commander until 1997 (and his civilian successors are powerless to remove him). Allende was dead, and the once-fearsome Chilean left had disavowed Marxism-Leninism in the wake of the Soviet Union's collapse. Chileans began groping to find their way in the dazzling light of free expression after two decades in the darkness of intimidation. The media were no exception.

When Pinochet bestowed the presidential sash on Aylwin on March 11, 1990—sixteen years and six months to the day after the coup—the press-freedom clause of the 1980 constitution began to have genuine meaning. Even during the interregnum between Pinochet's plebiscite defeat and Aylwin's ascension to power, controls were relaxed to allow more weekly and monthly periodicals, many of the stripe that had been banned. After the transfer of power, this proliferation of reading material became a torrent. *El Siglo*, the long-proscribed Communist Party daily, reemerged as a weekly; *Punto Final* returned as a fortnightly. They were counterbalanced on the far right by a weekly called *País*. Specialty magazines appeared for hobbyists of all sorts.

The print media have wallowed in unaccustomed liberty. What many would call pornography reappeared on the street-corner newsstands, with graphic or offensive covers in full view of passersby of all ages. Although the rhetoric on the editorial pages of newspaper and magazines today has been lively and colorful, it has not degenerated into the tawdriness characteristic of the Allende period. Apparently, lessons have been learned.

Media owners also learned quickly that they all faced a common new enemy—not political forces this time but economic ones. The media market had become glutted for a relatively small country of thirteen million people, highly literate and increasingly affluent as they may be. Advertising revenue is a finite resource. In addition to the explosion of publications, two privately owned television franchises were granted late in the Pinochet regime: Megavisión on Channel 9, owned by steamship magnate Ricardo Claro, and La Red on Channel 4, launched by banker-economist Alvaro Saieh, who has created a multimedia empire. The new stations had to compete with the four existing ones in Santiago, which are relayed by repeater antennas throughout the country. Whether supported by the government or a university, all stations depend on commercial advertising for survival. Teletrece, owned by Catholic University of Chile, still enjoyed the country's highest ratings and in late 1991 accounted for 49.3 percent of television ad revenue; the government's TV Nacional was a distant second with 32.8 percent.[50]

In 1991, well-known print media began succumbing to the new market reality. *Fortín Mapocho*, which won an eager audience when it was a novelty to be an opposition daily in Pinochet's Chile, apparently lost its luster with the return to democracy and ceased publication. The fifty-one-year-old photo-picture magazine *Vea* also folded. The biggest shock came when the venerable *Ercilla*, its credibility in tatters after years of faithfully toeing the Pinochet line, published its last issue after fifty-eight years. Ironically, the cover of the last issue depicted General Manuel Contreras, the chief suspect in the Letelier assassination, once a forbidden topic and now the focus of a media feeding frenzy, who finally had been arrested after fifteen years. Another irony in the final issue was a house ad boasting that *Ercilla* held 25.2 percent of the newsmagazine circulation, compared with 17.7 percent for *Qué Pasa*, 17 percent for *Hoy*, and 15 percent each for *Apsi* and *Análisis*. Also in the final issue was a vignette in the *"Periscopio"* column alleging that, of the five newsmagazines, only *Ercilla* had been denied advertising revenue by the Aylwin government from such government-owned enterprises as the national lottery, the Santiago subway, and Coldelco, the copper company. Government minister Enrique Correa, once a militant Socialist, insisted that the government had been even-handed in its advertising expenditures.[51]

Filippi's once-successful *La Epoca*, no longer a gadfly to a dictatorial regime, was now just one of the pack of Santiago dailies. Circulation and advertising dwindled, and the paper soon found itself in a cash crunch, sometimes unable to meet its own payroll. To keep the paper from going under, Filippi entered into an agreement with an unlikely rescuer: Alvaro Saieh, the banker, who, in addition to starting Channel 4 from scratch, also had purchased *La Tercera* and *La Cuarta* from Germán Picó and had acquired the faltering *Qué Pasa*. The result was Chile's first U.S.-style joint operating agreement, whereby Saieh's umbrella company—Consorcio Periodístico S.A., or Copesa—assumed *La Epoca*'s distribution, advertising, printing, and administrative functions. Filippi, meanwhile, retained editorial independence. Three years later, *La Epoca* was still publishing.[52]

Television also felt the pinch. In October 1991, TV Nacional announced that it was assuming operational control of the University of Chile's television station, which had changed to Channel 11. Falling ratings and the resulting loss of advertising revenue had brought the pioneering station to the point of bankruptcy, and it was becoming a greater drain than the university could endure. At year's end, Ricardo Claro announced that the Mexican broadcasting giant Televisa had purchased a 49 percent interest in Megavisión. At this writing, all five Santiago-based stations remain on the air.

The principal mover and shaker in Chilean media now appears to be Saieh, grandson of a Palestinian immigrant and son of a businessman, who was born in Colombia in 1949 and came to Chile as a child. He received an economics degree from the University of Chile and a doctorate at the University of Chicago, earning an A in price theory under Milton Friedman. He returned to Chile and taught briefly at his alma mater, worked as a consultant for the United Nations, then accepted a position as head of the economics division of Pinochet's Central Bank, becoming one of the so-called "Chicago Boys," Pinochet's cadre of Chicago-trained economists. After a year, he returned to the university and became director of the economics department. After five years there, he went into private counseling. One of his clients was a group of investors headed by a fellow Palestinian-Chilean, Carlos Abumohor, which was seeking to buy a bank. Saieh recommended the Banco Osorno, of which he became a vice president. A close relationship developed between Saieh and the seventy-year-old Abumohor.

In November 1988, Saieh, Abumohor, and other investors took a gamble by assuming financial control of the Picó-owned Copesa, publisher of *La Tercera* and *La Cuarta*, which was heavily in debt to the Banco del Estado. Saieh was the largest stockholder with 33 percent; Abumohor held 16.6 percent. "We took Copesa in a very bad situation because we thought we could fix it up," Saieh told this author later. "In Chile, I think the way to handle communication is through professional work, trying to cut costs and to look at the product that [the public] wants, and that's our approach. I can tell you that now, today, Copesa, which was an absolutely broken chain . . . [is] a very sound enterprise. . . . I think that the information industry is going to be one of the industries of the future."[53]

Saieh chose not to alter either paper's format or editorial line. *La Tercera*, generally recognized as having the country's top circulation, which Saieh estimated at the time at about 130,000 daily and 180,000 Sunday, is a middle-brow tabloid with a fairly sound reputation for accuracy. As it had been under Picó, it is considered part of the conservative opposition to the center-left governments of Aylwin and his successor, Eduardo Frei, son of the president of the 1960s. Saieh, however, maintains that they are not predictably opposition. "You cannot use the newspapers to sell your personal ideas," he said. "You will lose your clientele."

However politically objective it may be, *La Cuarta* clearly has been the sleaziest daily in Santiago, probably in all of Chile. It appeals to working-class men with full-color, front-page pictures of topless models, with little stars tastefully superimposed over the nipples. It engages in unabashed sensationalism, complete with screaming headlines and lurid stories of crime and sex. For example, when a homosexual in Valparaíso severed his penis after a hospital refused him a sex-change operation in 1991, the other papers buried the story on inside pages with modest headlines. *La Cuarta* bannered it and went into graphic, painstaking detail. Yet, Saieh chose not to argue with success, and he placed *La Cuarta*'s circulation just behind *La Tercera*'s, at 120,000.

With his next acquisition only a month later, the weekly newsmagazine *Qué Pasa*, Saieh was eager to make changes. He transformed it from a hard-line conservative, general news magazine into an objective, business-oriented periodical. He enlarged the dimensions, changed the typeface, and dropped the question mark that had been part of the name for decades. "*Qué Pasa* was a magazine with a lot of [circulation] problems," he said. "We made a study of what people wanted. We put less politics in *Qué Pasa* and more business, and now it's selling very well."

In November 1989, one month before the presidential election, Saieh took an even bolder, and financially riskier, step. He entered into a seemingly unlikely partnership with a Jewish-Canadian financier, Albert Friedberg of the Toronto Trust Mutual Fund, and obtained the franchise for Chile's second privately owned television station, La Red. Saieh is the largest single stockholder with 15 percent. He appointed as station director a near legendary television veteran, Sergio Melnick, but after the first year's operational losses exceeded what Saieh was prepared for, he sacked Melnick and took a more hands-on approach.

Saieh has eschewed the imported programs that have been a mainstay for young Latin American television stations since the inception of the medium, and he also has had only a token news staff. Instead, he has emphasized live shows, claiming that La Red has more hours of live programming than any of Chile's stations. As with *Qué Pasa*, he conducted a market survey and found that the public did not want any more of the cultural programming for which Chilean television had been renowned.

La Red is not the only channel with live shows, however. Although most entertainment programming still is imported, such as action dramas, sitcoms and the ever popular *telenovelas*, or soap operas, the share of U.S. programs has diminished in favor of Spanish-language imports from Argentina, Mexico, Spain, and Venezuela. Dubbed *telenovelas* from Brazil also are popular. One of the most popular U.S. imports has been made-for-television movies, judging from what this author has seen during extended stays in 1991 and 1993–94. Regrettably, there also are some mindless imports from Fox, including *Casado . . . con hijos* (*Married . . . with Children*) and *Los Simpson*. Domestically produced programs are increasing, however. A popular sitcom in 1991 was *Condominio*, about the misadventures of neighbors in a condominium development. Another amusing offering was an imaginative local version of *Candid Camera* called *Luz, cámara . . . y usted* (*Lights, camera . . . and you*). Without a doubt the most popular and pervasive figure on Chilean television has been Mario Krützberger, better known by the stage name Don Francisco.

He has catapulted his fame as emcee of the mammoth Saturday variety show, *Sábado Gigante*, into a hemisphere-wide broadcast emanating from Miami.

Only two channels, Catholic University's Teletrece and the government's TV Nacional, offer serious news programing. Both have highly professional news staffs and impressive coverage of domestic and international events. TV Nacional, for example, pulled off a journalistic coup in August 1991 during the attempted military *putsch* in Moscow when its correspondent somehow managed to arrange a live satellite feed from Red Square at the height of the crisis. Patricio Bañados hosted a well-produced weekly magazine program on TV Nacional called *Mirador*, in the style of such U.S. programs as *60 Minutes* and *20/20*. Probably the most highly respected newswoman has been Teletrece's Raquel Correa, who also has specialized in interviews with prominent people in *El Mercurio*.

As a check on the power of government, adversarial journalism has returned to Chile, but it does not threaten to degenerate into an orgy of vituperation as it did under Allende. The government still has economic cudgels it can wield, such as advertising, but the private sector is booming and expanding and will play a far more important role in advertising than will the government. Pinochet's successors even have echoed his advocacy for privatizing TV Nacional and *La Nación*, although this has not taken place. The Aylwin government created some consternation among the media and the IAPA by proposing legislation that would require a journalism degree to belong to the *colegio* and, hence, to practice journalism (see Chapter 6). Such a law would have barred both Isabel Allende and Patricio Bañados from entering the field. Aylwin left office without the bill having been passed, and Frei does not appear to have it on his agenda. Ironically, there now are far more university journalism graduates than the field can absorb at any rate.

Despite a tenuous beginning in this new age of freedom, Chile's media appear to be finding their way. The economy is the envy of Latin America, and literacy is almost universal, assuring an expanding audience and advertising base for both print and broadcast media. Cable television offers several foreign channels and is growing. The Chilean educational system is excellent, capable of providing a continuous stream of new journalistic and technological talent. Freedom of expression is respected in a way that has not been seen here in a quarter of a century, and the diversity of viewpoints is a welcome change from the Pinochet era. In sum, the outlook is bright, far brighter than this author would have been willing to predict ten years ago when Chile was in the trough of a severe recession and draconian restrictions were in place on the media. Chile, once again, has become a model for others to emulate.

Father Camilo would be proud.

Notes

1. Hubert Herring, *A History of Latin America from the Beginnings to the Present* (New York: Alfred A. Knopf, 1968), 685.
2. Luis Galdames, *A History of Chile*, trans. Isaac Joslin Cox (Chapel Hill: University of North Carolina Press, 1941), 110.
3. Ibid., 141–42.
4. *La Aurora de Chile*, intro. by Julio Vicente Cifuentes (Santiago: Imprenta Cervantes, 1903), iii. All quotations from *La Aurora de Chile* are taken from this volume of reproductions.
5. Ibid., v.
6. Samuel Burr Johnston, *Letters Written during a Residence of Three Years in Chili* [*sic*] (Erie, PA: R. I. Curtis, 1816), 195.
7. *La Aurora de Chile*, v.
8. Ibid.
9. Alfonso Valdebenito, *Historia del periodismo chileno* (Santiago: Impresa Fantasia, 1956), 310.
10. *Colección de antiguos periódicos chilenos*, vol. I (Santiago: Imprenta Cultura, 1952), xi.
11. Guillermo Feliú Cruz, *La imprenta durante el gobierno de O'Higgins* (Santiago: Imprenta Universitaria, 1952), 5–7.
12. Raúl Silva Castro, *Prensa y periodismo en Chile* (Santiago: Ediciones de la Universidad de Chile, 1958), 62.
13. Galdames, *A History of Chile*, 217.
14. José Peláez y Tapia, *La historia del diario* El Mercurio (Santiago: Talleres de El Mercurio, 1927), 4–5.
15. Silva Castro, *Prensa y periodismo en Chile*, 93.
16. Ibid., 95–97.
17. Ibid., 104–5.
18. Brian Loveman, *Chile: The Legacy of Hispanic Capitalism* (New York: Oxford University Press, 1979), 133.
19. Galdames, *A History of Chile*, 274–75.
20. Ibid., 350.
21. Ibid.
22. Ibid., 351.
23. Robert N. Pierce, *Keeping the Flame: Media and Government in Latin America* (New York: Hastings House, 1979), 56.
24. Robert J. Alexander, *The Tragedy of Chile* (Westport, CT: Greenwood Press, 1978), 246.
25. Paul E. Sigmund, *The Overthrow of Allende and the Politics of Chile, 1964–1976* (Pittsburgh: University of Pittsburgh Press, 1977), 188–220.
26. Alexander, *The Tragedy of Chile*, 238–39; Pierce, *Keeping the Flame*, 62–63.
27. Marvin Alisky, *Latin American Media: Guidance and Censorship* (Ames: University of Iowa Press, 1981), 204.

28. Pierce, *Keeping the Flame*, 59.

29. Alexander, *The Tragedy of Chile*, 240; Pierce, *Keeping the Flame*, 67.

30. Sigmund, *The Overthrow of Allende*, 157.

31. Alexander, *The Tragedy of Chile*, 241–42; Pierce, *Keeping the Flame*, 67–68; Sigmund, *The Overthrow of Allende*, 157–58.

32. Pierce, *Keeping the Flame*, 62; Sigmund, *The Overthrow of Allende*, 142.

33. Alexander, *The Tragedy of Chile*, 240–241; Pierce, *Keeping the Flame*, 69; Tomás P. MacHale, *El frente de la libertad de expresión* (Santiago: Ediciones Portada, 1972), 197–206.

34. Tomás P. MacHale, *Poder político y comunicación en Chile* (Santiago: Instituto de Ciencia Política, 1973), 59.

35. Alexander, *The Tragedy of Chile*, 243.

36. Ibid.; Pierce, *Keeping the Flame*, 64–65.

37. Pierce, *Keeping the Flame*, 67.

38. Alexander, *The Tragedy of Chile*, 144–45.

39. Ibid.; Pierce, *Keeping the Flame*, 64.

40. Pierce, *Keeping the Flame*, 65.

41. Sigmund, *The Overthrow of Allende*, 162–63.

42. Arturo Valenzuela, *The Breakdown of Democratic Regimes: Chile* (Baltimore: Johns Hopkins University Press, 1978), 90.

43. *Covert Action in Chile, 1963–1973* (Washington, DC: GPO, 1975), 29; Pierce, *Keeping the Flame*, 60–61.

44. Pierce, *Keeping the Flame*, 58.

45. All information on Filippi was obtained during a personal interview with the author, December 1989, Santiago. See also Robert Buckman, "Survivor in Santiago," *Editor & Publisher*, May 5, 1990, 22–23, 38–39.

46. Interview with Bañados by author in October 1991, Santiago.

47. Dave Marash, "A Chilean Cronkite Awaits His Country's Liberation," *Washington Journalism Review* 11, no. 6 (July–August 1989): 25–26.

48. Bañados interview.

49. Ibid.

50. Robert Buckman, "Media Shake-up in Chile," *Editor & Publisher*, December 28, 1991, 16–17, 32.

51. Ibid.

52. Ibid.

53. All information on Saieh was obtained by the author in an interview in December 1991, Santiago. See also Robert Buckman, "Multimedia Conglomerate," *Editor & Publisher*, December 5, 1992, 16–17, 38.

10

The Media in Argentina: Struggling with the Absence of a Democratic Tradition

Omar Lavieri

Political stability has not been a common feature for most countries in Latin America. For the last decade, Argentina has had a democratic regime after years of military rule, but it still has many vestiges of an authoritarian society, which carry over to the mass media system and to government-media relations. The Argentine media have considerable freedom, and most are solvent financially. Indeed, some media make great profits for their owners. The government, however, has continued to intimidate the media with the threat of restrictive laws. At the mid-1990s these laws were under consideration: doubling the prison time to six years for a libel conviction, a right-of-reply amendment to the national constitution that would require a newspaper to publish a response from a person who believed that he or she had been wronged in print, a proposed Senate rule that would allow a congressman to arrest and detain for ten days a journalist who wrote or broadcast a story that the congressman found offensive, and a Senate-imposed journalistic code of ethics. Omar Lavieri's critical analysis of Argentina's media system shows how inherited attitudes have made it difficult for the media to achieve their proper role in a democracy.

Omar Lavieri is a journalist with Clarín, *the largest newspaper in Argentina, working at the national desk, mainly covering the judicial system and cases of government corruption. He is also an assistant professor in the School of Communication at the University of Buenos Aires. In 1994 he was the recipient of a Visiting Fellowship for Latin American Journalists at Duke University.*

In its 1993 human rights report the U.S. Department of State said that the most serious problem regarding freedom of expression in Argentina was "the heightened level of threats and overt aggression against reporters, radio and television stations, media personalities, union leaders and opposition politicians." But when Argentina's president, Carlos Menem, leader of the Peronist Party, was asked by a journalist about the aggression against reporters, he answered, "It's part of their jobs."

President Menem's reply is important because Argentina and the media have suffered a half-century of repressive authoritarian regimes. Ninety-one journalists were among the "disappeared" during the last era of military rule that ended in 1983. Since the military took office in 1976, fear has been accepted as part of a journalist's job; the coup d'état that brought the military to power was followed by the kidnapping, torturing, and killing of some thirty thousand people. Those people are referred to as *los desaparecidos* (the disappeared) because nobody knows what happened to them; it is assumed that they were murdered.

In 1993 two journalists were attacked physically, one of them twice. In July, Marcelo Bonelli, a reporter at *Clarín*—the newspaper with the largest circulation in all of the Spanish-speaking countries in the world—and at Radio Mitre—one of the main radio stations in Argentina—was assaulted by two men on his way to the station. Two nights before the assault, he had interviewed the secretary of state, Alberto Lestelle, who later would be under judicial investigation, suspected of increasing his personal fortune by $500,000 in less than two years while a government official. Deputy Interior Minister Gerardo Conte Grand claimed that the attack on journalist Bonelli was probably part of an "intimidation campaign" against freedom of speech. President Menem condemned the attack but denied any official involvement and attributed it to those who wanted to besmirch the government's reputation. One year later the identity of the assailants was still unknown, and Lestelle, the official in charge of drug control, was still in office.

On August 15, 1993, President Menem addressed the annual opening of the Sociedad Rural Argentina, the powerful farmers' association. The place swarmed with the president's supporters; it was so crowded that even some of the association's members who had made reservations were left out. One person, only one person, whistled during the president's speech, and the security crew and government supporters beat him. Television journalists and photographers tried to record what happened, but a group of the president's supporters attacked them. The government condemned the attack and denied all responsibility. Three people were arrested. Two days later the author of this chapter reported that Lidia Domsic, the secretary of state for retirees, was trying to set the aggressors free. In justifying her help to the aggressors, she cited "humanitarian reasons."

The second attack involved Hernán López Echagüe, a journalist with the Buenos Aires daily *Página/12*, the newest newspaper in Argentina.

He was investigating reports that a gang of troublemakers operating out of Buenos Aires's central market was being used to support Peronists and to intimidate opponents. Part of this gang attacked the journalists during the president's speech at the Sociedad Rural Argentina. Echagüe said that the attackers worked for Alberto Pierri, president of the Chamber of Representatives and a member of the official party.

Echagüe was first assaulted in front of his house on August 25 and suffered a scarred face. On August 30, Interior Minister Carlos Ruckauf announced that two men had been arrested. It was a lie. Those two people were picked up by police outside a soccer stadium and had nothing to do with the attack, but the government wanted somebody in jail. They were released two days later, however, when Echagüe was unable to make a positive identification. In a statement to the press, the two men accused police of planting incriminating evidence on them at the time of their arrest. Almost everybody was suspicious about what had happened and who had attacked Echagüe. On September 9, in a Buenos Aires suburb, Echagüe was assaulted a second time. Two men forced him into a car where, with the help of a third man, they beat him unconscious. He was then driven several blocks and dumped. President Menem and government officials strongly condemned both attacks and attributed them to unspecified enemies of the government who were attempting to undermine its support before the October elections, which the Peronists won. Menem appointed a special prosecutor to investigate the violence against journalists, but at year's end the identity of Echagüe's assailants was still unknown. By the end of June 1994, investigations by two opposition congressmen showed that Daniel Leguizamón, a former intelligence agent close to Pierri, had taken part in both attacks against Echagüe.

The journalists' unions and professional associations have complained against these and other attacks. The Unión de Trabajadores de Prensa de Buenos Aires (UTPBA), which is the union that represents journalists working in the capital of the country, Buenos Aires, has eight thousand members. The Federación Argentina de Trabajadores de Prensa (FATPREN, or Argentine Federation of Press Workers) represents twenty thousand journalists from all over the country. "The worst opinion is silence" was the slogan of the latest UTPBA's campaign against intimidation and threats to journalists. In 1993 the body of Mario Bonino was found floating in a river. He was the UTPBA person in charge of the files concerning attacks on journalists. What happened to him is unknown. President Menem was reelected in 1995, with an estimated 47 to 50 percent of the vote. He will be in office when the next century begins, and journalists working in Argentina in the new millennium may continue to view being beaten as "part of their jobs."

A country of thirty-three million people, Argentina is a federal, constitutional democracy. President Menem, of the Justicialist (Peronist) Party,
was elected in May 1989, through an electoral college, for a single six-
year term. The constitution provides for a bicameral legislature and an
independent judiciary. The executive traditionally is the dominant branch
at the federal level. Since the end of military rule in 1983, there have
been two national presidential elections as well as numerous midterm
elections for Congress and provincial governments, the most recent of
which took place in October 1993. The constitution was amended in August 1994, and it now allows the president to run for a second consecutive term. The president is the constitutional commander-in-chief, and a
civilian defense minister oversees the armed forces. Responsibility for
maintaining law and order is shared by the Federal Police, the Border
Police, and the Coast Guard, all of which report to the federal government. The provincial police report to provincial governments.

Argentina has a mixed agricultural, industrial, and service economy
that has grown rapidly and experienced significant changes in recent years,
including implementation of an economic reform program intended to
convert a centrally controlled economy into one more responsive to market forces. The program reduced inflation dramatically by sharply increasing revenue collection, fixing the exchange rate, privatizing virtually all
major state enterprises, and opening the economy to vigorous competition from imports. These changes forced the business community to increase productivity in order to stay competitive, often through significant
investment in labor-saving technology. But this process has had the negative effect of increasing the level of poverty in the lower classes. The
health care system is not working properly, the public education system
is losing money in the national budget, retirees earn only $150 per month,
there is virtually no investment in scientific research, and the public university is being attacked by people who want it privatized.

During all of these economic changes, the crime rate has increased,
including incidences of attacks on journalists. Unemployment has risen
higher than in the previous three years. According to the government, the
illiteracy rate is close to 4 percent, but the real rate is not that low because official statistics consider literate any person who can sign his or
her name. Almost 10 percent of the population lives in subhuman
conditions of poverty, which makes it exceedingly difficult to get an
education.

It is fair to say, however, that freedom of expression exists in Argentina, despite the assaults on journalists. The media can report almost everything that takes place in the country, but in many cases, media
enterprises that support Menem's economic policies forbid their journal-

ists to write or speak about a specific issue—the appalling rate (10 percent) of poverty, for example.

Argentina has a huge mass media system. In Buenos Aires, there are ten major newspapers, five television channels, twenty-six large radio stations, four important cable channels, and hundreds of small radio stations. There are many newspapers all over the country, as well as radio stations and television channels, all depending, in one way or another, on the media from Buenos Aires. In many cases, Buenos Aires television channels own media in the interior or sell programs to them. Many radio stations in the country relay programs from Buenos Aires via satellite. Argentina has a large and well-developed media system spread throughout the country, but the focus is on what happens in Buenos Aires, which with its suburbs has close to 33 percent of the country's population.

It is difficult to explain why censorship exists in a free country such as Argentina, but much of it comes from the media, not from the government. The media could speak about almost everything. In many cases, however, journalists obtain information that could be detrimental to powerful individuals, businesses, or groups. Such information often is not published. According to government officials, never has such freedom of expression existed as during Menem's government, and they are correct. It is worth noting, however, that these are the same officials who pay reporters and media owners to repress information about issues, such as poverty or corruption, which are scourges in Argentina. In a country of thirty-three million inhabitants, almost ten million exist in less than humane conditions. Most of the mass media do not report on that. Many media owners support Menem's economic policies and will not report how these changes affect the poor.

The 1853 constitution contained just two articles that mentioned something close to freedom of expression. Article 14 stated: "All the inhabitants have the right to . . . publish their ideas by the press without previous censorship," and Article 32 read: "The Federal Congress will not create laws which restrict the freedom of printing." In August 1994 a new constitution was approved, allowing the president to be reelected. Regarding the press, the constitution adopted the San José de Costa Rica Trade, also known as the American Convention for Human Rights. The Trade established the right to search for and publish ideas without any kind of restriction. Article 13 of the Trade forbids censorship and rejects controls on freedom of speech. This document specifically refers to not allowing official or private controls on newsprint or any other supplies needed by the media, and it also outlaws such official control as media licenses or other means to curtail the communication process or expression of ideas or opinions.

The Trade also provides a right to reply, which many media owners in Argentina oppose. They contend that the U.S. Supreme Court declared such a compulsory right of reply unconstitutional and thus an infringement on the freedom of the press, which was one reason why the United States did not sign the Trade. The right to reply gives the opportunity for a response to a person who considers that some information published by a medium about him or her was false. Media owners would prefer to restrict this right of reply, arguing that in Argentina there are many ways to sue a news organization if a person considers that the information was untrue or if there was intent to hurt.

The control exercised by media owners and the government ensure that it is not at all easy to be a journalist in Argentina. Not only do members of the media face possible attacks, but also governmental efforts to control what is published are a constant pressure. Of course, since Argentina has a democratic government, controls on the press are exercised in a "diplomatic" way. Regardless of who is in office, the national government attempts to control or restrain the media in various ways, including regulation of television and radio licenses, suits against journalists as intimidation, payments for advertising, and oversight of media group operations. The Argentine government has total control of the airwaves. If a person wishes to buy a radio or television license, the government has the last word. If officials say no, that person will never own a radio or television station. In countries around the world, this has been the case because of the limited spectrum of the airwaves. But in Argentina, a number of potential station owners who were unfriendly to the government in power have been denied licenses.

Through July 1994 the government, relying on powerful nongovernmental friends, had managed to build an informal network of newspapers and radio and television stations. The Buenos Aires daily *La Prensa* belongs to Ambassador Amalia Lacroze de Fortabat, a wealthy, right-wing businesswoman who agrees with President Menem's economic policies. In general, the upper class, to which the ambassador belongs, has supported the president's economic reforms. The owner of *La Razón*, another Buenos Aires newspaper, is Carlos Sapadone, a former government official accused of making his personal fortune while in public office. One of the major radio stations is owned by Gerardo Sofovich, a friend of the president and former chairman of the only state-owned channel in the country. He was accused of increasing his personal fortune by selling advertising on the public channel at very low prices to his family's enterprises. In 1995 he was trying to start a newspaper.

The government runs the public television channel, ATC (Argentina Televisora Color) and its cable channel. Moreover, many journalists say that the government used to give financial support to the media group America, which owns a radio station, television channel, newspaper, and cable channels in Buenos Aires and other cities in Argentina. Journalists who work on these media have to be careful in reporting on governmental issues; it is the best way for them to keep their jobs. The privatization project of the radio station that belongs to the city of Buenos Aires will result in that station's falling under federal government influence: two of President Menem's friends have wanted to buy the station. Menem's administration is trying to build a media network of its own, one that will ensure that its thoughts and ideas will be disseminated widely, even if Menem is no longer in office.

The government is not alone in amassing media power, of course. Several major economic groups already have built a strong concentration of power in the media market. Foremost among them is the group named for *Clarín*, the newspaper in Buenos Aires with a daily circulation of seven hundred thousand and a weekend circulation of about one million. In addition, the group owns Radio Mitre, the largest radio station in the country; Channel 13, a major television channel; Multicanal, one of the most important cable channels; a wire agency; and divers businesses. The most successful television station in the country, Channel 11, is owned by Atlántida, which also counts among its assets Radio Continental, one of the country's three most popular radio stations; widely read magazines such as *Gente*, a weekly entertainment and current affairs publication; *El Gráfico*, a sports magazine; and *Billiken*, a weekly for children, among others. Circulation of the magazines is nearly half a million per week. In mid-1994, Atlántida bought 29 percent of the daily *La Prensa* in Buenos Aires. Other media conglomerates have been expanding as well.

This situation can cause problems for journalists. If a journalist works for one group, he or she will probably not be hired by another group, so the possibility of getting other jobs is reduced. This is actually a policy in most media groups, which do not wish to have people from another group working in their enterprises. It also should be noted that journalists' salaries are relatively low in Argentina, and many journalists hold down two jobs at the same time. This is common in a number of Latin American countries. Many Argentine journalists receive payments from the government, politicians, or businesspeople. The envelope under the table is a common practice among many—but not all—journalists. Politicians, businesspeople, or others eager to be mentioned in newspapers or on television or radio often provide such payoffs or incentives for continued coverage of their interests or activities.

These practices will not end until journalists' salaries are raised. A journalist working part-time, six hours per day, earns between $1,000 and

$1,800 per month, depending on the medium in which he or she works. Many salaries are even lower. An entry-level position with a newspaper, for example, may pay only $200 per month for a six-hour-per-day job. The owner of a business newspaper, when asked by his staff for a salary increase, responded, "The salaries are low, but you receive an envelope from so and so, and so." That was the end of the discussion.

Thus, media owners, in paying low salaries, perpetuate such payoffs. After researching the media in Argentina, Craufurd Goodwin, a professor at Duke University in North Carolina, and Michael Nacht, a professor at the University of Maryland, have observed:

> A concern of many observers of the Argentinean media today is with the corrupt practices of society that have moved into the media as well. While journalists assiduously pursue corruption in government, they seldom report that it is present aplenty in their own midst. One businessman spoke eloquently and angrily about the media corruption he faces regularly. He claims that he is repeatedly presented by reporters with various forms of the "shakedown" or blackmail.
>
> He is asked to engage certain reporters as consultants, lest they carelessly print negative information about the firm, and present it to him before publication so that he may "correct mistakes."
>
> He admits that their bribes and payoffs are a reflection of a long-standing cultural heritage, but he is convinced that the practices cannot be consistent with the status of an efficient modern market economy and mature democracy to which the country aspires. The alleged corrupt practices of the media about which this and other businessmen complain and toward which they believe owners of the media are complacent because as a result they may pay lower salaries, seem somehow more venal than the practices in Mexico of payments to journalists that are at least more thoroughly institutionalized and aboveboard than those induced by a shakedown.[1]

In Argentina newspapers constitute a large market, and the relationship between government and press has often been stormy. One of the most famous cases, which drew interest around the world, concerned *La Prensa* when Juan Domingo Perón was in power in the 1940s and 1950s. *La Prensa* was one of the best-known and most respected dailies in all of Latin America, having been founded in 1869 by Dr. José Clemente Paz, who declared in the original issue that independence and reasoned criticism of public officials would be a major part of the newspaper's creed.[2] Early on, *La Prensa* offered free medical services to the public, set up a large public library, and established other such services. The paper came to be regarded throughout the world as trustworthy and as an independent voice.

When President Juan Perón came to power, he issued a decree limiting press freedom and restricting journalists' activities. Soon all journalists had to register with the government or be barred from practicing their craft, and the government took over newsprint distribution and even set the number of pages for each newspaper. *La Prensa* fought against the Perón government, and Perón urged readers to boycott the paper. It became a war. Police stopped *La Prensa* delivery trucks, the owner was arrested and released, threats and intimidation were constant, and, finally, the government-controlled union of news vendors demanded authority over the newspaper's circulation system. Violence erupted, *La Prensa* employees were not allowed to work, and then the Perón government took over the paper in 1951, turning it into a government propaganda organ. The owner, Dr. Alberto Gainza Paz, and a number of staff members fled the country. After five years of Perón domination, the paper came back to Dr. Gainza Paz's control on December 21, 1955, after the coup d'état against Perón. The rightful owners numbered that edition of the paper 29,476, ignoring all the issues printed and numbered during the previous five years.[3] As mentioned earlier, *La Prensa* now belongs to businesspeople close to the government.

In the mid-1990s, *Clarín* leads the market. Menem's government fought against the Clarín group and its powerful media holding in 1992–93. The president has admitted that allowing media concentration of ownership to increase was the biggest mistake he made since taking office. Before Menem became president, owners of print media were not allowed to buy electronic media. Menem changed that, and the *Clarín* newspaper built a large and independent media group which, in several instances, opposed some of Menem's government policies. As part of the fight against *Clarín* and other media, the government tried to regulate freedom of speech. The international press community condemned the government's attempt, thus forcing the government to back off.

Other newspapers, such as *La Nación* and *La Prensa*, the oldest daily in Buenos Aires, have presented a more conservative model in recent years, focusing on the interests of the most traditional aristocracy. They hardly deal with issues such as corruption in government. But a feisty newspaper, *Página/12*, changed the history of Argentine journalism. It first appeared in May 1987 and created shock waves with ironic headlines and a different perspective overall. On one occasion the president said that *Página/12* represented yellow journalism. The next day, the paper came out printed on yellow paper. In 1992 the government withdrew all public advertising from *Página/12*, which caused a journalistic scandal. Other news media condemned the measure. A newspaper that cannot print public advertisements will go bankrupt, for the state is the largest advertiser in the market. One official alleged that the government had withdrawn all advertising from *Página/12* because of a bureaucratic mistake. In truth, it was an attempt to silence one of the most important opposition voices in the political arena. *Página/12* is the newspaper that broke the story about a drug-money-laundering operation that involved President Menem's private secretary, Amira Yoma, who was also his former sister-in-law. When the article first appeared in *Página/12*, the president said that it was journalistic terrorism.

Two other newspapers, *Ambito Financiero* and *El Cronista*, share the market of financial news and have a good relationship with Menem. They do not carry stories detrimental to his image. Some media observers contend that *El Cronista*, as part of the media group America, used to be supported by the government financially.

One of the largest newspapers in Buenos Aires and in Argentina is *Crónica*. Second to *Clarín* in circulation, it is well read among the poorest people in the country. Many media analysts criticize *Crónica* for being the newsprint version of those television programs where rape, murder, and bloodshed are the main fare. Others criticize this newspaper as yellow journalism, but they do not consider its great popularity and importance as an information source for the lower classes. And its sports section, especially the coverage of Argentina's beloved soccer, is highly regarded among sports fans and the public.

Other newspapers, such as *La Razón*, which belongs to government supporters, and *Diario Popular*, which competes with *Crónica*, also have a share of the national market. And a newspaper in English, the *Buenos Aires Herald*, has an excellent reputation and was recognized during the military era for its reporting on murders and missing people. During the military regime, the *Herald* and one other paper, *La Opinión*, were the only newspapers reporting killing by the military. Jacobo Timerman, former chairman of *La Opinión*, was tortured during the military regime.

In Argentina the press is concentrated in Buenos Aires. Beyond the capital city, regional newspapers mostly belong to the traditional or business families of the provinces. Outside the city's downtown and suburbs, many newspapers belong to the same owners of the local radio and television stations. Concentration of media ownership exists both in the national and regional markets.

The first television program in Argentina aired on October 17, 1951, when President Juan Peron initiated public television. For four years, there was only public television in Argentina. But when Peron, popular among the poor people of the country, was ousted in a bloody coup d'état and the military took over the national government in 1955, the generals who led the coup began to talk about new and private channels. In 1958 private television began when the military government opened three television channels in Buenos Aires. The three channels began to air programs in 1960, after they became associated—one each—with ABC, CBS, and NBC, the most important U.S. television companies. In the 1970s, when the U.S. networks had already built the strongest television market in South America, they sold the channels to Argentine businessmen. The Americans alleged that the left-wing political movement and terrorism forced them to abandon their business in Argentina.

In 1973, when Perón returned after eighteen years of exile and political proscription, he took control of the television channels. When he died on July 1, 1974, his wife, Estela Martínez, who up to that point had been vice president, became president of the country. A military coup d'état ended her government on March 24, 1976. During the military era that followed, each one of the five television channels of Buenos Aires belonged to one of the armed forces. The army, navy, and air force each ran a channel, and the others were run from the desk of the president. Today, four of the channels are privately owned; only one is still operated by the government.

One feature of journalism in Argentina that seems firmly entrenched is political talk shows with right-wing hosts, former supporters of the military regime that killed thousands of citizens during the 1970s. Not many opportunities exist for people to give diverse points of view on television. Television plays an important role in a poor country such as Argentina, particularly shows about political and social issues. In 1994, two political shows were especially popular. The host of one was Mariano Grondona, a liberal who had supported the military regimes; he was generally respected because of the issues on the program. He has been one of the media's most important opponents of the government, appearing in prime time to a large, elite audience.

The other popular television political show has been hosted by Bernardo Neustadt, a well-known, right-wing journalist who strongly supported the last military regime, which has been accused of killing thirty thousand people between 1976 and 1983 for political reasons. Neustadt's program is called *New Time*, but it has been on the air for almost twenty years. The show is close to the government, and it does not say anything detrimental about President Menem's administration. The links between Neustadt and Menem are close, indeed. After the attack against a Jewish association on July 18, 1994, Menem's cabinet was called to an emergency meeting in which the secretary of intelligence explained the investigation. Neustadt was sitting close to Menem, at the same table with members of the government. The fact that Neustadt was sitting as part of the cabinet in an emergency meeting suggests that he would not be critical of the government. No other political talk shows are as important as

Grondona's and Neustadt's. Years ago they were cohosts of the same program, but during Menem's administration they parted.

Most television shows are reality shows or game shows offering prizes. News shows are generally good, but political issues are not dealt with thoroughly. As in the United States, news programs cover crime and violence more than other topics. Only a few news reports devote time to poverty, hunger, or government corruption. Interestingly, television news shows rarely cover breaking news. They follow the newspaper headlines and enlarge the issues a little, but they do not provide in-depth coverage, which is done more by newspaper and radio journalists.

Argentina also has a strong tradition of radio, which is both popular and an important source of news. There is no television during the early morning, which is a time for radio. Furthermore, television has not broadcast soccer games live, which gives radio a crucial role because soccer is the most important sport in the country and is followed with real passion.

There are thirteen AM stations in Buenos Aires, two of which are publicly owned. Most broadcast via satellite to the rest of Argentina. The thirteen FM stations primarily broadcast music. A majority of the AM shows are produced by journalists. During the morning, 90 percent of the radio shows are interviews. On any given morning, listeners may find the president talking, the foreign affairs minister being interviewed on another station, and politicians from all parties discussing a wide range of topics. A number of politicians pay to get on radio, and many journalists accept money for prearranged interviews. In this case, journalist and politician agree beforehand on what issues will be avoided and what questions will be asked. Every morning, news agencies disseminate news stories based on the speeches and interviews given by politicians on the radio. Many dailies turn to radio to obtain the news that will appear the following day.

One of the most important challenges the media face today is how to obtain free access to public records. Some journalists contend that there are no real public records in Argentina. The possibility of finding public information depends solely on the journalist's contacts. If a judge is a good source, the journalist could find the record that says something important on which to base a story. A judge, however, may choose to withhold information about a government official who is in trouble. Most of the judicial system is under close government control. The Menem administration installed many judges whose support is certain.

No law obligates the government to give information freely and fully. When a journalist finds an official record that discredits a member of Menem's administration, a federal judge sets out to find the name of the source. Facing the judge, the journalist will answer, "I protect my sources;

it is a professional right." The judge will end the prosecution. Daniel Santoro, a senior reporter at *Clarín* and a professor in the School of Communications of Buenos Aires University, has observed:

> Investigative journalism is no easy task in Argentina because journalists lack the legal resources to enable an automatic access to public records. There is no Freedom of Information Act, as exists in the United States. Most of the information Argentinean journalists obtain depends on the mood of the government sources. This situation punishes the journalists who are not supportive of the government viewpoints. Besides, officials classify as "Top Secret" any kind of document lying on their desks, even photocopies of foreign newspapers (as I once saw in the Foreign Affairs Ministry office). The most important example of hiding public records was the case of Nazi records made public in 1991, 46 years after World War II, due to pressure from the international community.[4]

In the last four years of President Menem's administration, several journalists in Argentina gained their greatest fame through investigative reports, very much like the *Washington Post*'s Watergate stories that brought down Richard Nixon's administration. Many of the stories that appeared in daily newspapers later were published as investigative journalism books. The first one, written in 1983, showed the secret negotiations and diplomatic maneuverings during the Islas Malvinas (Falkland Islands) War between Argentina and the United Kingdom in 1982.

During Menem's administration, these books began describing corruption in government. One of the most significant works was written by Horacio Verbitsky, a journalist with *Página/12*. The book was *Robo para la corona* (I steal for the crown), after a comment made by José Luis Manzano, the former interior minister in Menem's administration. Manzano made the comment in a private meeting, while trying to respond to allegations of corruption against him. That book was a best-seller in 1992 and triggered a number of other books that deeply affected the most sensitive areas of Menem's administration. In the preface, Verbitsky writes that "this book is not an encyclopedia of corruption episodes. Even though this information about corruption appears in numerous pages, its purpose is to give information and analysis for the reader to understand certain major issues. For example, as officials go up in the bureaucratic pyramid, the higher positions are not only formally responsible for the deeds of their subordinates, but also for what enables them to commit the crimes."[5] After the success of *Robo para la corona*, Verbitsky wrote another book, *Hacer la corte* (To build the court), in which he declared that Menem created a Supreme Court that favors his government's needs: "Apart from its loyalty, the Court of Menem is above all the court of the ruling classes, hierarchy-conscious even in its most subtle details. There is no conflict between both devotions when violating the rights of the working class or eliminating individual protections. Only under certain circumstances does it oppose the presidential will; for example, when the Holy Mother Catholic Church refused to grant legal status to a homosexual association."[6]

Another investigative book that became a best-seller in 1993 was about Menem's political and private life. *El jefe* (The boss) was written by Gabriela Cerrutti, a journalist with *Página/12*, and tells the story of Menem from behind the scenes. Cerrutti portrays Menem's life from his youth through his presidency, including private political deals within his closest circle during the beginning of his term. Cerrutti discusses the media's attempts to write about Zulema Yoma, whom Menem divorced in 1990 and with whom he had two children. One passage particularly illustrates Menem's attitude toward the press. According to Cerrutti, "Zulema, during a meeting with journalists, assured them that she knew of a picture in which Menem appears with Ramón Hernández, his private secretary, at a . . . party. Zulema also stated, demanding strict off the record from the journalists, that the photo had been in the hands of a photographer with *Diario Popular*. The photographer had reportedly been killed in an accident that had been orchestrated by the government."[7]

The president's private life, however, was not the only subject of investigative books. His economic policy is based on the theories of Domingo Cavallo, whose life was also portrayed in a book. In his *El hacedor* (The maker), Santoro says of Cavallo: "I tried to be objective, as far as possible, and from an independent standpoint, when describing both the achievements and errors of this neoclassical economist, holder of a doctorate degree from Harvard, who was able at the age of 47 to curb inflation after two hyper-inflationary periods. . . . When he quarreled with other members of the government accused of corruption and when he admits he needs $10,000 a month to live, he seems to be a Quaker in a brothel: he knows many of the officials cannot talk as freely about their income, and he can't help feeling irritated for living in a nest of snakes."[8]

Menem's personal secretary since he took office in July 1989 has been his former sister-in-law, Amira Yoma, who was accused of laundering drug money. The justice system, after a two-year process, found her innocent. The book that tells this story and the way the judges built up the evidence and overlooked important details is one of the most important of the decade. *Narcogate* was written by Román Lejtman, a journalist with *Página/12* who won the King of Spain's International Journalism Prize, the most important journalism prize in the Spanish-speaking world, for his articles about this case. The popularity of such investigative books as these show that the Argentine public wants to know more than what newspapers, magazines, radio, and television tell them. They want to read in-depth information and opinion about corruption in government.

As borne out in a 1994 national poll, people in Argentina trust journalists more than politicians. The country has a huge and well-developed media system, but the power and the decisions are in Buenos Aires. Freedom of speech and freedom of the press certainly exist, but with restrictions on the media and in many cases on journalists. In recent years numerous journalists have been threatened, and some have been beaten. Despite that, most journalists try to be as forthright as they can in their reporting. Salaries for journalists are low, often forcing newspeople to work at more than one job. Payoffs to journalists by government or business are common, and journalists often exercise self-censorship out of fear of reprisal from government or powerful private economic enterprises. Violence against journalists has been relatively rare in recent years but still did occur in the mid-1990s. In 1994, for example, one journalist was injured while covering a story about privatization.

Because television was owned by the state before President Menem took office in 1989, it has been going through a more thorough transition to independence and greater freedom than the print media or radio have. When television was owned by the state, a quick telephone call from a powerful government official kept television journalists in line. Today they have more freedom.

Like governments everywhere, the Argentine government often tries to hide facts and show itself in the best light. It has great power over the media, yet journalists are coming to be more independent. Although Argentina has just completed its first decade of democratic government after the military regimes, more time is needed to develop an independent, mature media system.

Notes

1. Craufurd D. Goodwin and Michael Nacht, *Talking to Themselves: The Search for Rights and Responsibilities of the Press and Mass Media in Four Latin American Nations* (Washington, DC: Institute for International Economics, 1995), 16–29.

2. John C. Merrill, *The Elite Press: Great Newspapers of the World* (New York: Pitman, 1968), 247–53.

3. Ibid.

4. Daniel Santoro, interview with the author, September 1994.

5. Horacio Verbitsky, *Robo para la corona: Los frutos prohibidos del árbol de la corrupción* (Buenos Aires: Editorial Planeta, 1991), 9–10, translation by Omar Lavieri.

6. Horacio Verbitsky, *Hacer la corte: La construcción de un poder absoluto sin justicia ni control* (Buenos Aires: Editorial Planeta, 1993), 29, translation by Omar Lavieri.

7. Gabriela Cerrutti, *El jefe: Vida y obra de Carlos Menem* (Buenos Aires: Editorial Planeta, 1993), 341, translation by Omar Lavieri.

8. Daniel Santoro, *El hacedor: Una biografía política de Domingo Cavallo* (Buenos Aires: Editorial Planeta, 1993), 10–11, translation by Omar Lavieri.

11

Controversies over Mass Communication and Professional Education in the Andean Countries

John Virtue and J. Arthur Heise

Instruction in journalism and mass communication in the United States has had more than eight decades of evolution at the college level, and evidence of its higher quality and more established position with respect to its Latin American counterpart in the educational hierarchy is overwhelming. What began soon after the turn of the century as a few courses in journalism today is often a conglomerate of departments called a school or college of mass communication. Such units frequently have the largest enrollments in their universities. In 1995 roughly 140,000 students were journalism-mass communication majors in more than four hundred schools, departments, or programs at U.S. colleges. In addition, mass communication is a promising field for the future because of the many new forms of media and the increasing need for different peoples and subgroups of the population to communicate with each other.

Typically, in U.S. colleges journalism-mass communication education requires about three-quarters of a student's overall curriculum to be in broad liberal arts and sciences and general education, and about one-quarter to be in specialized journalism-mass communication courses. The specialized education comes in two components: substantive courses on the role of mass communication in society, law, ethics, history, and other areas; and skills courses in reporting, editing, graphics, photojournalism, broadcasting, public relations, advertising, or another professional field of the student's choosing. Overall, the education is fact based rather than ideological and aims at instilling in the student the inclination and ability to produce full, fair, and accurate reports.

In Latin America, education in journalism-mass communication has had a far different history and less time for development. Today it is often centered in schools of social communication and is much more theoretical and conceptual than professional; frequently it is much more ideological than fact based. In this chapter, the authors report results of their survey of mass communication practices in five Andean Pact countries: Bolivia, Colombia, Ecuador, Peru, and Venezuela. Although they discuss differences among the countries, they found more basic similarities than differences in overall professionalization.

John Virtue is the associate director of the Latin American Journalism Program at Florida International University. A graduate of Carleton University in Ottawa, Canada, he spent twenty-five years with United Press International (UPI), most of the time based in Latin America. After leaving UPI, he was executive editor of the Spanish-language daily newspaper El Mundo *in San Juan, Puerto Rico, for almost six years.*

J. Arthur Heise is founding dean of the School of Journalism and Mass Communication at Florida International University and director general of its Latin American Journalism Program. He has worked for the Associated Press in Berlin and for the Buffalo News. *He has published two books and more than fifty articles, monographs, and papers. He holds a Ph.D. from Syracuse University.*

W hen the passenger boarded the taxi in Guayaquil, Ecuador, and asked the driver if he knew where the University of Guayaquil was located, the cabby replied, "Of course. I graduated in social communication from the university." The passenger asked if it was unusual for a journalism graduate to be driving a taxi. "No," the cabby said. "The drivers of the next three taxis waiting in line at the stand are also journalism graduates." The School of Social Communication at the university, which belongs to the state system, had a student enrollment of sixteen hundred when an assessment team from the School of Journalism and Mass Communication at Florida International University (FIU) made a visit in 1993.[1] The enrollment surpassed the number of journalists employed at the time in all of the media in Ecuador.

As the team traversed the campus, members saw slogans about Cuba and Sandinista Nicaragua written on walls. The office of the dean of the School of Social Communication was decorated with pictures of Latin American revolutionary Ernesto "Che" Guevara. Associate dean Germán Cobos Herrera cautioned the team that the graphic display might be misleading. He conceded that the school had been influenced by Marxist philosophy in the past but insisted that things had changed since the end of the Cold War. He described the displays as folkloric.

In Venezuela, when the team tried to make an appointment with the dean of the School of Social Communication at the Central University of Venezuela, it could not. All of the telephones had been out for several weeks. A member went to the university on the off-chance of finding Dean Guillermo López in. He was. The lack of functioning telephones seemed symptomatic of the university as a whole. Newspaper accounts published while the team was in Venezuela told of severe funding problems at the state university. López complained of a lack of computers, television cameras, microphones, recorders, mixers, and other equipment.

In Ecuador, a newspaper executive told of interviewing a young journalism graduate to fill a reporting vacancy. "What do you think of Aristide?" he asked, referring to the exiled president of Haiti who had been very much in the news. The candidate looked confused, hesitated, and then beamed when an answer to the question came to mind. "Oh, you mean the new perfume they are announcing?" he asked. "My degree is not in journalism, yet I run a newspaper," the executive said. "But even if I had the time and the inclination, I would never go to a journalism school in my country. They are real monuments to stupidity."

The four incidents mentioned above reveal fundamental problems facing journalism or social communication schools in Latin America, not just in the Andean region:

1) Many professors, especially in the state schools, have been philosophically adrift since the New World Information Order died with the end of the Cold War. The order, promoted by the former Soviet Union and Cuba, saw the role of the press as being supportive rather than questioning of government and visualized journalists as social communicators.

2) There are too many students, and they have little hope of finding employment in the media.

3) The schools have little money, especially the state institutions, which are free or have only nominal tuitions.

4) Many media executives find the graduates ill trained in the professional skills they need.

Owners, publishers, and top editors complain that the schools—by law, most of the region's news media can hire only journalism or social communication graduates for their newsrooms—do not adequately educate. They say most graduates lack the elemental skills of interviewing and writing and that editors have to devote time to teaching them. They attribute a socialist or even Marxist agenda to many faculty members, which conflicts with the market-driven economies taking root in many countries.

While some schools are adopting a more professional approach to journalism education, others maintain that there is no need to change. The deans at those schools say that their role is to teach students to think and that skills can best be learned in the newsroom. Others say that they emphasize theory over practice because their universities lack the funds to buy equipment for hands-on teaching. Comments from top management, working journalists, and educators were similar in all five countries, even though there is great disparity in this region of almost one hundred million inhabitants. The poorest country, Bolivia, has an annual per capita income of $630 and an illiteracy rate of 22.5 percent, compared to $2,560 and 7.3 percent in oil-rich Venezuela.

Because television sets are costly and most newspapers are aimed at educated readers, many people depend on radio for their news. Bolivia, for example, boasts nearly six hundred radios for every one thousand residents, but just fifty-five television sets. Its 7.5 million residents buy fewer than one hundred thousand newspapers per day. Venezuelans, on the other hand, have 256 television sets for every one thousand residents, while one in ten buys a newspaper. Colombia, with its two newspapers of international renown, *El Tiempo* and *El Espectador*, both in Bogotá, is considered to have the highest level of journalism. Furthermore, it has the two biggest radio networks in Latin America, Caracol and Radio Cadena Nacional, which between them had 88 percent of the audience in Bogotá, Medellín, and Cali in 1990.[2]

Peru has one of the most prestigious, and oldest, newspapers in Latin America, *El Comercio*, founded in Lima in 1839. Peru's weekly newsmagazines are the most aggressive of any in the Andean region. One media family in Peru, the Delgado Parkers, established regional networks for radio and television called SOLAR (Sociedad Latinoamericana de Radiodifusión) and SUR (Sistema Unido de Retransmición), respectively. Finally, Ecuador is unique among Andean countries inasmuch as it has two cities of equal importance, Quito, the capital, and Guayaquil, the commercial center. The country's two leading newspapers are *El Comercio* of Quito and *El Universo* of Guayaquil. All five Andean countries have substantial native Indian populations. Some radio stations in Bolivia, whose population is 60 percent Indian, and in Ecuador broadcast in native languages.

To determine if there was a need for further training of journalists, the assessment team from FIU sought to evaluate the news media in the five Andean Pact countries. Operating in Central America, FIU's Latin American Journalism Program trained 2,200 of the region's journalists between 1988 and 1994 through a contract with the U.S. Agency for International Development. The assessment team interviewed 461 working journalists, media executives, and academics from 104 organizations and eighteen schools in fourteen cities in the five countries. Of those interviewed, 328 answered a twelve-page questionnaire that dealt with the journalists' perception of the press and their role in society.[3] The 328 respondents consisted of 318 journalists and 10 journalism educators.

Some of the journalists also taught as adjunct professors. Slightly more than 60 percent were men, 39 percent were women. That breakdown probably reflects the gender distribution in the media as a whole in the five countries. The average age of the respondents was 33.6 years, which is likely close to the average age of those working in the Andean news media. Men averaged 36.1 years and women 29.7. The average age of journalists in the United States, according to a 1981 survey, was 32.4 years.[4]

All of the interviews took place in the newsroom or an adjacent conference room. The team usually interviewed all of the reporters or editors available at the time of the visit. Two newspapers, one in Colombia and the other in Bolivia, selected those to be interviewed. One managing editor in Bolivia summoned all his newsroom personnel near deadline and told them they had to drop what they were doing and answer all of the team's questions. Only one newsroom executive, in Medellín, refused to allow the assessment team to interview his personnel, although he talked openly himself. He said all of his reporters and editors were busy, although about eight people were observed milling around the newsroom and chatting. Only one journalist refused to talk to the team, a reporter-announcer in his sixties at a small radio station in Lima.

The assessment team determined that, throughout Latin America, news media executives are practically united in their opposition to the obligatory licensing of journalists. It has been twenty years since the requirement of a degree in social communication was introduced in the Andean countries in order for people to be able to work legally as journalists. Legislation was passed in 1974 in Colombia requiring journalists to have a degree before being given a *carnet* (identification card) by the education ministry allowing them to work in the media or government. The following year, legislation covering *colegiación*—as this practice is known in Spanish—was passed in Venezuela and Ecuador, followed by Peru in 1982 and Bolivia in 1984. Since then, many media executives contend that *colegios*, or licensing, has caused a drop in the level of professionalism. They say that the pool of potential new journalists has been reduced to those graduating from the schools of social communication, which fail to train them properly. Previously, media executives would hire the best candidate, regardless of what he or she had studied. One executive named a group of journalists from his country who had gained recognition abroad working for international news agencies and foreign newspapers. He noted that none had been graduated from a school of social communication but had studied other disciplines. Another executive even said that no outstanding journalists have been produced in the generation since *colegiación* began.

Colegiación advocates throughout the hemisphere contend that journalism is a profession and, as such, demands a high level of training and a code of ethics that can only be enforced by a *colegio*. They liken journalists to doctors, engineers, and architects who belong to a college of medicine, engineering, or architecture. Opponents say that licensing infringes on freedom of the press because it limits access to newspapers and airwaves. While *colegiación* might be well intentioned, opponents say that in fact government approval for the existence of the *colegios* opens the door for government manipulation of the press.

Only in Venezuela is licensing strictly enforced in the Andean region. The requirement is ignored in varying degrees in the other four countries. Several executives in Bolivia expressed surprise that there even was licensing legislation in that country. The fight over licensing in Venezuela has moved to that nation's Congress, where twenty journalists and media executives were elected in December 1993. Five members of the Colegio Nacional de Periodistas were elected to the Senate and eight to the Chamber of Deputies. Media managers held three Senate seats and four in the Chamber. The president of Congress and first in line of succession after President Rafael Caldera was Senator Eduardo Gómez Tamayo, publisher of *El Informador* of Barquisimeto.

In 1994 the *colegio* was trying to strengthen legislation in Venezuela that would prevent nonmember newspaper editors and owners from writing in their own publications and would keep nonmember radio and television journalists from conducting interviews. As well, journalists involved in the selection of news would have to be Venezuelan citizens. The licensing issue has affected journalism training in Venezuela. *Colegio* president Eduardo A. Orozco told the assessment team that many media companies refuse to give journalists time off to attend seminars sponsored by the *colegio*. But one media executive replied, "The *colegio* has a political agenda." Said a radio executive, "The *colegio* doesn't represent the philosophy of most journalists."

The *colegio* dispute also appears to affect the professional loyalty of journalists, at least in Venezuela. During the assessment, a team member gave an ethics seminar in Barquisimeto for fifty-seven journalists. He used a case study which identified journalists' loyalties as being in favor of the public, their media, or their colleagues. All fifty-seven said that their loyalty was with their colleagues.

Heads of *colegios* and associations in two other countries indicated they would seek additional legislation if *colegiación* is not better respected. "We can't permit the existence of a law if it is not obeyed," said Lupe Cajías, president of Bolivia's Association of Journalists. And Miguel Calderón, president of the Colegio de Periodistas in Peru, said that legislation is being prepared to define what the practice of journalism means and what freedom of expression means. Licensing is not enforced in Peru because the law says *colegiación* cannot infringe on the constitution, which guarantees freedom of expression. This issue of *colegios* is discussed in detail in Chapter 6 of this volume.

While media executives complain about the training of their personnel, the assessment team found that the journalists themselves complain about their employers. The lack of independence in the newsroom was the major grievance except in Colombia and Peru, where it was second after personal safety. The following breakdown shows how the journalists' complaints rated regionwide: independence in the newsroom, 28 percent; low salaries, 19.8 percent; personal safety, 15.5 percent; training and professionalization (discussed later in this chapter), 11.2 percent; lack of respect, 7 percent; and professional ethics, 4 percent.

One Latin American publisher provided a good example of how strongly journalists feel about the need for independence in the newsroom. He would point to the floor outside the entrance to the newsroom and claim that there is an invisible line that no one but the journalists working inside could cross. He stated that policy in order to shield his editors and reporters from pressure from the newspaper's business side and, by extension, from advertisers, politicians, government officials, and anyone else who wanted to influence news coverage.

Many journalists told the assessment team of having written stories only to have them killed by management, either because they affected outside economic or political interests of the owner, his family, or his friends, or because they involved important advertisers, the military, or the government. Media executives who commented on the issue dismissed the complaints as those of politicized journalists who were being misled by the *colegios* and other journalistic associations in demanding rights that belonged to management.

"The most serious problem is censorship by management itself," said a twenty-eight-year-old reporter in Ecuador. "The media are in the hands of powerful economic and political monopolies. The news can be well documented, but if they don't want it to come out, it won't come out." A business writer in Colombia told of writing about a major advertiser who had been accused of not paying all the income tax he owed. The story was killed. A reporter in Ecuador had a similar experience with an article that touched on the family of the owners of the magazine where he worked. That story also was killed, and the reporter subsequently quit. Still another reporter on a Caracas newspaper was assigned a series on the city's subway system. She wrote five articles dealing with kickbacks and other illegal activities, but the series was reduced to three articles, then to one.

Nothing was ever published, the belief being that management checked the series with the companies involved, which also had other interests that advertised in the newspaper. She told of her experience during an investigative reporting seminar organized by the Colegio Nacional de Periodistas.

Typical, too, is the story told by a twenty-eight-year-old photographer on a major Venezuelan newspaper. When he had come upon an angry demonstration outside a government office, he knew his pictures would be exclusive. No other photographer was in sight, and the police were about to break up the demonstration. But he was not happy. "I knew when I took the pictures that they would not be used by my newspaper," he said. He anticipated, correctly, that someone from the government office had recognized him and that pressure would be put on the newspaper not to publish the pictures. If the call from the government official had not worked, the official would have called an important advertiser and had that person pressure the newspaper's management.

"The big problem is the 'gag law' imposed by a medium that has a political or business agenda you have to follow," said a veteran reporter in Caracas. "You practice self-censorship because you can't write what you want to." "It's easy for the government or politicians to pressure the media not to touch some stories," added a twenty-eight-year-old Peruvian reporter; "they have the power of the military and police behind them."

Next to the journalists' concern for the constraints placed on their independence is their dissatisfaction with the low salaries that they are paid. A radio station owner in Ecuador was asked how much a family of three (with aspirations to at least the lower middle class) would need to be able to live reasonably well. He responded with $500 per month, a figure with which others in and out of the media agreed. The top salary paid by this owner was $300 per month. The assessment team then tried to determine what a reasonable salary would be in the other countries as well and found the monthly pay to be $400 in Bolivia, $1,000 in Colombia, $700 in Peru, and $1,000 in Venezuela. The lowest salary encountered by the assessment team was $45 per month, which Sandro Vaca, executive secretary of the Press Workers Union, stated was being paid in some areas of the province of La Paz, Bolivia. The lowest salary received by someone interviewed by the team was $55 per month, which a radio reporter in Lima said that she earned. Salaries of $200 per month were found among radio workers in Venezuela and Colombia. Sometimes the owners of radio stations pay even less but then give the reporter the opportunity of selling advertising on commission. This system, of course, leads to the possibility of the reporters tailoring their news stories to help their sales campaign.

Several section heads of newspapers in Colombia and Venezuela said that they earned the equivalent of $1,000 or more per month, with the starting salary for a reporter at *El Tiempo*, the leading newspaper in Bogotá, just under $400 per month. In contrast, salaries of television personnel interviewed ranged up to $4,000 per month, although one well-known political reporter earned only $500 per month. Of those interviewed, 61.8 percent earned $400 per month or less.

While salaries are low, the assessment team was told that they are in line with others within the private sector. Respondents to the questionnaire were asked to compare the salaries of journalists and engineers, policemen, accountants, car salesmen, politicians, university professors, medical doctors, and high school teachers. They said that all but high school teachers are paid better. Furthermore, male journalists are increasingly no longer the sole wage earners in the family. Of those interviewed, 72 percent said that their wives work, many (17 percent) as journalists, more than in any other profession or activity.

Many journalists, of course, are far more intensely concerned for their personal safety than for their journalistic independence or their salaries. During the last decade, more than 50 journalists have been killed in Peru and about 250 in Colombia. Most of the deaths have been attributed to guerrillas, drug traffickers, the armed forces, and police. "When the antibomb squad opened the package addressed to me, they found the head of a chicken with my picture attached to it with a black ribbon," said the twenty-nine-year-old investigative reporter in Lima. "I've received bouquets of flowers with death threats included. All told, I received eight death threats last year, besides obscene telephone calls at 3 A.M. and other harassing calls."

"Professional risk is the biggest problem facing journalists in Peru," explained Miguel Calderón, president of the Colegio de Periodistas. "If the paramilitary believes you're a subversive, you can be arrested and tried and jailed, or worse. If you're considered a leftist or a progressive, you can easily be disappeared. If the Shining Path [the revolutionary group Sendero Luminoso, which uses terrorism to try to destabilize the government] thinks you're promoting the government, you can become a target." At the time of the assessment, Calderón had given refuge in the Colegio's building to the families of two jailed journalists from the interior.

Personal safety is also the number one worry of journalists in Colombia, although Medellín cartel leader Pablo Escobar was killed the week before the assessment team made its visit. A veteran journalist explained how the drug traffickers, responsible for many of the killings, operate. "First comes the offer of bribes, especially in Cali, where the cartel is very intelligent. The cartel will have three or four 'public relations men' among journalists in each medium in Cali to try to influence their colleagues. If that doesn't work, you can get a call complaining about a story. Gilberto Rodríguez of the Cali cartel has called me personally to complain. If the complaints don't work, you start getting threats. If you receive a package with a small coffin inside, it's time to get a bodyguard. The final stage is the kidnappings and killings." Personal safety was also an issue in Ecuador but was not mentioned by any of those interviewed in Bolivia or Venezuela.

In all of the Andean countries except Ecuador, journalists said that they are not respected enough by owners, by those they report on, or by the public as a whole. "The most serious problem we face is the lack of respect from politicians and the owners," complained a thirty-two-year-old reporter from a Bolivian newspaper. "They treat us like laborers."

Respondents to the questionnaire also were asked to compare the prestige of journalists with that of engineers, policemen, accountants, car salesmen, politicians, university professors, medical doctors, and high school teachers. The results show that journalists think that they have more prestige than policemen, car salesmen, and high school teachers and almost as much as politicians.

In Colombia, some journalists link what they feel is a lack of respect to the image created by veteran colleagues who accept bribes and payoffs. "We have to fight to overcome the bad impression left by the old-time journalists," noted a twenty-seven-year-old section head in Bogota. And in Lima, according to a twenty-three-year-old female magazine reporter, "journalists get no respect from society."

Nearly 60 percent of those interviewed by the assessment team said that they know a colleague who has accepted a bribe. Just over 26 percent noted that corruption is extensive among journalists in the media, and they pointed to governments and politicians as the main corrupters of the press. One executive in Ecuador told the assessment team that last year a politician showed him a list of journalists that he claimed he was buying off. The low level of salaries was often cited as justification for accepting bribes. In fact, one editor in Ecuador said that he had to change the beats of his reporters every few months because they would start accepting payoffs from their sources.

Some journalists admitted that the amount of money offered depends on where one is in the hierarchy. "The higher you rank, the more likely you are to be bribed," said a thirty-one-year-old reporter in Colombia.

"Editors are worth more than buck privates." The assessment team also was told of a publisher who ordered a full-page investigation of a scandal in the social security administration in Ecuador. A top editor pulled the story just before the presses were to roll, cut it in half, and watered it down. When confronted, the editor stated: "Think of our good friends at the social security administration." He kept his job. And another journalist in Lima claimed that bribe-taking has reached a "dangerous level" in Peru, telling the assessment team that he is proud of the fact that he has traveled around the world three times without spending a cent. He said that all of the bills were paid by sports federations or athletic teams.

The assessment team asked journalists in the five countries their opinions about the media. The following replies show that the majority of those surveyed have a clearly defined view of the role of mass media in a democracy. They also believe that the media should be independent of political parties, and that journalists should be able to write impartially on ideological issues, even though many of them work for organizations that are identified with a particular party.

- *Does the government have the right to censor political and economic news?*
  No (97 percent).
- *Should the news media report on errors or abuses by the government?*
  Yes (99 percent).
- *Should the news media defend the right to disseminate news?*
  Yes (99 percent).
- *Does the government have the right to censor news about the armed forces?*
  No (90 percent).
- *Should the news media be independent of political parties?*
  Yes (94 percent).
- *Should journalists write impartially even if the news conflicts with their ideology?*
  Yes (90 percent).
- *Does the credibility of a news medium depend on its journalists?*
  Yes (86 percent).
- *Is it the function of the news media to stimulate honesty in government posts?*
  Yes (68 percent).
- *Do journalists in the region have little prestige?*
  Yes (only 18 percent).

The assessment team also noted a trend in the Andean region similar to one in the United States: ownership of several media outlets by the same individual or group. But unlike in the United States, there is no legislation restricting multiownership in the same market. The two largest business groups in Colombia are actively involved in the media. The Santodomingo group, which owns Avianca airlines and the Bavaria brewery, among other holdings, bought the Radio Caracol network in 1986. Caracol is the whole or partial owner of 75 stations, while another 100 are affiliated. The Santodomingo group also owns *Semana* magazine and was expected to be granted a television channel when Congress breaks the state television monopoly, as it has indicated it will. The Santodomingo group's rival, the Ardila Lulle group, owns the leading textile and soft drink companies in Colombia, as well as the Radio Cadena Nacional network of 103 stations. Like the Santodomingo group, it expects to get a television channel.

The Isaías family in Ecuador owns television stations in Quito and Guayaquil and a newspaper in Guayaquil, a national magazine, and about a dozen radio stations. Moreover, individual members of the family have investments in other media companies. In Venezuela, the Radio Caracas group operates radio and television networks as well as owning a newspaper, *Diario de Caracas*. Its rival, Venevisión, has a newspaper as well as its television network. Venevisión hopes to obtain a channel in Colombia and will probably buy an Ecuadorian channel. And in Peru the Delgado Parker family owns Channel 5 as well as Radio Programas del Perú, the leading radio outlet.

The assessment team tried to determine whether journalists were being properly educated to carry out the traditional watchdog role of the press. It can be argued that the media in Latin America have a greater responsibility to safeguard democracy than do the media in the United States and in other developed, Western countries. This is due to the lack of an effective system of scrutiny of government in many countries and to the weakness of civil society as a whole. Although equivalents of the U.S. General Accounting Office exist in Latin American countries, those agencies are often intimidated or accommodating.

More than 84 percent of the journalists who responded to the questionnaire said that the media should report on errors and abuses by government. But with few exceptions, that role was not being fulfilled by the news media in the Andean region. Sometimes there is little tradition to do so, as in Bolivia and Ecuador. Sometimes the political situation inhibits the media, as in Peru, where only the opposition press, at considerable sacrifice, regularly questions the government. Sometimes the media decide, for one reason or another, to rally around the government, as seemed to be the case in Colombia during the administration of President Cesar Gaviria, who left office in 1994. Sometimes the media join forces with those they should be scrutinizing, as in Venezuela, where twenty journalists or media executives sit in Congress.

The main weapon of a vigilant press in a democracy, that is, investigative journalism, is used only sporadically in the Andean countries. Very little investigation is done in Bolivia and Ecuador. Investigation in Peru is limited mainly to the three weekly newsmagazines—*Caretas, Ojo*, and *Sí*—and the newspaper *La República*. Colombia's investigative teams have not been as active as they were in the past, when *El Tiempo*'s Daniel Samper, now working for *Cambio 16* in Madrid, was making a reputation for himself. *El Espectador*'s drug investigative team was broken up through assassination and the exile of its members. Venezuela's leading investigative reporter, Juan Vicente Rangel, is not really a journalist but a politician. He was the one person responsible for revealing the alleged corruption that brought down President Carlos Andrés Pérez in 1993.

The assessment team also discovered that with the expansion of democracy in the Andean region have come significant changes in the roles and opportunities of women. There now appear to be more women than men in the schools of social communication in the five Andean Pact countries. Women also make up half of the newsroom personnel in some media, but they do not hold management positions commensurate with their numbers. The reason given is that most are relatively new arrivals in the newsroom and are still moving up the corporate ladder. For instance, 96.8 percent of the women interviewed had less than ten years' experience in journalism.

Most women who serve as publishers or editors are on newspapers owned by their families. However, the assessment team met one female editor in Caracas who had been hired for the post and several in Ecuador who held key jobs in television. Many women, especially in radio, are hired at lower salaries than men. Married women run the risk of being dropped because of lengthy paid maternity leaves written into law. Surprisingly, men and women interviewed agreed that women are more responsible than men because of their life-style. A male television executive said he preferred hiring women to men because women never miss work due to excessive socializing. A female editor said women have to be more serious than men because of Latin customs. She said, for instance, she cannot linger over a cognac at lunch as a male editor can, or go to a bar by herself for a relaxing drink.

When the assessment team asked about the nature and quality of the preservice education of journalists, it discovered considerable dissatisfaction with the schools of social communication. Nearly all of the media executives interviewed criticized the curriculums of these schools for being too theoretical and not practical enough and, in many instances, for having an ideological bias to the left. The media executives find the faculties peopled by professors with little or no professional experience in the media. "Journalism education is very theoretical, not practical, and a lot of time is wasted trying to teach graduates to be journalists," the editor of a Bogotá newspaper said. "Too many of the professors have never worked in the media," noted a female executive in Caracas who was an adjunct professor herself. "The students spend five years at university learning everything and then enter the media and know nothing."

Graduates working in the newsrooms were often as harsh as the executives in their criticism of the schools. "It's possible to graduate knowing everything about Karl Marx but not knowing how to write a lead," said a thirty-one-year-old reporter in Quito who never finished his journalism studies. "You graduate and go out into the street, and you're lost," said a twenty-seven-year-old television reporter in Caracas. "You don't know about reality because you weren't introduced to it in school."

Some educators were divided over the issue of practice-versus-theory. Raúl Rivadeneira, dean of the School of Social Communication at the Catholic University in La Paz, said he was in the midst of revising the study plan in order to place more emphasis on practice and less on theory. Courses on "Theory of Interpersonal Communication," "Theory of Mass Communication," "Philosophy of Communication," and "Psychology of Communication" were still on the books.

Dean Joaquín Sánchez of the Social Communication Faculty of the Jesuit Javerian University in Bogotá said his program is committed to the general philosophy of the largely theoretical social communication concept. For him, the practical skills can be learned on the job once the students are graduated. His opposite number at the University of the Valley in Cali, Alejandro Ulloa, agreed. He said that too many schools overemphasize technology and how-to-do-it skills without teaching the students to think, and that his school does a better job of the latter. One journalism professor conceded that courses were theoretical rather than practical for a simple reason: "We don't have enough money to equip newsrooms and studios to give practical training. So we teach theory, which is cheaper." While most schools were criticized, two—the University of Lima and the University of Piura in Piura, Peru—were generally praised by media executives and graduates. Both are private schools.

Some of the dissatisfaction with journalists' education was directed at CIESPAL (Centro Internacional de Estudios Superiores de Periodismo para América Latina, or International Center of Advanced Studies in Journalism for Latin America) both for the influence it had on curriculums in the past and for its training efforts at its Quito headquarters. Many faculty members throughout the Andean region had adopted the philosophy of UNESCO (United Nations Educational, Scientific, and Cultural Organization) and its New World Information Order, whose champions included CIESPAL. Western organizations such as the Inter American Press Association and governments, including that of the United States, saw the free flow of information endangered by UNESCO's policies. "There's a Marxist tendency, including support for the New World Information Order, and this tends to confuse young journalism students," a Bolivian publisher said. "They're told that journalism should have a social character, that journalists should change the world and be promoting causes."

"In my opinion, we have to return to the pre-CIESPAL stage," said Antonio Peredo, vice-dean of the School of Social Communication at the University Mayor de San Andrés in La Paz. "The CIESPAL philosophy of communication was too theoretical and represented a loss of many years, so we have to clean the slate and start again." "CIESPAL has not fulfilled its role," said Galo Martínez Merchán, then president of the association of newspaper owners in Ecuador. "The courses are not good; they're too theoretical."

Apprised of these comments made to the assessment team, CIESPAL officials replied that it had acted as a catalyst when schools of social communication were originally redesigning their programs. Edgar Jaramillo, the organization's technical director, said that CIESPAL played a pioneering role in research, professional training, publication of books on journalism, and assistance in radio and television programming in Latin America. According to CIESPAL figures, it has trained eight thousand Latin American journalists, including fifty-seven hundred Ecuadorians, since its inauguration in 1954. CIESPAL states that less than 1 percent of its funding comes from UNESCO, with the rest coming from the Ecuadorian government, Germany, the Low Countries, the Organization of American States, foundations such as Germany's Friedrich Ebert Foundation, U.S. foundations, and others. It has seventy-five people on its payroll in Quito.

Given the level of dissatisfaction with the professional education of journalists in the Andean region, it may be surprising that few media organizations have set up programs in newsrooms to educate their personnel or to send them abroad to attend seminars or universities. Colombia is the leader in education. *El Tiempo* of Bogotá has its own school and sends journalists abroad to study. Radio Caracol and Radio Cadena Nacional have education programs. So does *El Colombiano* of Medellín. Venezuela's Radio Caracas group contracts the services of instructors, as does the newspaper *Panorama* of Maracaibo, which also sends its journalists to the United States for education. *El Comercio* of Lima brings in an instructor from Spain's University of Navarra every other year. Several Ecuadorian newspapers also bring in instructors.

The *colegios* and journalism associations give seminars, but they usually depend on instructors willing to work for nothing. The *colegio* in Venezuela has an institute with its own director that gives up to twenty seminars a year. Many journalists interviewed blame their low salaries on their lack of professionalization. "Our low salaries are a result of our poor education and training," said a thirty-six-year-old female reporter in Guayaquil. A publisher in Guayaquil more or less agreed. "We want to pay the journalists better when they better themselves," he said. "We have already begun with some basic writing and grammar classes, but the problem is a human one."

Media executives in all five countries, but especially in Bolivia and Ecuador, expressed a desire to educate their journalists better. Asked what seminars they would schedule for themselves, the journalists overwhelmingly chose investigative reporting, followed by writing, newsroom management, television production, and ethics. Because television personnel represented 12.7 percent of those interviewed, it can be concluded that many print and radio journalists would like to go into television for the perceived glamour and higher salaries.

Because the professional education of journalists in the Andean Pact countries is inadequate and their on-the-job training unsupported, it is not surprising that there are still many self-taught journalists who have never taken a course in journalism or mass communication. Edwin Tapia, president of the National Chamber of Social Communication media in Bolivia, estimated that slightly more than half of the country's journalists had never attended university journalism schools. The figure is lower elsewhere.

The assessment team noted friction in some countries between journalists with journalism degrees and *empíricos* (self-trained or self-educated journalists). Young journalism graduates tend to blame unethical behavior on their older, empirical colleagues. "The big difference between the *empírico* and the graduate is that the self-taught journalist will demand payment for a story," said a young copyeditor in Piura, Peru. As a thirty-seven-year-old journalist in Venezuela explained, "One great defect in the law setting up *colegiación* is that self-taught journalists were admitted in the first place." The possibility of tension exists when a reporter who is a graduate has to report to an editor who is self-taught. "The graduates feel superior to an editor who is an *empírico* until they sit down at a typewriter and realize they don't know how to write," said a self-taught managing editor. "The graduates have more prejudices against us than we have against them."

Based on interviews and observations of the media, the assessment team reached the following conclusions about the education of journalists in the Andean region:

- Journalists do not have many of the required professional skills and tools, especially in investigative reporting. They are often unfamiliar with investigative techniques and the resources available to them.
- News stories are often a mixture of fact and opinion, misleading readers, listeners, and viewers. Publishers and owners complain that reporters do not know how to conduct interviews or produce well-written stories.
- Professionals in the mass media blame the schools of social communication for the poor performance of journalists. Owners, publishers, editors, and many working journalists say the courses are too theoretical and often politicized to the left.
- Journalists recognize the need for more education, but few media companies invest in programs to improve the skills of their news staffs.
- Journalists blame poor education and training for their low salaries.
- Unethical behavior is common and accepted or tolerated in many newsrooms.
- Journalists often lack a clear vision of their professional obligations to the public. Too often, they feel that their first loyalty is to their colleagues.
- Women are fast gaining numerical equality with men in the newsroom but still lag behind in management positions.

Notes

1. Besides John Virtue, a coauthor of this chapter, the assessment team consisted of Roy E. Carter, Ph.D., retired University of Minnesota professor of journalism and sociology; Mario Diament, Spanish-language journalist-in-residence at Florida International University; Ana Cecilia With, coordinator in FIU's Latin American Journalism Program (LAJP) office in San José, Costa Rica, and a veteran of three previous assessments; and Sandra Navarro, a Venezuelan-born Panamanian who heads the LAJP office in Managua, Nicaragua.

2. María Teresa Herrán, *La industria de los medios masivos de comunicación en Colombia* (Bogotá, Colombia: Fescol, 1991), 78.

3. The 235-page assessment report contains 40 pages of charts and graphs based on the questionnaire, which was answered by 328 working journalists, media executives, and professors to whom the sixty-four questions were read. The report also contains a list of all those interviewed and a description of the 104 media organizations for which they work. As well, there is a background section

on the media in each of the five countries and details on newspaper circulation and the number of radio and television sets. The report is available from: Latin American Journalism Program, School of Journalism and Mass Communication, Florida International University, 3000 NE 145 Street, North Miami, FL 33181-3600.

4. David H. Weaver and G. Cleveland Wilhoit, *The American Journalist* (Bloomington: Indiana University Press, 1986), 19.

12

The Electronic Media in Brazil

Joseph D. Straubhaar

Television reigns supreme in Brazil. In this nation of nearly 160 million people, 77 percent of the population watches television habitually, and the average daily household viewing time exceeds five hours, leading the country's own media observers to label Brazil "the country of television." Audiences in one survey rated television more powerful and prestigious than any other institution, surpassing multinational companies, the president, the armed forces, and the print media.

Some prominent newspapers do exist and are respected nationally, including two in São Paulo—Folha de São Paulo and O Estado de São Paulo—and two in Rio—O Globo and Jornal do Brasil. But in a country with such a huge population, the largest circulation newspaper, Folha de São Paulo, prints fewer than four hundred thousand copies per day. There are more than three hundred dailies and about seventeen hundred weeklies and biweeklies, but their total circulation comes to less than seven million, or some 4.5 percent of the nation's population. In contrast, TV Globo reaches about half Brazil's people. Said to be the fourth-largest network in the world, after the big three in the United States, TV Globo has been owned by Roberto Marinho, the wealthy owner of the O Globo newspaper and other media outlets. Several prominent families have large media holdings and dominate Brazil's media ownership. This is often true in Latin American countries.

Joseph Straubhaar traces the development of commercial Brazilian radio and television, which mirrored that of U.S. broadcast media and at times was directly assisted by them. U.S. formats and genres—rádio-novelas, telenovelas (soap operas), and shows de auditório (variety shows)—were adopted and adapted, acquiring a distinctive Brazilian flavor over the years. The theme subir na vida (to rise in life) played out on telenovelas emerges in popular desires to own a home, buy on credit, and open savings accounts.

Despite similarities in the electronic media of the two nations, however, important differences exist. In the United States, a handful of television networks traditionally have vied for the top position. In Brazil, one competitor has long dominated both the entertainment and news arenas:

TV Globo. Some observers attribute this success in part to TV Globo's close relationships with a succession of governments, both military and civilian. And Brazil's consumer-oriented media play to a far more stratified audience. Wealth and power are concentrated in the hands of a small elite. As Straubhaar points out, increasing audience segmentation brought about by new television technologies may widen this gulf.

Straubhaar is director of the Communications Research Center at Brigham Young University's Department of Communications, having taken a leave from his position as professor in Michigan State University's Department of Telecommunications. He earned his Ph.D. in international communication from Tufts University's School of Law and Diplomacy and formerly worked as a foreign service officer and research analyst for the U.S. Information Agency. He has published extensively on television and politics in Brazil and Latin America, new video technologies in the Third World, television flows between countries, and privatization of telephone systems in the Third World. His work includes "The Decline of American Influence on Brazilian Television" (1984), "Television and Video in the Transition from Military to Civilian Rule in Brazil" (1989), and "The Brazilian Case: Influencing the Voters" (1993).

The United States of Brazil occupies most of the eastern coast of South America. Close to 160 million people live in Brazil, more than one-third of the total population of Latin America. The majority of the population resides along the Atlantic Coast and in the south of the country. Geographical barriers to broadcasting have been overcome for most regions, and commercial radio stations have proliferated to cover most small towns. Television has been extended via the EMBRATEL (Empresa Brasileira de Telecomunicacões, or Brazilian Telecommunications Company, a government telecommunications monopoly) microwave and satellite system to most of the population. Even most rural dwellers in the more populous south are covered by both commercial radio and television. Nevertheless, a significant minority of Brazil's population is still involved in subsistence or small-scale agriculture. Particularly in the west and north or Amazon regions, the extensive distances to be covered and the low attractiveness of the population as an advertising market have restricted the extension of commercial broadcasting. So, in these areas, government radio is considerably more important than in the rest of the nation.

Even more significant in shaping the development of Brazil's electronic media is the fact that the economy has been industrializing and the population has been rapidly shifting to the major cities: São Paulo has an estimated sixteen million people, Rio de Janeiro seven million, and seven other cities have more than one million each. From 1940 to 1990 the population shifted from 70 percent rural to 75 percent urban (including "urban" residents in small towns). This change is important for electronic media, as almost all urban households have radio and an estimated 85 percent to 90 percent have television. In contrast, probably only one-third of rural residents has television, although most now watch it fairly regularly in public places. According to estimates based on 1991 census data, 80 percent of households have television sets. Most rural people have radios.

Income is highly stratified. According to World Bank data on forty-six nations, Brazil has among the world's highest concentration of income in the upper classes. The wealthiest 10 percent held 48 percent of national income in 1985, up from 40 percent in 1960. While the Brazilian economy as a whole grew 385 percent from 1940 to 1987, the actual value of a minimum salary (currently $60 to $70 per month) declined by 64 percent. In 1988, 53 percent of the work force earned less than a total of two minimum salaries.[1] Regional differences are strong in income distribution as well: the average salary in the industrialized southeast (including Rio de Janeiro and São Paulo) was more than twice that of the more rural, less industrialized northeast (including Salvador and Recife).[2]

This concentration of income by class and region is thought by various experts interviewed by the author to have increased in the 1980s and 1990s, which seems to have greatly limited the impact of new technologies. Income concentration has even restricted the spread of television into rural areas, although television viewing (beyond set ownership) is widely diffused in rural areas due to patterns of collective viewing in friends' homes and in public places. In the 1980s and 1990s the continued concentration of income and stagnation in the economy also shifted advertising revenue from television and radio toward more targeted print media.

According to the Instituto Brasileiro de Geografia e Estatística (Brazilian Institute of Geography and Statistics, or IBGE), at least 80 percent of all adults are literate, but studies of functional literacy tend to lower that estimate to around 60 percent. Illiteracy is less of a problem in Brazil than in some other Latin American countries, but it tends to emphasize the broadcast media as the true mass media. Perhaps more than literacy per se, poverty excludes many people from access to print media, which cost more as a proportion of the average salary than in most developed countries. Poverty excludes fewer from access to broadcast media because there is extensive group viewing and listening in many rural communities and villages,[3] and because purchases of radios and television sets are extremely high consumer priorities, according to market surveys.[4]

Brazil has a diverse ethnic makeup. The major stock comes from Portuguese colonists and descendants of their black and Indian slaves, frequently mixed together, because Portuguese settlers tended to intermingle more with indigenous and slave populations than did many Spanish colonists.[5] Since the 1800s these populations have been supplemented by other Europeans, particularly Germans and Italians, and more recently by Japanese and other Asians. In certain regions, one group or another predominates, such as blacks and mulattoes in Bahia, and Germans in Santa Catarina. In broad terms, however, Brazil is a remarkably homogeneous culture, at least by Third World standards. The diverse groups share a common language and, particularly since the increasing unification of the country by broadcasting, a common notion of Brazilian culture.

While television production does incorporate some aspects of various regional cultures, most television content reflects the dominant cultures of São Paulo and especially Rio de Janeiro, the production base of TV Globo, the main national network. While many believe that an interesting popular culture is being synthesized, others are concerned about its commercialism and its repressive effects on other local cultures.[6]

Radio broadcasting began as a private, not government, initiative and took a strong commercial orientation in its early development, following the model of U.S. broadcasting. There had been a tradition in the Brazilian press for both commercial and political party-owned newspapers.[7] Party newspapers had been suppressed by several governments, including that of President Getúlio Vargas (1937–1945) and the military regimes (1964–1978). Commercial newspapers gradually gained complete ascendancy. Even after 1978, when the military government removed the ban on party-related newspapers, the only significant party paper is that of the Communist Party of Brazil (Partido Comunista do Brasil, or PCdoB). The Brazilian government historically has not invested directly in the ownership of media.[8] Since private capital took the initiative to create and build media companies in most parts of the country, the government tended to reserve its capital for other sectors in which private investment was inadequate. There was thus little tradition of party- or government-owned media for radio to follow.

Brazilian radio began with amateur, experimental clubs in the early 1920s. Commercial stations began in the late 1920s and increased in number as advertising revenue began to flow to them. Most programming was live, emphasizing news, variety programs (*shows de auditório*), and comedy. The number of broadcasters and receivers grew dramatically in the 1930s and 1940s, with recorded music and *rádionovelas* (radio serials or soap operas) becoming popular.

The minimalist approach of the Brazilian government toward media changed in the late 1930s. Earlier governments had been somewhat ambivalent about commercial radio, but President Vargas found it a useful tool for mobilizing support for his "populist" regime. Vargas encouraged the development of commercial radio and used it extensively to promote his government from 1937 to 1945.[9] After Vargas, from the 1940s to the late 1950s, commercial broadcasting was fostered by the government as it stressed a consumer economy.

Commercial radio was successful because it fit into the market economy. Radio stations were relatively cheap to start and operate, and, given the advertising market, they were profitable. As elsewhere in Latin America, small private radio stations proliferated rapidly throughout Brazil from the 1920s on, in every town large enough to support one. Some research indicates that U.S. corporations that wanted to advertise in Brazil played a direct role in promoting commercial radio.[10] The country's extensive trade and investment ties with the United States encouraged the adoption of the advertising-based approach.

Commercial radio networks also developed in the 1940s and 1950s in the pattern common to Latin America. Radio stations were associated with newspaper chains, which were owned by a few rich families. Networks developed as the commercial advantages of sharing program and news material among stations in different cities became clearer. Network growth also had a strong political motivation. Favors and patronage came more often to media owners who could provide geographically extensive, multimedia coverage to politicians.[11]

The major radio network was Diários e Emissoras Associadas. By 1938 it consisted of five stations, twelve newspapers, and one magazine in a chain, led by Assis Chateaubriand.[12] Also notable were Rádio Bandeirantes (part of the Grupo Carvalho) and Rádio Globo (linked with the newspaper *O Globo* and Roberto Marinho). Hundreds of local stations also emerged. The number of mediumwave or AM stations increased from 440 in 1956 to 1,557 in 1990, while FM stations went from zero in 1956 to 617 in 1988 and 1,215 in 1990.[13] Furthermore, most stations have developed in states with many small- and medium-sized towns not within broadcast reach of the capital cities: Pernambuco, Minas Gerais, São Paulo, and Rio Grande do Sul. Most of these stations are independent. In the major cities, network-affiliated stations such as Rádio Globo and Rádio Bandeirantes are the most popular, according to research done in 1982 by the U.S. Information Agency.

Most broadcast media in Brazil are privately owned and operated. The federal government runs an extensive shortwave broadcasting system in the Amazon region and also some other radio and television stations, as do some state and provincial governments. But these government media have much smaller audiences and less impact than private media. Radio sets, however, are available widely. As of 1987 there were about fifty-seven million of them in Brazil, or about 2.3 per household, but at least 50 percent were concentrated in the most affluent southeast region.[14] The 1980 Brazilian census showed that radios were in 79 percent of urban households and 68 percent of rural households. The reach of radio, however, extends beyond those who actually own one, as noted. Probably 95 percent or more of the populace can listen to radio.

Radio set a pattern for broadcasting in Brazil: a dominance of entertainment over education or cultural programs, advertiser-supported stations, a tendency to import a good deal of material and program ideas, and a countervailing tendency to use a great deal of Brazilian material as well. A few stations, owned by state or national governments, have a more educational, developmental, or even political focus.

Rádionovelas developed from several sources. Serialized French novels that were popular in Brazil in translation in the 1800s planted the seeds of interest in serial drama on radio.[15] *Rádionovelas* were also imported from other Latin American countries such as Cuba, Mexico, and Argentina in the 1940s and translated from Spanish into Portuguese. Particularly important were the scripts imported from Cuba, where *rádionovelas* were first developed as a Latin American form of the soap opera, sponsored by Colgate, a U.S. corporation wanting to sell soap in the region with the same advertising vehicle that had proved so successful in the United States.

Many aspects of the U.S. radio variety show were probably also copied by Brazilian programs. Live interviews, singers, show hosts, audience participation, amateur performances, and games were all used but with distinctly Brazilian cultural elements: characteristic personality types, situations and references to history, popular music, literature, and folklore.[16] As in other Latin American countries, these variety shows evolved into a distinctive format, the *show de auditório*, with a charismatic host broadcasting live in front of a studio audience. These shows were often long and went from games to music to interviews and news. Some writers on Brazilian mass culture have thought this to be one of the few formats in which traditional oral folk culture—storytelling or song challenges (*repentistas*), circus-type patter, and folk music (albeit commercialized into mass culture forms)—has been brought into mass communication media. Similarly, television has proved a good medium for the visual elements of folk culture.[17]

Radio content remains diverse. In fact, market segmentation and competition are making it more diverse in major cities. Much time is given on many stations to sports, particularly soccer, in live coverage and on talk shows. Depending on the political climate, a good deal of political discussion also takes place on radio talk and variety shows. Local talk shows are in many cases the format that best reflects local culture and issues.

Audience surveys rate radio as the most popular source of musical entertainment, but it is less preferred than television or newspapers as a source of news.[18] Still, studies of the 1989 presidential elections showed that radio news and radio commentators were an important source of information for people, particularly for the less and middle-level educated (see Table 1).[19]

Table 1. 1989 Brazilian Presidential Election Sources of Information by Respondents' Level of Education

	Primary *(percent)*	Middle *(percent)*	Secondary *(percent)*	University *(percent)*
Talking with friends, family	41	43	40	34
Political ads on radio/TV	30	35	39	42
Talking to colleagues	23	29	33	30
Television news	21	20	19	23
Candidates' TV debates	13	28	41	55
News in newspapers	8	17	22	42
Seeing candidates in rallies	12	18	18	14
Radio news	12	11	6	6
Radio commentators	4	6	6	4
Information by the Church	6	5	4	0
Labor leaders	3	6	9	3
Neighborhood associations	4	10	7	3
Poll results	4	6	7	6

Source: Joseph Straubhaar, Organ Olsen, and Maria Cavaliari Nunes, "The Brazilian Case: Influencing the Voters," in *Television, Politics, and the Transition to Democracy in Latin America*, ed. Thomas E. Skidmore (Washington, DC: Woodrow Wilson Center; Baltimore: Johns Hopkins University Press, 1993), 118–36.

The results in Table 1 show that in Brazilians' selection of information sources for the 1989 presidential campaign, lower-class, less-educated respondents relied more on family and friends and on radio. They relied less on political advertising (on radio and television), and much less on the television debates and newspapers.

As in the United States, radio in Brazil has moved toward fairly extensive segmentation of formats and audiences in the 1980s and 1990s. AM and FM have developed differently. AM is still more widely available in both transmitters and receivers, particularly in rural areas, smaller towns, and lower-class suburbs of cities. Even within cities, AM remains focused on formats and musical genres that appeal primarily to lower-class audiences, which include a large number of recent migrants from rural areas. Genres include country music, Brazilian popular music, sports, and talk. AM talk shows and a slowly increasing number of all-news stations do cross class boundaries, particularly during commuting hours.

FM tends to be primarily urban, although it is expanding into smaller towns. The number of FM stations grew rapidly in the 1980s and 1990s. As in the United States, FM stations have become even more segmented, primarily in musical format or genre. Pop, jazz, and classical formats are mostly on FM stations. While FM stations play more imported music, particularly pop, rock, jazz, and classical, Brazilian popular music is apparently more popular, even on FM, than imported music. A survey of playlists on São Paulo FM stations in 1989 showed that seven of the ten most widely played songs in that year were Brazilian, including the top four.[20]

One result of radio competition has been increasing audience segmentation. Particularly in larger cities, the twenty or thirty radio stations serve specialized audiences: all-news formats, talk and sports, classical music, light rock, heavy rock, Brazilian rock, Brazilian pop, and Brazilian samba/jazz. Aside from the continuing popularity of Brazilian rock, pop, and samba, the evolution of formats strongly resembles that of U.S. radio markets.

In contrast to the development of radio, television has grown more systematically. The development of Brazilian television may be divided into:

- An elitist phase (1950–1964), when it was limited to the upper and upper-middle classes in cities.
- A populist phase (1964–1975), when the audience expanded rapidly and programming became more popularly oriented.
- A technological development phase (1975–1985), when broadcasting expanded via microwave and satellite and the number of networks increased.
- A transition and international expansion phase (1985–1990), when civilian government returned and TV Globo and other powerful entities began to export to the world.[21] Since 1990 a fifth phase seems to be characterized by the advent of cable, Direct Broadcast Satellite (DBS)

and Satellite Master Antenna TV (SMATV), and further segmentation of the audience.[22]

Brazilian television broadcasting began on September 18, 1950. Assis Chateaubriand of Diários e Emissoras Associadas opened a commercial station in São Paulo—the beginning of the TV Tupi network, which was the largest network for some time, covering twenty-three cities by 1976. But TV Rio, TV Excelsior, and TV Globo were more innovative in programming and network organization.[23] Of these latter two, TV Excelsior's parent group was crippled by economic regulations put forward by the post-1964 revolutionary governments, and Excelsior went bankrupt. TV Rio prospered for a while, but most of its staff was raided by TV Globo, which developed a favorable relationship with the government and expanded to cover virtually all urban areas of the country.[24]

TV Tupi lost organizational coherence after founder Chateaubriand died in 1966. The network went bankrupt in 1980. Its licenses were broken into two groups and given to TV Manchete, which was linked with the weekly magazine *Manchete*, and to TVS, owned by Sílvio Santos, a variety show host who had worked on Globo and other stations. TV Bandeirantes had also acquired more stations to become a major network.

By 1992, four national commercial networks competed over most of Brazil. TV Globo (seventy-nine stations) was the largest, followed by SBT/TVS (forty-six stations), TV Manchete (thirty-six stations), and TV Bandeirantes (thirty stations). Two regional networks also were in operation: Rede Brasil Sul in the south, which carried TV Globo programming but supplied local news and other shows; and TV Record, which consisted of loosely affiliated independent stations in Rio and São Paulo and a few other cities in the heavily populated southeast. Some educational television stations have developed. The most productive is TV Cultura, run by the Padre Anchieta Foundation and financially supported by the state of São Paulo.

TV Globo has dominated in audience size and development of programming. In its heyday as a quasi-monopoly (1968–1985), it had a 60-to-70 percent share of viewers in the major cities at any given time, and sometimes more than 90 percent. TV Globo was accused during this period of being the government's mouthpiece. It still dominates in audience size but has had more competition in the 1980s and 1990s. In 1991 it drew an average 66 percent of the nationwide audience. SBT/TVS had 18 percent, TV Manchete 7 percent, TV Bandeirantes 5 percent, and all others (TV Record, public television, and independent stations) 4 percent.[25]

Other networks have had difficulty competing with TV Globo for big general audiences. Efforts by several—first TV Tupi, then TV Bandeirantes and TV Manchete—failed. So the oligopolistic, imitative competition among commercial networks that occurred in the United States never took place in Brazil. Instead, other television networks pursued smaller, more specific audience segments largely defined by social class. The developing segmentation by social class of the main television networks and other media is shown in Table 2.

SBS (owned by Sílvio Santos) targeted a lower-middle-class, working-class, and poor audience, which gave it a consistent second place in ratings in most of the 1980s and early 1990s. Advertisers, however, were not always attracted to that audience.[26] Initially, TV Manchete targeted a more elite audience but found it too small for adequate advertising.[27] TV Bandeirantes tended to emphasize news, public affairs, and sports.

Table 2. Patterns of Brazilian Media Use by Social Class

Social Class	TV Networks	Radio	Print Media
Elite (5–10 percent)	Manchete, Globo	FM music	Elite papers, News magazines
Middle (15–20 percent)	Globo	FM music, talk	Elite papers, News magazines
Working Class (10–15 percent)	Globo, SBT	FM music, AM music, talk	Popular newspapers
Poor (50–60 percent)	Globo, SBT	AM music, talk	
Marginal (10 percent)		AM music, talk	

Source: Luiz G. Duarte, Joseph Straubhaar, and James Stephens, "Audiences, Policy and 'Cable' Technology," International Communication Association, Miami, 1992

Brazil's military governments (1964–1985) were far more active and interventionist in media than the civilian governments. Military governments financed microwave, satellite, and other television network infrastructure. They favored certain networks, particularly TV Globo, in placing advertising, which was crucial, since government corporations, banks, trading companies, mines, steel mills, and the like constituted nearly half the gross national product for two decades. The state was the main advertiser.

Television networks formed since 1964 had a close relationship with government officials, communicating their messages in informal and sometimes subtle ways. TV Globo has often been said to be favorable to the government in power. It was very supportive of the first two postmilitary civilian governments, those of José Sarney and Fernando Collor. In fact, many scholars attributed Collor's 1989 election victory in large part to TV Globo's support,[28] although others felt that its support was but one factor among several.[29]

In 1984, TV Globo initially supported the military government against a campaign for direct election of a civilian government, while other media—including other television networks, many radio stations, and most major newspapers—supported the campaign. Perceiving that it might literally lose its audience to the competition, TV Globo also switched sides and supported transition to a civilian regime, which came about. This immediately reduced political censorship and pressure on broadcasters, although some censorship on moral issues remained.[30] The role of television, particularly TV Globo, as the regime's banner carrier was also diluted by the creation and effective growth of new networks. Increased television competition was characterized by market segmentation, in which most other networks positioned themselves around the programming strengths of the dominant TV Globo.[31]

As in many other Latin American countries, television stations in Brazil have often been started or bought out by radio station owners, particularly by those who have had national or regional networks. Because of this and because of the lack of a Hollywood-type film industry, television tended to draw on radio for mass-culture formats, personnel, and traditions.

As with radio, the first decade of Brazilian television in the 1950s was essentially live. Most program genres and even a number of programs were brought over from radio. Television took most of radio's best talent: the top writers, actors, and directors for *telenovelas* as well as comedians, musicians, and dramatic scriptwriters.[32] The television audience was mostly the wealthier upper and middle classes in a few major cities.

By the mid-1960s the situation had changed. The country's economy had grown rapidly, which led to a consumer economy. Television's audience embraced the middle and lower-middle classes in many cities. The number of television sets grew apace: 760,000 in 1960, 6.7 million in 1970, 19.6 million in 1977, and 33 million in 1990.[33] This mass audience attracted advertising.

Several stations, particularly TV Rio, TV Excelsior, and TV Globo, responded to this commercial opportunity by aiming programming at a mass audience. They began to create or import programs to sell soap, tobacco products, textiles, foodstuffs, and appliances.[34] Advertising for elite products began to shift to magazines and a few television stations such as TV Bandeirantes and later TV Manchete, which continued to target the upper-class audience.

This trend accelerated in the 1980s and 1990s, when advertising began to shift visibly from television to newspapers and magazines, as the decade-long recession of the 1980s eroded consumption among the working class and poor. Television still retained considerable advertising, however, especially for products still purchased by the lower classes, such as soap, soft drinks, beer, small radios, watches, and clothes.[35] The mass market and mass audience led to a major shift in domestic programming, with the focus on mass-audience genres such as *telenovelas, shows de auditório*, game shows, popular music, and comedy. All of these had been present during the 1950s, but the shift in emphasis was clear.

Introduced in 1952, *telenovelas* became popular quickly. TV Excelsior in São Paulo and TV Globo in Rio made these soap operas more sophisticated in the 1960s, when their average broadcast period was increased to about nine months. The shows were aired regularly (usually daily) in prime viewing time, the plots were increasingly nationalized, and sophistication was added by bringing in writers, actors, and directors from theater and cinema. A key turning point was the 1968 *telenovela, Beto Rockefeller*, which was well produced and reflected a singular Brazilian personality, the Rio bon vivant, or *boa vida*. *Telenovelas* increasingly drew on popular novels, such as those by Jorge Amado. The dominant themes were upward mobility and consumer consumption. Thus, by the 1970s, *telenovelas* were the most popular programs and dominated prime time on the major networks, TV Globo and TV Tupi. TV Globo, in particular, began to attract major writers and actors from film and theater to work on *telenovelas*.[36]

Throughout most of this period, TV Globo and the other networks and major independent stations produced virtually all of their own programming (except for what was imported). For example, TV Globo produced twelve to fourteen hours of programming per day. Brazil did not have independent production companies such as those that supply programs to television broadcasters in the United States, Great Britain, or even Egypt and India. At TV Globo, the production values in *telenovelas* became high enough to rival programs imported from the United States or Europe. Brazilian *telenovelas* are good enough, as commercial television entertainment, to be exported throughout Latin America and even recently into Europe and Africa.[37]

In the 1980s other networks attempted to break into *telenovela* production to compete with TV Globo. Neither SBT nor TV Bandeirantes had much commercial success, but TV Manchete achieved fairly high ratings for an ecology-oriented serial, *Pantanal*, set in Brazil's western subtropics. SBT resorted to importing *telenovelas* from Mexico instead of producing them. TV Globo had also begun coproduction of *telenovelas* with international partners to lower costs and reach other markets. Building upon the *telenovela* industry, TV Globo also successfully created a few series consisting of self-contained one-hour episodes with a continuing cast and theme, patterned after series exported by the United States. The contents are adapted to Brazil, however: a crime reporter focuses on abuses of *favela* or slum dwellers, truck drivers traverse the country's roads and encounter local characters, a newly separated woman tries to be independent in Rio. TV Globo also successfully exported these series, particularly the one about the unmarried woman, which was shown on Spanish International Television in the United States as *Malu Mujer*.

Another major genre of the 1960s was the *show de auditório*, also adapted to television from radio. The *shows de auditório* were extremely popular with the lower-middle and lower classes and drew them to television viewing.[38] They featured entertainment that was *popularesco* (vulgarized or extreme versions of popular culture). Some topics were scandalous by the previous middle-class standards of television and, for a combination of moral and political reasons, the military government of the early 1970s forced many *shows de auditório* off the air. After the relaxation of censorship in the late 1970s, the genre expanded again, particularly on the new network of Sílvio Santos, who had gained fame and wealth as a *show de auditório* host. His network appeals primarily to the lower-class audience and draws enough advertisers to be very profitable.[39]

Music programs were either general or centered around one type of music, such as current Brazilian pop or more traditional *bossa nova*. Comedy programs were sometimes dominated by a single ensemble such as *Os Trapalhões* (The clodhoppers) or by individuals such as Chico Anisio's *Chico City* or Jô Soares's *Viva o Gordo* (Viva fatso). Nearly all of TV Globo's major music and comedy programs were quite popular in prime time.

Although Brazilian television is clearly entertainment oriented, certain kinds of news and information programs have been widely liked and have prospered. The evening news on TV Globo, *Jornal Nacional*, is always popular, even among working-class viewers.[40] News interviews have been popular as well, particularly among the upper-middle class. Relaxed censorship since 1978 permitted more open discussion of public issues, but self-censorship persisted until the civilian regime of 1985 and even into the 1990s. News is still often shaped to fit political interests. For instance, TV Globo news was charged with editing its coverage of the final debate of the 1989 presidential campaign to favor Collor.[41]

A study of prime-time network news (on Globo, Manchete, SBT, and Bandeirantes) for February 1992 showed that stories were dominated by the federal government (28 percent), economics (20 percent), sports/leisure (19 percent), violence (17 percent), police (16 percent), courts (12 percent), companies (12 percent), and health (12 percent). Other subjects covered were the United States (10 percent), state governments (10 percent), Europe (10 percent), environment (10 percent), inflation (9 percent), recession (8 percent), Latin America (7 percent), foreign policy (6 percent), fraud (6 percent), science and technology (6 percent), and armed forces (6 percent). Critics noted that crucial topics concerning children (3 percent), women (2 percent), Indians (1 percent), and blacks (0.4 percent) were underrepresented on network news.[42]

Among other kinds of programming, educational programs have been the major fare of the state and federally owned television stations. The most widely seen educational programs, however, are jointly produced by the Padre Anchieta Foundation and TV Globo: *Curso Primeiro Grau* (Primary course) and *Curso Segundo Grau* (Secondary course). More recently these programs are produced solely by the Roberto Marinho Foundation, controlled by Globo's owner.[43]

The new channels vary considerably in how much foreign, particularly American, programming they bring in. While TVA and GloboSat have similar lineups, TVA's material is almost entirely imported in the original languages. That may well limit its appeal over time. In contrast, GloboSat is drawing on TV Globo's resources to fill about 25 percent of its time with national material and to dub or subtitle 90 percent of the programming. The latter has its own correspondents and resources in journalism, a film library of ten thousand dubbed titles, and other resources to fill its channels.[44]

Advertising has heavily influenced the programming of commercial television. TV Globo augmented its advertising in the 1980s by "merchandising," especially in *telenovelas*. Specific products were shown or mentioned in dialogue on programs in return for a fee. From 1983 on, for example, a number of *telenovelas* on TV Globo carried propaganda for Banco Itaú. In the *telenovela Tieta* in 1989–90, a modern branch of the bank was frequently shown in the middle of a small, traditional northeastern town. The branch opening was shown, and characters later did business there and used its credit cards and other banking services. In a 1990 *telenovela* called *Top Model*, a fashion show featured the real-life designer lines of a company partially owned by the daughter-in-law of Roberto Marinho, owner of TV Globo.[45]

TV Globo has also used its various media branches to promote each other's products. *Telenovela* soundtracks are released as records, and key songs are promoted on radio, so all three media reinforce each other. In particular, television and radio help sell the records, and hearing the songs tends to keep the audience thinking of the television program.

Brazil has been characterized in its own media as the "country of television" because the television audience is so large. Critics note that while a large majority of people can afford a television set or get communal access to one, many, if not most, Brazilians are too poor to have other leisure options. That is why they watch so much television. In a 1983 survey by the newspaper *Folha de São Paulo* in São Paulo, 24 percent of the respondents said that they watched television because it is "the cheapest form of entertainment," and 17 percent because they "lacked other leisure options."[46] In 1990 there were an estimated thirty-six million television sets and sixty million radio sets for Brazil's population of 157.9 million.[47]

A 1992 study by the market research firm Marplan noted that in the Brazilian national audience, 77 percent "habitually" or regularly watch television, 62 percent listen to radio, and 51 percent each read newspapers and magazines (see Table 3).[48] These overlapping numbers are slightly lower in metropolitan São Paulo, which includes a large number of poor people, and slightly higher in the rest of the state of São Paulo, which is actually wealthier in terms of distributed income than metropolitan São Paulo.

Table 3. Penetration of Mass Media in Brazilian Households

	Magazines (percent)	*Television (percent)*	*Newspapers (percent)*	*Radio (percent)*
Brazil	51	77	51	62
Metro São Paulo	47	74	42	59
State of São Paulo	65	83	63	68

Source: Nelson Blecher, "Leitura de jornal cresce no interior de SP," *Folha de São Paulo*, January 1992.

Both radio and television transmitters and receivers are concentrated in the more affluent south and southeast of Brazil. The southeast had 40 percent of the radio transmitters; 81 percent of households there had radios as of 1990–91. Radio penetration is even higher in the south (84 percent), which is somewhat more affluent overall, but lower in the center-west (68 percent), northeast (64 percent), and north/Amazon (58 percent).[49] Regional growth patterns have been uneven, and the economic growth in the south of Brazil and the interior of the state of São Paulo have been exceptionally high. So while penetration into other rural and small-town areas is likely to have grown, it is unlikely to have matched the growth in the interior of the state of São Paulo, as noted in Table 4.

Table 4. Penetration of Mass Media in Households in the State of São Paulo Interior

	Magazines (percent)	Television (percent)	Newspapers (percent)	Radio (percent)
1985	42	75	47	56
1991	65	83	63	68

Source: Nelson Blecher, "Leitura de jornal cresce no interior de SP," *Folha de São Paulo*, January 1992.

Brazilians watch a lot of television. Average household daily viewing is generally more than 5 hours. A study of young people in São Paulo found that sixth-graders watched 5 hours per day and tenth-graders 3 hours. Sixth-graders also listened to 2.1 hours of radio and tenth-graders 2.4, indicating that radio is relatively more important for adolescents than for younger children, who also watched television more with their parents. On television, young people preferred comedies, movies, rock music, *telenovelas,* and action/adventure programs. On radio, they preferred rock and international music, although girls also preferred more Brazilian pop.[50]

TV Globo has dominated television audiences. This is especially true on weekdays, when a May 1990 São Paulo survey showed that TV Globo had a 70 percent share of the audience, TV Manchete 12 percent, SBT 7 percent, and others 5 percent. The weekend audience is slightly different. TV Globo had 53 percent on Saturdays, while SBT (emphasizing variety shows) and TV Bandeirantes (emphasizing sports and talk) each had 9 percent and TV Manchete 8 percent. On Sundays, TV Globo had 43 percent, SBT 26 percent (revealing a higher Sunday audience for variety shows), TV Bandeirantes 9 percent, and TV Manchete 4 percent.[51]

TV Globo's hold is being challenged, however. It is interesting to notice that in the same survey, two non-Globo programs achieved a higher spontaneous recall than any Globo program: the SBT variety show *Programa Sílvio Santos* (53 percent recall) and the TV Manchete *telenovela Pantanal* (51 percent), compared to the TV Globo news program *Jornal Nacional* (37 percent).

TV Globo also has dominated television news audiences. In 1987, 79 percent of the São Paulo audience watched news on TV Globo, while 30 percent watched news on TV Manchete, 25 percent SBT/TVS, 15 percent TV Bandeirantes, 12 percent TV Record, 7 percent TV Cultura, and 4 percent TV Gazeta.[52] A 1982 study found that, in four major cities, the evening news on TV Globo was the only common information source among those interviewed, other media being more localized.[53] Other networks have made inroads since then, but in 1987 the Globo evening news was still preferred by 84 percent of the national audience, in part because it is considered easy to understand by 90 percent.[54]

The traditional electronic media are being affected by newer technologies. The first new video technology to diffuse widely in Brazil was the home videocassette recorder (VCR). The proportion of homes with VCRs increased from less than 1 percent in 1980 to about 8 percent in 1989.[55] That growth was slower than in many other Latin American countries but has accelerated in recent years. The number of video rental outlets increased from 200 in 1982 to 4,669 in 1989.[56] Nearly all videos available in rental catalogs surveyed by the author were from the United States. A survey of rental stores to establish the ten most widely rented videotapes of 1989 showed that all ten were from the United States: three adventure films, three police dramas, three comedies, and one drama.[57]

Satellite television has been quite effective. Stations first used Intelsat and then the first and now the second generation of BrasilSat to reach into rural areas and small towns of the interior and Amazonian north. In the 1980s thousands of small towns purchased satellite dishes and low-power repeaters. Many times the systems were bought by local mayors or political candidates as public works. In one month of the 1990 local and state political campaign season, six hundred such systems, all bought by local politicians, were installed in just one state, Bahia.[58]

Four main technological approaches have arisen so far: advertising-supported UHF, over-the-air pay-television systems, cable television, and DBS (direct-broadcast satellite) systems. These systems are competing with conventional VHF television and with each other in programming and technological platforms.

A number of UHF licenses have been issued, and several UHF television operations have entered the market. The principal one is a Brazilian adaptation of MTV (Music TV), owned by the Editora Abril publishing group. It uses a great deal of programming from U.S. MTV, with local announcers, local ads, and some Brazilian music videos[59] (Table 5). So far MTV is the only UHF channel to gain even a small share of the audience. There is one major scrambled UHF/SHF/MMDS (multichannel multipoint distribution system) operation: TVA. It is a combination of earlier separate offerings by the TVA Group, Editora Abril, and the Machline industrial group. In 1992 it offered five channels (films, CNN, ESPN, a superstation-type channel, and TNT) at about $25 per month. Its technological approach and marketing are targeted at individual upper-middle-class households in major cities, probably about 1.5 million potential users.[60] In contrast, GloboSat is a DBS and SMATV satellite channel aimed at some rural viewers and condominium owners in major cities, probably about five hundred thousand potential users.[61] Its programming is similar to TVA's, with four channels (films, news, sports, shows) for about $25 to $30 per month (see Table 5). Cable television development had been limited by uncertain government regulation, but in 1995 the government was simplifying regulation and liberalizing rules on foreign ownership, which seemed likely to increase cable development in major cities. Competing "overbuild" systems were already being built in affluent neighborhoods in São Paulo in 1995.

Table 5. Television Hours Added by New Channels in Brazil

Company/ Channel	Program	Daily hours	Nationality
Pay-TV			
TVA	Film	24	USA (99 percent), European (1 percent)
	News (CNN)	24	USA
	Sports (ESPN)	24	USA
	Superchannel	18	USA (99 percent), Italian (1 percent)
	Classics (TNT)	24	USA
Total		**114**	
GloboSat	Film (Telecine)	24	USA (99 percent), European (1 percent)
	News (GNT)	16	USA/Europe (99 percent), Brazil
	Sports (Top Sports)	16	USA & Europe (99 percent), Brazil
	Shows (Multishow)	18	German, Japanese, French
Total		**74**	
PluralSat		12	German, French
Open Channels			
MTV-Abril		24	USA (50 percent), Brazilian (50 percent)
Jovem Pan		16	Mainly foreign
Grand Total		**240**	

Source: Abril, GloboSat, and Jovem Pan, January 1992, compiled by Luiz G. Duarte, 1992.

The general trend seems to be toward more segmentation. Some of the main television networks are already segmenting by social class. New television systems seem to be trying to segment by interest within the upper and upper-middle classes. As Duarte observed:

> Several different factors are leading Brazilian television toward target marketing. First, among the new entrants in the industry are old communication conglomerates, barred from television by the government, due to their traditional opposition standpoint. These groups have not only contributed with significant new capital but have used their lobbying power to accelerate and concentrate a political basis for the regulation of new television services. . . .
>
> Second, the TV production technology available today in the international market has evolved to provide quality video at cheaper costs. The technology made it easier for Brazilian companies to produce their own programming or to buy it from local independent producers, which turns the fulfillment of more channels into a feasible and less expensive task. . . . Many of the American segmented (cable) channels have invested in the creation of new programming and networks, which presently provide the bulk of the schedule for the new Brazilian channels that await the amortization of the initial investments to increase or start national production.
>
> Third, and most important, Brazilian advertisers have grown more interested in narrowing the target of commercials as the percentage of the population with significant acquisitive power has been consistently reduced in the last years due to the severe economic recession in the country.[62]

New video technologies are arriving in Brazil but real questions exist as to their audiences. One respected analyst, Homero Icaza Sanchez, former research director for TV Globo, expects the segmented channels to draw a third of the audience from conventional broadcast television within ten years.[63] A more modest industry estimate is that most of the two million prospective viewers of STV/DBS will be upper class, raising the prospect that new technologies will isolate elites from the rest of the country in access to information.[64] Until the 1990s, television had been a common source of information for all and a force for national identity.

Income and social class limit the penetration of new technologies. As of 1992, even broadcast television (UHF or VHF) program or format segmentation was limited because only 45 percent of Brazilian television households had a second television.[65] With only one set, viewers tend to tune to general audience channels, not those segmented by age, interests, and so on. This is a limit on Brazil's MTV audience, for instance. Younger people may wish to watch MTV but they may not control family viewing decisions. Furthermore, there is always the question of what people choose to watch. A sample week in 1991 in São Paulo showed that of the 45 percent of viewers with more than one set, the main set accounted for an average of 78 percent of household viewing hours. Furthermore, two or more sets were turned on simultaneously only 13 percent of the time.[66] This indicates that even households that could choose to watch potentially segmented channels on different sets seldom do so.

Both television and radio are thought to have considerable impact on Brazilian audiences. In a 1987 survey in São Paulo, television was rated both "more powerful" and "more prestigious" than any other institution. Radio was rated second most prestigious and seventh most powerful (behind multinational companies, banks, the president and ministers, the print press, and the armed forces), while the print press was tied for fourth most powerful and third most prestigious.[67]

Three major anthropological studies have found evidence of impacts of long-term viewing on values such as male-female roles, social mobility goals, social permissiveness, views of what it is to be Brazilian, and social class identity (see Table 6).[68] Consumption and mobility goals seem to be among the most affected.

> In addition to spurring savings accounts and installment purchases, Brazilian TV has honed viewers' wishes to own a home—and to be upwardly mobile. We have seen that *subir na vida*, "to rise in life," is one of the main *telenovela* themes, and home ownership is a constantly expressed goal of lower-middle-class *novela* characters. . . . With its fashionable society women and powdered milk ads, Brazilian TV promotes early weaning and bottle feeding. Both our main TV variables correlated negatively with breastfeeding. . . . The public health effect is likely to be negative.[69]

Table 6. Effects of Long-term Viewing and Correlates of Current Viewing in Brazil

Brazilians with long-time home exposure are more likely to:	*Brazilian current heavy viewers are more likely to:*
Be skin-color conscious • Say they have a favorite performer of their own skin color	Be skin-color conscious • Say they have a favorite performer of their own skin color
Be liberal • Have liberal social issue views • Do less sexist job stereotyping • Use informal "you" terms • Let their children address them informally	Be liberal • Have liberal social issue views • Do less sexist job stereotyping • Use informal "you" terms • Let their children address them informally
Consume • Have many household possessions • Give birthday gifts • Give and receive presents	Consume • Have household possessions • Give Christmas gifts

Value (inter)national holidays and the external world • Say they like Carnival • Say they value what you learn in the street	Have savings accounts
Use print media	Read • Use print media generally • Read widely
Devalue work • Say they would stop working if they won the lottery • Say kids should wait to start working until they are older	Devalue work • Say they would stop working if they won the lottery • Say kids should wait to start working until they are older
Focus on the nuclear family of procreation • Value spouse over parents	Consider their siblings important Have many visitors
Perceive danger • Score high on the danger index • Consider their town dangerous	Worry about safety • Have a high fear-danger index • Say the community needs more police
	Admit hitting someone Say that TV has changed their life
Less exposed Brazilians are likely to:	*Light-viewer Brazilians are more likely to:*
Trust • Trust government • Score high on the trust index	Consider TV addictive
Value local festivals	Trust members of their personal network
Value school learning	Say they consider family important
Use corporal punishment	Say they value "what one learns in the family"
Fear for their children	Say they consider marriage important
Focus on the family of orientation and the extended family • Value parents over spouse • Value siblings	

Source: Conrad P. Kottak, *Prime-Time Society: An Anthropological Analysis of Television and Culture* (Belmont, CA: Wadsworth, 1990), 186–87.

Although the importation of programming into Brazil has led some to fear cross-cultural impacts of U.S. and other programs, two anthropological studies found that the most impact seemed to come from domestic programming, particularly *telenovelas*.[70] It also seemed clear from these studies and a 1982 survey by the author that social class was the primary factor in people's choice of programs (see Table 7). Furthermore, the ethnographies indicate that class is the most crucial variable in how viewers interpreted what they saw, but that even lower-class viewers were fairly independent in their interpretations.[71]

Table 7. São Paulo Audience Preference for Television Genres, by Education

Genres	No schooling (percent) (n=9)	Primary (percent) (n=37)	Secondary (percent) (n=35)	University (percent) (n=27)
U.S. Programs				
Miniseries	22	40	46	41
Series	22	37	43	48
Rock music	20*	32*	49*	58*
International programs				
Movies	30*	68*	60*	84*
Mexican comedies	22*	18*	17*	4*
Cartoons	56	54	62	39
Japanese heroes	22*	22*	14*	4*
Brazilian programs				
Telenovela	80	66	63	56
Miniseries	44	38	60	59
Comedies	78	66	66	48
Variety	44***	66***	34***	27***
Pop music	80*	78*	91*	77*
Rock music	40*	30*	46*	62*
News	20***	84***	89***	93***
Debates	40*	54*	69*	85*
Films	56**	50**	71**	73**
Political ads	33**	40**	71**	73**
Sports	11**	57**	83**	60**

Source: Joseph Straubhaar, "The Development of the *Telenovela* as the Paramount Form of Popular Culture in Brazil," *Studies in Latin American Popular Culture* 1 (1982): 138–50.
Statistical significance: * indicates P<.05, **P<.01, ***P<.001.

Brazilian radio and television are well established as major cultural industries in economic terms. Fears of a direct foreign takeover of cultural industries leading to both economic and cultural dependence have been muted since the 1960s. Extensive mass culture programming is produced by Brazilian television, and Brazilian music continues to be prominent on radio. Some Brazilian scholars see much of this programming as innovative and as reflective of the national culture, although many Brazilian critics see national programming as far too imitative of world pop culture, particularly that from the United States.[72]

The programming, including news, is clearly commercial, and all of the criticisms of commercial, industrialized culture can be addressed to it. Furthermore, some critics accuse Brazilian mass media of furthering economic and cultural dependence through integration of Brazilian consumers into the world economy, particularly through their prominent advertising of American, Japanese, and other consumer goods.[73]

Because a thriving industry with a largely nationalized content exists, the critical question about Brazilian radio and television as mass culture concerns the character of "national" programs. The major issues are effects of formats and techniques borrowed from abroad, the continuing influence of multinational advertisers, and, until recently, control of content by the government. In their close cooperation with the government through the mid-1980s, industry owners produced programs depicting Brazil as picturesque, dynamic, and developing. The chief vehicles for this were *telenovelas*, described in 1984 as "shot through with materialism, empty of political content and laced unfailingly with forward-looking optimism."[74] A good deal more material about Brazil's problems appears on television and radio now, even in *telenovelas*, but television and radio are still powerful collaborators in imagemaking for governments and political candidates.

Concern can also be raised about foreign programs flowing into Brazil via the new technologies (VCRs, STV, cable, and DBS). So far their audiences seem limited to the upper-middle and upper classes. That raises a new concern: Will the new television technologies further elevate an elite population that has been elevated in almost everything but television already? Radio is more local and more difficult to characterize as a medium. It is under considerable influence and control by advertisers and government. Through pop music, it conveys both foreign cultures and Brazil's own national identity.

For now, in Brazil's world of mass communication, television is king, and radio is ubiquitous and powerful. Although a few noted newspapers exist, the press is not nearly as pervasive as either radio or television; that hierarchy will not change. In the future, the electronic media will likely remain pervasive and powerful. New interactive media will grow as the information superhighway reaches Brazil and spreads from city to city. Although the influence of the mass media of other nations, especially the United States, will continue to be readily apparent, the overall media system of Brazil will continue to have its unique character.

Notes

1. "O 'bolo' cresceu mas renda não foi distribuida," *Folha de São Paulo*, October 12, 1989.
2. "Os números do IBGE (Census)," *Mercado Global* (January 1990), 6–9.
3. C. P. Kottak, *Prime-Time Society: An Anthropological Analysis of Television and Culture* (Belmont, CA: Wadsworth, 1990).
4. "60 anos de radio," *Propaganda* (January 1983): 1–56.
5. Gilberto Freyre, *The Masters and the Slaves* (New York: Knopf, 1964).
6. Omar Souki de Oliveira, "Mass Media, Culture, and Communication in Brazil: The Heritage of Dependency," in *Transnational Communications: Wiring the Third World*, ed. Gerald Sussman and John A. Lent (Newbury Park, CA: Sage, 1991), 200–213; Joseph D. Straubhaar, "The Decline of American Influence on Brazilian Television," *Communication Research* 11 (April 1984): 221–40.
7. Nelly de Camargo and Virgilio Pinto, *Communication Policies in Brazil* (Paris: UNESCO Press, 1975), 16.
8. Ibid., 23.
9. Sergio Caparelli, *Comunicacao de massa sem massa* (São Paulo: Cortez, 1980); Miriam Goldfeder, *Por tras das ondas da TV Globo* (Rio de Janeiro: Paz e Terra, 1980).
10. Fred Fejes, "The Growth of Multinational Advertising Agencies in Latin America," *Journal of Communication* 30, no. 4 (Autumn 1980): 36–49; James Schwoch, *The American Radio Industry and Its Latin American Activities, 1939–1990* (Chicago: University of Illinois Press, 1990).
11. Rodolpho Valentini, interview with the author, 1978, São Paulo.
12. "Dez anos apos Chateaubriand," *Visão*, April 17, 1978.
13. *Meio de comunicação* 2 (1991): 14–15; Jair Borin, "Rádios e tvs crescem com o festival de concessões," *Comunicação e sociedade* 10, no.18 (1991): 19–24.
14. Borin, "Rádios e tvs crescem com o festival de concessões."
15. Muniz Sodré, *O monopólio da fala* (Petrópolis, Brazil: Vozes, 1981).
16. Idem, *A comunicação do grotesco* (Petrópolis, Brazil: Vozes, 1972).
17. Ibid.
18. Joseph D. Straubhaar, "Media Use by the Better Educated in Four Major Brazilian Cities," Research Report R-19-82 (Washington, DC: USIA, Office of Research, November 29, 1982), 66–68.
19. Joseph D. Straubhaar, Organ Olsen, and Maria Cavaliari Nunes, "The Brazilian Case: Influencing the Voters," in *Television, Politics, and the Transition to Democracy in Latin America*, ed. Thomas E. Skidmore (Washington, DC: Woodrow Wilson Center-Johns Hopkins University Press, 1993).

20. José Carlos Camargo, "Lista dos mais consumidos só revela quantidade," *Folha de São Paulo,* December 30, 1990.

21. Sergio Mattos, *Um perfil da tv brasileira (40 anos de história: 1950–1990)* (Salvador, Brazil: Associação Brasileira de Agências de Propaganda, 1990).

22. Luiz Duarte, "Television Segmentation: Will Brazil Follow the American Model?" (M.A. thesis, Michigan State University, East Lansing, 1992).

23. Alcir H. da Costa, "Rio e *Excelsior*: Projetos fracassados?" in *Um país no ar* (São Paulo: Editora Brasiliense, 1986), 123–66; Joseph D. Straubhaar, "The Transformation of Cultural Dependency: The Decline of American Influence on the Brazilian Television Industry" (Ph.D. diss., Tufts University, 1981).

24. Alcir H. da Costa, "Rio e *Excelsior*: Projetos fracassados?"; Sergio Mattos, "The Brazilian Military and Television" (M.A. thesis, University of Texas, Austin, 1982); Straubhaar, "The Transformation of Cultural Dependency."

25. José Marques de Melo, "Lecture on Brazilian Television," Michigan State University, East Lansing (May 22, 1991).

26. Mattos, *Um perfil da tv brasileira*; Duarte, "Television Segmentation."

27. Mattos, *Um perfil da tv brasileira*; Duarte, "Television Segmentation."

28. Venício A. de Lima, "Television and the Brazilian Elections of 1989," in *Television, Politics, and the Transition to Democracy in Latin America,* ed. Thomas E. Skidmore (Washington, DC: Woodrow Wilson Center-Johns Hopkins University Press, 1993), 97–117.

29. Carlos Eduardo Lins da Silva, "Indústria da comunicação: Personagem principal das eleições presidenciais brasileiras de 1989," *INTERCOM - Revista Brasileira de Comunicação* 18 (1990): 121–28; José Marques de Melo, "Mass Media and Politics in Brazil: The Collor Phenomenon," in *Brazilian Communication Research Yearbook,* ed. Marques de Melo (University of São Paulo, 1992), 122–39; Straubhaar, "The Role of Television in the 1989 Brazilian Presidential Election."

30. Joseph D. Straubhaar, "Television and Video in the Transition from Military to Civilian Rule in Brazil," *Latin American Research Review* 24, no. 1 (1989): 140–54.

31. Luiz G. Duarte, Joseph D. Straubhaar, and James Stephens, "Audiences, Policy, and 'Cable' Technology," paper presented at International Communication Association, Miami, 1992.

32. "60 anos de rádio," 10–56.

33. Octavio Getino, *Impacto del video en el espacio audiovisual latinoamericano* (Lima, Peru: Instituto para América Latina, 1990).

34. Muniz Sodré, interview, *Folha de São Paulo,* July 8, 1978, *Folhetim* section.

35. Oliveira, "Mass Media, Culture, and Communication in Brazil."

36. Joseph D. Straubhaar, "The Development of the *Telenovela* as the Paramount Form of Popular Culture in Brazil," *Studies in Latin American Popular Culture* 1 (1982): 138–50.

37. José Marques de Melo, *As telenovelas da Globo: Produção e exportação* (São Paulo: Summus, 1988).

38. Sergio Miceli, *A noite da madrinha* (São Paulo: Editora Perspectiva, 1972).

39. Joseph D. Straubhaar, "Brazilian Variety Television Programs: Popular Culture, Industry, and Censorship," *Studies in Latin American Popular Culture* 2 (1983): 71–78.

40. Sarah da Via, *Televisao e consciencia de classe* (Petrópolis, Brazil: Vozes, 1977).

41. Humberto D. Souza, "A tv dio pais das maravilhas," *Imprensa* 5, no. 55 (1992): 12–18.

42. Ibid. Viewing figures for the Brazilian news audience add to more than 100 percent because respondents could indicate viewing of more than one news program.

43. Ciro Marcondes Filho, "O monopôlio da teleeducacão nas mãos da Globo," *Crítica da informação* 1, no. 2 (1983): 14.

44. Duarte, "Television Segmentation."

45. "Merchandizing," *Isto E/Senhor*, July 2, 1990.

46. Inagio Araujo, "Paulistano, um prisoneiro da televisão," *Folha de São Paulo*, 1983.

47. "Os números do IBGE (Census)," 6–9.

48. Nelson Blecher, "Leitura de jornal cresce no interior de SP," *Folha de São Paulo*, January 12, 1992.

49. Jair Borin, "Rádios e tvs crescem com o festival de concessões"; José B. Pinho, "O rádio Brasileiro dos anos 90 e o estatuto do fonograma publicitário," *Comunicação e Sociedade* 10, no. 18 (1991): 25–37.

50. Bradley Greenberg, Russell Alman, Rich Busselle, Joseph D. Straubhaar, Fred Litto, and Nazira Gait, "Young People and Their Orientation to the Mass Media—An International Study—Brazil" (Department of Telecommunication, Michigan State University, East Lansing, July 1992).

51. Gustavo Venturini, "Zapping," DataFolha relatório de pesquisa de opinião 938, *Folha de São Paulo*, May 16, 1990.

52. "O que sobra do telejournal depois do boa noite," *Imprensa* 1, no. 3 (1987): 67–70. Viewing figures for the São Paulo television news audience add to more than 100 percent because respondents could indicate viewing of more than one news program.

53. USIA Office of Research, "Media Use by the Better Educated in Four Brazilian Cities."

54. "População considera tv instituição mais poderosa do país," *Folha de São Paulo*, March 29, 1987.

55. "Consumer Report" (São Paulo: Instituto Brasileiro de Opinião Pública e Estatística [IBOPE], 1989).

56. Cristina Maiello, "Setor de vídeo está de olho no grande público," *Folha de São Paulo*, February 12, 1990.

57. José Carlos Camargo, "Lista dos mais consumidos só revela quantidade."

58. Ibid.

59. José Flesch, "MTV altera programação depois de um mês no ar," *Folha da Tarde*, November 20, 1990.

60. Ana Cecilia Americano, "TVA contabiliza 33 mil assinantes," *Gazeta Mercantil* (São Paulo), September 12, 1991.

61. Cristina Iori, "TVA e Globosat brigam por assinaturas," *Folha de São Paulo*, May 12, 1992.

62. Duarte, "Television Segmentation," 23–24.

63. Gerson Sintoni, "Entrevista—Homero Icaza Sánchez—O bruxo da telinha," *Imprensa* 4, no. 47 (1991): 77–79.

64. Duarte, "Television Segmentation," 124.

65. Ibid., 255.

66. Ibid., 256–57; "Consumer Report"; "Data from 2/18–3/3/91" (São Paulo: IBOPE, 1991).

67. "População considera tv instituição mais poderosa do país."

68. Conrad P. Kottak, *Prime-Time Society;* Ondina Fachel Leal, *A leitura social da novela das oito* (Petrópolis, Brazil: Vozes, 1986); idem, "Popular Taste and Erudite Repertoire: The Place and Space of Television in Brazil," *Cultural Studies* 4, no. 1 (1990): 19–29; Nico Vink, *The Telenovela and Emancipation: A Study on TV and Social Change in Brazil* (Amsterdam: Royal Tropical Institute, 1988).

69. Kottak, *Prime-Time Society*, 162–63.

70. Ibid.; Vink, *The Telenovela and Emancipation.*

71. Vink, *The Telenovela and Emancipation.*

72. Oliveira, "Mass Media, Culture, and Communication in Brazil."

73. Ibid.

74. Alan Riding, "Brazilian TV Challenges U.S. Hold on Soap Operas," *Washington Post*, May 3, 1984.

Conclusions: Toward the
New Millennium

Richard R. Cole

Photographs and mementos of all kinds fill the walls of Richard Cole's office, but visitors are frequently drawn to two small glass-and-brass cases with miniature skeleton men inside. Red blotches mar the figures' clothing, showing where each man was shot. The skeletons represent eighteen Mexican journalists who were murdered in recent years, most because of their reporting on drug traffic or sensitive political issues, including the famous case of Manuel Buendía, the crusading front-page columnist on Mexico City's Excélsior *newspaper, who was gunned down on the street there in 1984. They are a terrible and real part of the practice of journalism in Latin America, yet they are atypical. Most journalists do not cover drugs, and the vast majority of professional communicators live and work in safety. Mass communication throughout Latin America has grown enormously in recent years, and prospects for the future—for more growth and more freedom—are bright.*

Professor Cole, dean of the School of Journalism and Mass Communication at the University of North Carolina at Chapel Hill since 1979, has researched mass communication in Mexico and Cuba for years. A frequent visitor to both countries, he also has taken several classes to Mexico City and Havana. He has been president of both the Association for Education in Journalism and Mass Communication and the Association of Schools of Journalism and Mass Communication, and vice president of the Accrediting Council on Education in Journalism and Mass Communications. For further information about Professor Cole, see About the Editor.

As the twentieth century draws to a close, the days of the stereotypical Latin American military dictator may be over. Democracy is in ascendance. In the mid-1990s, in all the twenty Latin American countries except Cuba, democratic political regimes are in power. The degree of democracy and freedom varies from nation to nation, of course, but the overall picture bodes well for journalism and all forms of communication after the turn of the new millennium. Freedom of the press is a function of political development; they are inextricably interlocked. So as long as democracy holds sway, the future of freedom of expression and the free exercise of mass communication in Latin America looks promising.

Cuba, however, is the exception. In virtually all categories in Latin America these days, Cuba is in a sad state. Since the fall of the Soviet Union, which had propped up the island nation economically, the country has been in tatters. The picture in the mid-1990s is one of its people suffering mightily. Almost everything, including fuel, food, and medicine, is in short supply. Ironically, in Fidel Castro's once-vaunted socialist state, begging and prostitution are rampant. At the end of 1995 there were some signs of slight improvement in the economic situation, but the people still suffered.

Cuba is the only Latin American nation without a democratically elected national leader, and its Leninist political system forbids freedom of expression. Media are owned, operated, and tightly controlled by the state. No serious criticism of basic tenets of politics or the Castro government is permitted at all. If people violate that rule, they are apt to be thrown into prison for spreading enemy propaganda. Castro has been at the helm of government for three and one-half decades. Change is inevitable; the only question is when. Surely significant change will have arrived by the dawn of the twenty-first century. For the rest of Latin America, the following points hold generally in the mid-1990s as the new millennium nears.

Latin America's past is filled with tightly controlled press systems, often under military dictatorships. But those systems are gone today; the press of the region is much healthier and more open. The media systems of Latin American countries, Cuba excepted, are basically free, although each nation has at least some limits on that freedom. Indeed, no country in the world, including the United States, has an absolutely free and unfettered media system, and none ever will. There always will be safeguards against irresponsibility, including laws against libel and falsely shouting "Fire!" in a crowded theater.

Certain controls in Latin America have been debated for years, including the *colegios*, as in Costa Rica, where a law requires journalists to belong to the College of Costa Rican Journalists and have college degrees in journalism (see Chapter 6). In Brazil, a right-of-reply law requires a newspaper to publish a rebuttal in the same place in the paper where the offending story was printed. This, too, is easily debatable. Newspapers obviously should correct errors, but what is offensive can get political, and a reply to correct an error in a story need not receive the same play as the whole original story. In Venezuela, the government grants a special exchange rate for importing newsprint, thereby subsidizing newspapers. This obviously helps the newspapers economically, yet it is a

Sword of Damocles hanging over their heads. Many other specific controls vary from country to country.

The Latin American media, especially television and radio, historically have been more likely to hesitate in criticizing the political powers-that-be and to show more respect for people in powerful positions than have the media in the United States. One of the biggest problems in Latin American media coverage remains the reporting of government corruption. Journalists often practice self-censorship out of wariness or fear of criticizing the government. Worse, bribes or payoffs to journalists have been common in several countries, including Mexico, where for many years officials in the government and ruling political party routinely have handed out *embutes*, or payoffs, to reporters for their coverage. But such payoffs must be considered in light of the culture. They are common in several occupations and, indeed, in life in Mexico, and the extra money has supplemented the reporters' very low salaries. But the payoffs obviously have inhibited critical reporting, and, at worst, they have corrupted the practice of ethical journalism throughout the system. Today in Mexico, however, journalism is changing for the better. Important agents for this change are Alejandro Junco de la Vega's newspapers, *El Norte* in Monterrey and, especially, *Reforma*, the new trendsetter in Mexico City, which is establishing a strong ethical example for other newspapers and mass media in the capital and therefore in the rest of the nation. Reporters and other staff members there earn good salaries and are forbidden to accept payoffs from anyone (see Chapter 7).

One terrible danger to certain crusading journalists comes mainly as a result of the drug traffic. Of the thousands of journalists in Latin America, most practice their craft safely; they certainly do not go to work every day in fear of life or limb. But some, especially those covering drugs or highly sensitive political activities, are murdered each year. In 1994, according to the Inter American Press Association (IAPA), which keeps careful watch, 18 journalists were killed. Furthermore, by year's end not one arrest had been made and no one had been charged for any of the crimes. Unfortunately, in such cases most of the culprits are never caught. In the past six years, the IAPA has counted 144 murdered journalists. The vast majority—57—were in Colombia, where much of the drug activity is centered, followed by Peru with 18 and El Salvador and Mexico with 16 each.[1]

As terrible as this is, it, too, must be put into some global perspective. Around the world at least 115 journalists were killed in 1994, according to the International Federation of Journalists, which called that year the bloodiest on record for reporters: "a year of media slaughter on an unprecedented scale."[2] As one might expect, many of the journalists died in wars; 48 Rwandan journalists were killed in the war in that tiny African country, and numbers also died in the conflicts in Algeria and Bosnia. The International Federation of Journalists cited Russia and Latin America as the world's most dangerous areas for reporters covering corruption and criminal gangs, which would include drug traffic. Here, then, are other capsule summaries of elements of the Latin American communication scene as the new century approaches.

~ More Latin Americans receive their news from radio than from any other mass medium because radio is so pervasive and is free, once a person has at least an inexpensive transistor receiver. Virtually everyone has access to radio. In urban areas, television provides much of the population with at least headlines of the news, but newspaper readership is fairly small, much less than in the United States. In huge Brazil, for example, only about 4 percent of the more than 160 million people subscribe to newspapers, although a higher percentage reads them when street sales and multiple readership are considered. Throughout Latin America, radio and television, with their great proportion of entertainment content including the ever-popular *telenovelas*, or soap operas, draw immense audiences, whereas newspapers are read more by the highly educated and by those attuned to politics. Traditionally, Latin American newspapers have been more literary and more political than their counterparts in the United States.

Private ownership of the media is the norm for Latin America, and in many countries several powerful, wealthy families have large and influential media holdings. These families are national media barons. Most financial support for the media comes from advertising. In a number of countries, however, governments have owned a portion of the broadcasting stations, although such public ownership is decreasing. In Argentina, for example, when President Carlos Saul Menem took office in 1990, he immediately transferred ownership of television and radio stations to the private sector.

Another change will occur in the role that women play. Although they have not achieved equality with men in the top positions in the mass media, women have dramatically increased their presence overall. They constitute a strong presence in newspapers and magazines and on radio and television. In the future, there is no doubt that women's role in the media will continue to improve (see Chapter 2).

~ In Latin American universities, most education for would-be journalists comes from schools of social communication, which provide more theory than practical, hands-on reporting, gathering information, and other professional skills. The schools have tended to be left-of-center politically, at the least, and to emphasize ideology and critical studies. Recent years, however, have seen a healthy increase in nonuniversity educational efforts: more short-term seminars and workshops for working journalists put on by professional associations. In the future, journalism-mass communication education in Latin American universities will probably come closer to that in their U.S. counterparts, where professional skills courses are married with substantive courses in such areas as communication history, law, and the media's role in society. Indeed, a university in Puerto Rico and one in Santiago, Chile, have been working toward accreditation of their mass communication programs by the U.S.-based Accrediting Council on Education in Journalism and Mass Communications.

~ The flowering of democratic government in Latin America promises a future for journalism and mass communication that is brighter than the past: freer communication and more communication channels as the information superhighway and new, interactive media link individuals and nations. Throughout history, technology has outstripped government efforts to censor or stifle freedom of expression. With the great velocity of technological development today, in Latin America as elsewhere, new media will continue to foster not only more communication but also freer communication.

~ One bright development came in March 1994 with the historic Declaration of Chapultepec, a bill of rights for mass communication that was adopted by the Hemisphere Conference on Free Speech at Chapultepec Castle in Mexico City. Asserting that "no law or act of government may limit freedom of expression or of the press, whatever the medium," the Declaration lists ten basic principles of press freedom:

Declaration of Chapultepec[3]
Principles

A free press enables societies to resolve their conflicts, promote their well-being, and protect their liberty. No law or act of government may limit freedom of expression or of the press, whatever the medium. Because we are fully conscious of this reality and accept it with the deepest conviction, and because of our firm commitment to freedom, we sign this declaration, whose principles follow.

1. No people or society can be free without freedom of expression and of the press. The exercise of this

freedom is not something authorities grant; it is an inalienable right of the people.

2. Every person has the right to seek and receive information, express opinions, and disseminate them freely. No one may restrict or deny these rights.

3. The authorities must be compelled by law to make available in a timely and reasonable manner the information generated by the public sector. No journalist may be forced to reveal his or her sources of information.

4. Freedom of expression and freedom of the press are severely limited by murder, terrorism, kidnapping, intimidation, the unjust imprisonment of journalists, the destruction of facilities, violence of any kind, and impunity for perpetrators. Such acts must be investigated promptly and punished harshly.

5. Prior censorship, restrictions on the circulation of the media or dissemination of their reports, arbitrary management of information, the imposition of obstacles to the free flow of news, and restrictions on the activities and movements of journalists directly contradict freedom of the press.

6. The media and journalists should neither be discriminated against nor favored because of what they write or say.

7. Tariff and exchange policies, licenses for the importation of paper or news-gathering equipment, the assigning of radio and television frequencies, and the granting or withdrawal of government advertising may not be used to reward or punish the media or individual journalists.

8. The membership of journalists in guilds, their affiliation to professional and trade associations, and the affiliation of the media with business groups must be strictly voluntary.

9. The credibility of the press is linked to its commitment to truth, to the pursuit of accuracy, fairness, and objectivity and to the clear distinction between news and advertising. The attainment of these goals and the respect for ethical and professional values may not be imposed. These are the exclusive responsibility of journalists and the media. In a free society, it is public opinion that rewards or punishes.

10. No news medium or journalist may be punished for publishing the truth or criticizing or denouncing the government.

The struggle for freedom of expression and of the press is not a one-day task; it is an ongoing commitment. It is fundamental to the survival of democracy and civilization in our hemisphere. Not only is this freedom a bulwark and an antidote against every abuse of authority, it is society's lifeblood. Defending it day upon day is honoring our history and controlling our destiny. To these principles we are committed.

By the end of 1994 the presidents of eleven countries—Mexico, Guatemala, Panama, Argentina, Uruguay, Paraguay, Bolivia, El Salvador, Honduras, Nicaragua, and Colombia (in that chronological order)—plus the secretary general of the Organization of American States and the governor of Puerto Rico had signed the Declaration. No doubt others will follow. The Declaration is a promise of better days to come for communication within each Latin American nation and throughout the region. And better days are coming.

Notes

1. Inter American Press Association, *Press Freedom in the Americas: 1995 Annual Report* (Miami: Inter American Press Association, 1995), 90.
2. Associated Press report, December 28, 1994.
3. Inter American Press Association, *Press Freedom in the Americas,* 84.

Suggested Readings

Alexander, Robert J. *The Tragedy of Chile*. Westport, CT: Greenwood Press, 1978.

Alisky, Marvin. *Latin American Media: Guidance and Censorship*. Ames: Iowa State University Press, 1981. Discusses free and government-controlled press systems and professional organizations in eight major nations.

Allen, Cheryl. "Una Prensa . . . Libre? Freedom of the Press in Mexico from 1968 to 1991." Senior honors thesis, University of North Carolina at Chapel Hill, School of Journalism and Mass Communication, 1992.

Argudín, Yolanda. *Historia del periodismo en México: Desde de virreinato hasta nuestros dias*. México, D.F.: Panorama Editorial, S.A., 1987.

Betancourt, Enrique C. *Apuntes para la historia: Radio, televisión y farándula de la Cuba de ayer*. Hato Rey, Puerto Rico: Ramallo Bros., 1986. This important Spanish-language book covers the state of Cuban broadcasting before Castro.

Castellón, Lucía, and Alejandro Guillier. "Chile: The Emerging Influence of Women in Journalism." *Media Studies Journal* (Winter/Spring 1993): 231–39.

Cole, Richard. "The Mass Media of Mexico: Ownership and Control." Ph.D. diss., University of Minnesota, 1972. This source is old but it provides considerable background; many of the issues are still pertinent.

Cuadernos de Información. Catholic University of Chile, Santiago. Edited by Tomás MacHale, this annual scholarly journal contains articles by working journalists and international scholars about media issues, professionalism, and legal matters affecting the press in the region.

Dorschner, John, and Roberto Fabricio. *The Winds of December*. New York: Coward, McCann, and Geoghegan, 1980. Dorschner and Fabricio provide an extensive historical overview of the pre-Castro era in Cuba.

Duzán, María Jimena. *Death Beat: A Colombian Journalist's Life Inside the Cocaine Wars*. New York: HarperCollins, 1994. A woman journalist recounts experiences on dangerous assignments.

Gallimore, Tim. "Radio and Television Broadcasting in Cuba: U.S. Communication Policy and the International First Amendment." *Gazette* 52 (1993): 43–56. This scholarly article examines the international legal, regulatory, and policy questions raised by U.S. government broadcasting over Radio and TV Martí.

Garrison, Bruce, and Julio E. Muñoz. "The Free and Not-So-Free Press of Latin America and the Caribbean." In *Current Issues in International Communication*, ed. L. John Martin and Ray Eldon Hiebert, 257–63. New York: Longman, 1990.

Herrán, María Teresa. *La industria de los medios masivos de comunicación en Colombia*. Bogotá, Colombia: Fescol, 1991.

Hester, Albert L., and Richard R. Cole. *Mass Communication in Mexico: Proceedings of the March 22–25, 1974, Seminar in Mexico, D.F.* December 1975. This special publication was distributed by the International Communication Division of the Association for Education in Journalism (now the Association for Education in Journalism and Mass Communication), University of South Carolina, Columbia, SC 29208.

Hora de cierre. Inter American Press Association. Edited by Harry Caicedo, this quarterly, Spanish-language IAPA publication provides current technical and professional discussions of international interest.

Huesca Rebolledo, Sabás. "New Press-State Relations in Mexico." *Mexican Journal of Communication* 1 (September 1993): 113–18. Huesca, coauthor of a collection of essays on the mass media, *Spaces of Silence*, and a newspaper and magazine writer, reviews the background and intentions of press regulations issued by the government in 1992.

IAPA News and *NotiSIP*. Inter American Press Association. Managing editor, Harry Caicedo. These English-language and Spanish-language bimonthly newsletters are intended primarily for IAPA members but offer extensive discussions of issues of interest to this leading professional organization and to the region in general.

Inter American Press Association. *Press Freedom in the Americas. 1995 Annual Report*. Miami, 1995. This edition of a yearly publication of the IAPA reviews the status of press freedom in twenty-four nations, including the United States and Canada. It contains the full text of the Declaration of Chapultepec; details of a follow-up campaign on the declaration; statistics on murders, kidnappings, assaults, and restrictions placed on journalists over the preceding six years. It also reports on IAPA activities.

Johnson, Owen V. "Cuba: An English-Language Mass Communication Reading List." *International Communication Bulletin* 29 (Spring 1994): 6. Published by the International Communication Division of the Association for Education in Journalism and Mass Communication, University of South Carolina, Columbia, SC 29208, the list contains seventy-two suggested readings on Cuba.

Kennedy, Paul P. *Middle Beat: A Correspondent's View of Mexico, Guatemala, and El Salvador*. New York: Teachers College Press, 1971. Published three years after the death of the author, a distinguished foreign correspondent for the *New York Times*, *Middle Beat* describes the period from 1954 to 1964 in "Middle America," the area from the northern border of Mexico to the northern border of Colombia.

Kunale, D. "Nicaragua's *La Prensa*: Capitalist Thorn in Socialist Flesh." *Media, Culture, and Society* 6 (April 1984): 151–76. This article details the assassination of *La Prensa*'s owner and editor, which galvanized support for the Sandinistas, and discusses press restrictions placed on the paper after its criticisms of the new government.

Lent, John A. *Bibliography of Cuban Mass Communications*. Westport, CT: Greenwood Press, 1992. This book includes many difficult-to-find sources in English and Spanish.

———. *Mass Communications in the Caribbean*. Ames: Iowa State University Press, 1990. Lent devotes substantial attention to the pre-Castro era in Cuba.

López, Oscar Luis. *La radio en Cuba: Estudio de su desarrollo en la sociedad neocolonial*. Havana: Editorial Letras Cubana, 1981. This Spanish-language book offers an interesting portrait of the state of the broadcast media before Castro; it has a decidedly Marxist tone.

MacHale, Tomás, ed. *Problemas contemporáneos de la información*. Santiago, Chile: Corporación de Estudios Contemporáneos, 1980. This volume contains articles by internationally recognized scholars describing press freedom, press organizations, and government interaction with the press.

Matta, Fernando Reyes. "The Latin American Concept of News." In *Current Issues in International Communication*, ed. L. John Martin and Ray Eldon Hiebert, 251–57. New York: Longman, 1990. Matta discusses press groups, *colegios*, and unions.

Miller, Tom. *Trading with the Enemy: A Yankee Travels through Castro's Cuba*. New York: Atheneum, 1992. This travelogue/discussion details encounters with ordinary people, well-known personalities, and the landscape and culture of Cuba during a seven-month excursion.

Nauman, Talli. "Communications Media." In *Mexico: A Country Guide*, ed. Tom Barry. Albuquerque, NM: Inter-Hemispheric Education Resource Center, 1992, 245–50. This chapter by an Associated Press correspondent provides a brief overview of the Mexican print and electronic media, including censorship, history, and industry leaders.

Nichols, John Spicer. "Cuban Mass Media: Organization, Control, and Functions." *Journalism Monographs* 78 (November 1982): 1–35.

Oliveira, O. S. "Mass Media, Culture, and Communication in Brazil: The Heritage of Dependency." In *Transnational Communications: Wiring the Third World*, ed. Gerald Sussman and John A. Lent, 200–213. Newbury Park, CA: Sage, 1991.

Oppenheimer, Andres. *Castro's Final Hour: The Secret Story behind the Coming Downfall of Communist Cuba*. New York: Simon and Schuster, 1992. Oppenheimer interviewed more than five hundred people in Cuba over a two-year period. He describes "how Castro's Socialist revolution destroyed itself after the collapse of world communism."

Padula, Alfred A. "The Fall of the Bourgeoisie: Cuba, 1959–1961." Ph.D. diss., University of New Mexico, 1974. This historical overview offers insights about the press before Castro.

Pérez, Louis. *Cuba between Reform and Revolution.* New York: Oxford University Press, 1988.

Pierce, Robert N. *Keeping the Flame: Media and Government in Latin America.* New York: Hastings House, 1979. Pierce opens with a series of country-by-country case studies of relationships between media and government; he then compares and analyzes the situations from a hemispheric viewpoint. Rather than offering a complete history, Pierce talks about predominant media patterns visible throughout Latin America.

Poniatowska, Elena. *Massacre in Mexico.* Columbia: University of Missouri Press, 1991. Translated by Helen R. Lane from *La noche de Tlatelolco.* New York: Viking Press, 1975. Poniatowska interviewed students, workers, parents, professors, maids, and others in Mexican society who witnessed the events of October 1968.

Pulso del periodismo. Latin American Journalism Program, Florida International University, Miami. Edited by John Virtue, this bimonthly publication focuses on problems faced by the Latin American press. Recent articles have analyzed the problem of *colegios* and other restrictions on press freedoms.

Randall, Margaret. *Sandino's Daughters Revisited: Feminism in Nicaragua.* New Brunswick, NJ: Rutgers University Press, 1994. Randall covers how women, including journalist Sylvia Montenegro, fared during the Sandinista revolution in Nicaragua.

Riding, Alan. *Distant Neighbors: A Portrait of the Mexicans.* New York: Knopf, 1985. This is a classic, well-received book on Mexico and its people.

Salwen, Michael B. *Radio and Television in Cuba: The Pre-Castro Era.* Ames: Iowa State University Press, 1994. Salwen offers an exhaustive overview with a thorough index.

Salwen, Michael B., and Bruce Garrison. *Latin American Journalism.* Hillsdale, NJ: Lawrence Erlbaum Associates, 1991. This overview analyzes major topics concerning Latin American news media in the beginning of the 1990s, as the region moved toward democracy and press freedom. It includes a discussion of professional organizations, particularly the Inter American Press Association, that wield significant influence in the region.

Salwen, Michael B., Bruce Garrison, and Robert T. Buckman. "Latin America and the Caribbean." In *Global Journalism: Survey of International Communication,* 2d ed., ed. John C. Merrill, 267–310. New York: Longman, 1991. This chapter describes the role of the Inter American Press Association and covers the status of press freedom in each of the major Latin American countries.

Seaton, Edward. "Latin America: After Communism, New Foes, New Challenges." *Media Studies Journal* 4, no. 4 (Fall 1993): 123. The former president of the Inter American Press Association argues that the United States should assist the development of a free press in Latin America, saying that "for democracy to survive . . . , so must a free, pluralistic and unfettered press."

Shea, Donald R., and William L. Jarrett, eds. *Mass Communication in the Americas: Focus on the New World Information and Communication Order.* Milwaukee: Center for Latin America, University of Wisconsin-Milwaukee, 1985. Based on a symposium in Racine on October 7–9, 1984, this book examines implications of the New World Information and Communication Order, ownership and control of media, North-South communication imbalances, licensing and protection of journalists, prospects for the future, and other topics.

Sigmund, Paul E. *The Overthrow of Allende and the Politics of Chile, 1964–1976.* Pittsburgh: University of Pittsburgh Press, 1977.

Skidmore, Thomas E., ed. *Television, Politics, and the Transition to Democracy in Latin America.* Washington, DC: Woodrow Wilson Center; Baltimore: Johns Hopkins University Press, 1993. This book resulted from a June 22–23, 1990, conference at the Woodrow Wilson Center and includes chapters on the influence of television on the 1989 Brazilian presidential election.

Smith, Wayne S. *Portrait of Cuba.* Atlanta: Turner Publishing Inc., 1991. The author was for years head of the U.S. Interests Section in Havana and now is a professor at Johns Hopkins University. He has been a critic of U.S. policy toward Cuba, advocating that the embargo be lifted. This book provides a thoughtful and cogent analysis of Cuba and of President Fidel Castro. It is illustrated with many beautiful photographs by Michael J. Walsh.

Soderlund, Walter C., and Stuart H. Surlin, eds. *Media in Latin America and the Caribbean: Domestic and International Perspectives.* Windsor: Ontario Cooperative Program in Latin American and Caribbean Studies, University of Windsor, 1985. Proceedings of a conference at the University of Windsor, October 26–27, 1984. Fourteen papers are included, covering the New World Information Order and the MacBride Report, media performance in Latin America and the Caribbean, media coverage of the region in the North American press, and the 1983 U.S. military invasion of Grenada.

Thomas, Hugh. *Cuba: The Pursuit of Freedom.* New York: Harper and Row, 1971. Thomas provides a historical overview that devotes attention to the state of journalism before Castro.

Timerman, Jacobo. *Cuba: A Journey.* New York: Knopf, 1990.

———. *Chile: Death in the South,* trans. Robert Cox. New York: Knopf, 1987. A social activist talks about human rights under President Augusto Pinochet.

Verbitsky, Horacio. *Robo para la corona: Los frutos prohibidos de árbol de la corrupción.* Buenos Aires: Editorial Planeta, 1991. This best-seller by a journalist with a crusading newspaper analyzes the causes of political corruption in Argentina. The title (I steal for the crown) comes from a statement by an interior minister accused of corruption.

————. *Hacer la corte: La construcción de un poder absoluto sin justicia ni control.* Buenos Aires: Editorial Planeta, 1993. This follow-up to Verbitsky's earlier book on President Carlos Menem's government argues that the president created a Supreme Court to serve his political needs.

Vila, Hermino Portell. *Medio siglo de* El Mundo: *Historia de un gran periódico.* Havana: Editorial Lex, 1951. This book by one of the leading historians of Cuba, himself a host of educational television programs in the pre-Castro period, offers a case study of a leading Havana newspaper.

————. *Nueva historia de la república de Cuba.* Miami: La Moderna Poesía, Inc., 1986. In this Spanish-language history, Vila devotes some attention to pre-Castro-era journalism.

Virtue, John, ed. *Guía de medios centroamericanos de comunicación.* Miami: Latin American Journalism Program, Florida International University, 1994. Virtue has compiled a directory of newspapers, radio stations, television stations, and journalists in Costa Rica, El Salvador, Guatemala, Honduras, Nicaragua, and Panama.

Suggested Films

Campaign for Cuba. Executive producer, Churchill L. Roberts; writer/producer, Sandra H. Dickson; narrator, Daniel Schorr, 58 min. Aired on PBS October 14, 1992. Produced by the nonprofit Documentary Institute, University of West Florida, Pensacola, FL 32514.

Last Days of the Revolution (1994) examines the U.S. Cold War policy toward Cuba (particularly the embargo), the reasons for the island's economic crisis, and the mass exodus to the United States. In this documentary, shot primarily in Cuba, people of different races and socioeconomic backgrounds tell of their nation's economic and political deterioration. The hour-long show was directed by Sandra H. Dickson and Churchill L. Roberts of the nonprofit Documentary Institute at the University of West Florida, Pensacola, FL 32514. José de Córdoba, who left Cuba in 1960 and covers Latin America and the Caribbean for the *Wall Street Journal*, narrates.

Mexico: Revolution: 1910–1940. Public Media Inc., 1988. This hour-long video explores people and events during three decades of revolutionary turmoil, a period that created institutions with enduring impact on Mexican life. Part one of a three-part series.

Mexico: From Boom to Bust: 1940–1982. Public Media Inc., 1988, 57 min. Part two of a three-part series examines the 1940s to mid-1970s, a period of rising prosperity marked by political stability. But political unrest returned as the economy suffered from excessive spending and the oil industry crisis.

Mexico: End of an Era: 1982–1988. Public Media Inc., 1988, 57 min. Part three of a three-part series on Mexican history, this video covers the time leading up to the 1988 elections when opposition parties made historic gains against the monopoly party.

Portrait of Castro's Cuba. Hosted by James Earl Jones. New York: Ambrose Video, 1991. 2 cassettes, 91 min. Written by William E. Duggan, Jr., and Sherry Abaldo; directed by Kirk Wolfinger and Roger Mills. Part of the "Portrait of the World" series. This film takes viewers to the former Pearl of the Antilles and explores what Cuba became under Fidel Castro. It considers the fate of the nation and its people after the crumbling of the Communist bloc that for so long had backed Castro financially and ideologically.

About the Editor

Since 1979, Richard R. Cole has been dean of the School of Journalism and Mass Communication at the University of North Carolina at Chapel Hill (UNC-CH). In 1992, at age fifty, he became the youngest person to receive the Freedom Forum Medal for Distinguished Accomplishments in Journalism-Mass Communication Administration. He was national president of the Association for Education in Journalism and Mass Communication in 1982–83, and national president of the Association of Schools of Journalism and Mass Communication in 1986–87. For ten years, he also served as the book review editor (or coeditor) of *Journalism Quarterly*.

Professor Cole holds a university-wide teaching excellence award at UNC-CH and has been a member of many national and international boards and task forces. He chaired the Freedom Forum's National Scholarship Committee for years and is now chairman of the National Steering Committee of the Hearst Foundation's journalism awards program. He was vice president of the national Accrediting Council on Education in Journalism and Mass Communications in 1987–1995, has chaired or been a member of accrediting teams to more than thirty schools, and has acted as a consultant to two state governments and more than thirty universities in the United States, Mexico, Puerto Rico, Russia, and Cuba. For eight years, Professor Cole was a vice president of the worldwide International Association for Mass Communication Research. He is the coauthor of *Gathering and Writing the News: Selected Readings* (1975) and has written articles that have appeared in *Journalism Quarterly, Gazette: The International Journal for Mass Communication Studies, American Behavioral Scientist, Journalism Educator*, and other scholarly publications.

ISBN 0-8420-2558-8

90000>

9 780842 025584